CALIBRATING COLONIAL CRIME

Reparations and the Crime of Unjust Enrichment

Joshua Castellino

First published in Great Britain in 2025 by

Bristol University Press
University of Bristol
1–9 Old Park Hill
Bristol
BS2 8BB
UK
t: +44 (0)117 374 6645
e: bup-info@bristol.ac.uk

Details of international sales and distribution partners are available at bristoluniversitypress.co.uk

© Bristol University Press 2025

British Library Cataloguing in Publication Data
A catalogue record for this book is available from the British Library

ISBN 978-1-5292-4182-2 hardcover
ISBN 978-1-5292-4186-0 paperback
ISBN 978-1-5292-4187-7 ePub
ISBN 978-1-5292-4188-4 ePdf

The right of Joshua Castellino to be identified as author of this work has been asserted by him in accordance with the Copyright, Designs and Patents Act 1988.

All rights reserved: no part of this publication may be reproduced, stored in a retrieval system, or transmitted in any form or by any means, electronic, mechanical, photocopying, recording, or otherwise without the prior permission of Bristol University Press.

Every reasonable effort has been made to obtain permission to reproduce copyrighted material. If, however, anyone knows of an oversight, please contact the publisher.

The statements and opinions contained within this publication are solely those of the author and not of the University of Bristol or Bristol University Press. The University of Bristol and Bristol University Press disclaim responsibility for any injury to persons or property resulting from any material published in this publication.

Bristol University Press works to counter discrimination on grounds of gender, race, disability, age and sexuality.

Cover design: Liam Roberts Design
Front cover image: iStock/bucky_za

Bristol University Press' authorised representative in the European Union is:
Easy Access System Europe, Mustamäe tee 50, 10621 Tallinn, Estonia,
Email: gpsr.requests@easproject.com

Warning: Objects in the rear-view mirror
may be closer than they first appear

Contents

Table of cases   vii

Introduction   1
    Caveats   8

PART I   Colonial Crime: Challenges, Classification and Cures

1   **Combatting the Challenge of Colonial Crime: Ten Hurdles**   21
    The intertemporal rule of law   22
    Legal personality   24
    Statutes of limitations   26
    The right to property   27
    Validity of contracts   28
    Establishing victimhood   29
    The general versus the specific   29
    Historical verification   30
    Calculating colonial tort   31
    Remedies wider than compensation   32

2   **Classifying Colonial Crime: Seven Deadly Sins**   34
    Subjecthood and objecthood   35
    Acquisition of title to territory   40
    Episodic colonial crime   49
    Systemic and widespread practices   57
    Decolonization-oriented crimes   64
    Legacy crimes   69
    Collusion in the commitment of crime   72

3   **Curing Cancer: A Five-Point Plan to Address Colonial Crime**   74
    Acceptance of wrongfulness   76
    Reparations   81

		Restitution	85
		Compensation	88
		Solidarity-oriented remedies	93

PART II Extraction, Enrichment and Exploitation: Addressing the Tipping Point of Climate Change through Colonial Crime

4	Colonial Crime, Environmental Destruction and Indigenous Peoples: A Roadmap to Accountability and Protection	97
	Colonial crime and environmental degradation	99
	Law as the enabler of colonization	107
	Conclusion	118

5	Financing System Change: A Recovery-Based International Law Response to Colonial Crime	120
	Drawing on science to understand the nature, impact, victimhood and responsibility for environmental crime	124
	Sharpening legal tools to address accountability and remedy structural discrimination	131
	What an international crime of unjust enrichment could look like	133
	Conclusion	139

6	From Vicious Cycle to Virtuous Circle	141
	Disrupting the cycle	143
	Undermining global and national governance	145

Bibliography	151
Annex: Regional Groupings of Countries	166
Index	169

Table of cases

African Commission of Human and Peoples' Rights v. Kenya, Judgment, 17 May 2017, Application No. 006/2012, and its subsequent reparations judgment on 23 June 2022.
Factory at Chorzów Case (Germany v. Poland), 25 May 1926, PCIJ Reports (1926) Series A, No. 7
Factory at Chorzów Case (Germany v. Poland), 13 September 1928, PCIJ Reports (1928) Series A, No. 17.
France, Court of Cassation, Civil Chamber 1, Judgment, 25 June 2013, 12–12.341.
France, Court of Cassation, Civil Chamber 1, Judgment, 4 April 2001, 98–13.285.
Indigenous Peoples' Alliance of the Archipelago (AMAN) et al v. Government of Indonesia & Ors (2013) Decision number 35/PUU-X/2012.
International Centre for Settlement of Investment Disputes, ADC Affiliate Limited and ADC & ADMC Management Limited v. The Republic of Hungary, Award, ICSID Case No. ARB/03/16, 2 October 2006.
Lena Goldfield Arbitration Award, in The Times (London), 3 September 1930, p 13, col. 2.
Ndiku Mutua, Paulo Nzili, Wambugu Nyingi, Jane Muthoni Mara and Susan Ngondi v. The Foreign and Commonwealth Office [2011] EWHC (1913) QB.
Separate Opinion of Vice President Judge Ammoun, *ICJ Reports* (1975) 86.
Jota v. Texaco, Inc., Judgment, 5 October 1998, 157 F.3d 153 (2d Cir. 1998) Court of Appeals, Second Circuit, USA.
National Coalition Government of Burma v. Unocal, Inc., Judgment, 5 November 1997, 176 F.R.D. 329 (C.D. Cal. 1997) District Court for the Central District of California, USA.
Doe v. Unocal Corp., Judgment, 25 March 1997, 963 F. Supp. 880 (C.D. Cal. 1997) District Court for the Central District of California, USA.
Beanal v. Freeport-McMoRan, Inc., Judgment, 10 April 1997, 969 F. Supp. 362 (E.D. La. 1997) District Court for the Eastern District of Louisiana, USA.
Sequihua v. Texaco, Inc., Judgment, 27 January 1994, 847 F. Supp. 61 (S.D. Tex. 1994) District Court for the Southern District of Texas, USA.

Vekuii Rukoro, David Frederick, *The Association of the Ovaherero Genocide in the USA Inc. and Barnabas Veraa Katuuo, v. Federal Republic of Germany*, 1:17-cv-00062 (S.D.N.Y.).

Western Sahara (Advisory Opinion) *ICJ Reports* (1975) 39.

Wi Parata v. The Bishop of Wellington SC Wellington [1877] NZ Jurists Report 183; (1877) 3 NZ Jur (NS) 72 (SC); 1 NZLRLC 14 (17 October 1877).

R v. Speaker of the National Assembly, the President of Namibia. The Cabinet and the Attorney General on behalf of Bernadus Swaartboi, the Ovaherero Traditional Authority and 11 Nama Traditional Authorities (High Court of Namibia Case number HC-MD-CIV-REV-2023/0023).

Primary legislation and official reports

American Law Institute, *Restatement of the Law of Restitution* (St. Paul, MN, 1937).

Basic Principles and Guidelines on the Right to a Remedy and Reparation for Victims of Gross Violations of International Human Rights Law and Serious Violations of International Humanitarian Law, General Assembly Resolution 60/147 (16 December 2005), UN Doc. A/Res/60/147.

Build America Buy America Act (15 November 2021).

Intergovernmental Panel on Climate Change ('IPCC'.), *Climate Change 2022: Impacts, Adaptation and Vulnerability* (Cambridge: Cambridge University Press, 2022) 3056.

Report of the United Nations Special Rapporteur on Contemporary Forms of Slavery, Including Its Causes and Consequences, UN Doc. A/77/163, 14 July 2022.

On Building a United Front to Advance the Course of Justice and Reparations to Africans (14–17 November 2023), Accra, Ghana.

Ordinance from 10/02/2016 created Article 1303.1–4

Papal Bull Inter Caetera, AD 1493.

Parl. St. Kamer 2019–2020, nr. 1462/001.

Article 9, *Statute of the International Court of Justice*, 18 April 1946 (33 UNTS 993, UKTS 67 (1946) Cmd 7015, 3 Bevans 1179, 59 Stat 1055, 145 BSP 832, TS No 993), OXIO 95

UK Government, *Colonial Laws Validity Act 1865* (29 June 1865).

UK Parliament, *Amritsar: Minutes of Evidence taken before the Hunter Committee* (London: UK Parliament, 1920) Parliamentary Archives, DAV/123.

United Nations Population Fund, *Asia and the Pacific: Population Trends*, October 2022.

Montagu–Chelmsford Report (HC Deb 06 August 1918, Vol 109 cc1125–236).

Rudd Concession (30 October 1888, British South Africa Company).

Anarchical and Revolutionary Crimes (also known as Rowlatt Acts) (Act No. XI, 1919).

Report Amritsar: Minutes of Evidence Taken before the Hunter Committee (London: UK Parliament, 1920) Parliamentary Archives, DAV/123.

Reuters Concession 1872 (Persian Government Concession to Baron de Reuter, Vol. 217, Monday 14 July 1873).

Treaty of Tordesillas (7 June 1494, agreement between King Ferdinand II of Aragon and Queen Isabella I of Castille and King John II of Portugal).

Introduction

Surely not another book on colonial crime? All this decolonization talk everywhere. It can be so tiresome. These people will not stop until they rewrite history ...

Colonization has been an important facet of global history and can be directly attributed to the fact that human beings have always craved more. Trying to account for colonial crime may sometimes appear like an exercise in trying to punish human nature itself. Besides, unlike in previous eras of human history, the 'global community', already united in the aftermath of the devastation of World War II, took a firm stance against colonial rule and sought to decolonize the planet on an unprecedented scale. This immense transfer of power, through the creation of new institutions and new norms, oversaw what is likely to be the single biggest transfer of power from colonial to more local rule. In the process, it articulated decolonization as an important theme in the laws governing the international community. That transfer of power led to the birth of new States, relying on an older principle of self-determination that originated in the writings of some of the earliest published thinkers in the field of public life, giving substance to the notion of action in support of freedom from oppression (*jus resistendi secessionis*, or the right to resistance). Of all the myriads of episodes and aeons of colonization throughout history, this last bout was probably the only one that warranted such a large-scale response.

Yet there is considerable evidence to suggest that seven and a half decades after the forces of decolonization changed the global map, the world may be in a worse state in terms of the mass oppression of communities. Rather than the decolonization project resulting in a freedom from oppression and the positing of political authority in the hands of more representative forms of government across the globe, it may have transferred power in most cases from one set of privileged rulers to another. The post-colonial State has now had close to seven decades to overcome the worst ills of colonization but has had, at best, only mild success in overcoming its inherited colonial legacies. This book is not arguing that all the wrongs that currently exist in post-colonial States are the fault of colonial powers. Nor is it arguing that the current lack of representation of all the diverse communities within a State is exclusively the fault of the structures inherited from colonial rule. The post-colonial State and its governors must face the blame: they have been as culpable of dominating communities far from sites of power as their colonial predecessors were. Many issues that were planks for mobilizing people against colonial rule have persisted, not least the inequality of land tenure systems and the failure to recognize the inherent dignity and equal worth of all who live within the State. Yet there are several elements of colonial rule that merit further scrutiny and action in those States, as this book will seek to demonstrate.

Equally pressing and socially disruptive issues have also arisen in the territories of former colonial powers since their abdication of colonial power, many that bear direct correlation to colonial adventurism. These States changed dramatically through the questionable acquisition of foreign wealth, followed by decades of forced and voluntary immigration. The consequences flowing from this are deep, with the intermixing of populations making the use of simple tags such as 'victim' and 'perpetrator' meaningless. The extent to which these former colonial States are changing is dramatic and is proving disconcerting to many within their electorates. It has led to significant identity-based tensions between those who view these States as homogenous and based on a dominant, perhaps pure ethno-religious, identity and the incredible swathe of populations that now call these countries their home. This tension is impacting the politics in the former colonial powers, growing xenophobia and rupturing the social fabric that makes up these now multicultural States.[1] These tensions simmer against the steady drumbeat of an environmental catastrophe that needs urgent action.

This book seeks to substantiate the following arguments. First, that persistent inequality is increasingly dividing populations in former colonial powers as well as in those that came within its remit through colonization. Second, that there are key reasons, including the narrating of history itself, that reify and aggravate these issues impacting inequality, alienating significant parts of the population and deepening social breakdown. Business as usual models work on a number of deeply embedded assumptions – that societies are already merit-based, that growth must be venerated, that increased consumption is good for the economy – which remain unconcerned about wealth acquisition among the few while dismissing inequality as a symptom of laziness. Attempts at seeking accountability and fairness through the construction of human rights based on non-discrimination as a route to

---

[1] See Beth S. Rabinowitz, *Defensive Nationalism: Explaining the Rise of Populism and Fascism in the 21st Century* (Oxford: Oxford University Press, 2023).

empowering all segments of the population have not been fully effective in creating egalitarian societies, neither in disrupting undue privilege nor in empowering masses far from access to justice. The token talented individuals from these masses who break through the system and achieve success are used as evidence that the system is fair and meritocratic. In addition, any discussion of human rights itself has become discredited by criticism from within the human rights movement as well as by those who view it as 'soft' in giving rights to those who do not 'deserve' it. Defanging human rights at a time when need has deepened while power and wealth has become concentrated has limited the extent to which a route to equality can be constructed.

A more obvious route to social harmony would lie in recognizing that diverse individuals and communities have far greater commonalities rather than differences. This idealistic notion has floundered in the face of scarcities and adversities generated by the extent to which the dominant socio-economic system has been able to generate adequate employment and satiate growing demands for consumption. The growing concentration of immense wealth in a few hands, and the fact that 'economic growth' no longer features people or generates jobs in the way it used to thanks to the technological revolution, has added a significant complexity to the equation, rendering global politics into a race to the bottom between the haves and the have-nots. The threat of climate change, generated by a wanton destruction of finite resources that has yielded significant parts of this immense wealth, has added further urgency to the project of reconciliation and recalibration.

Identity politics before, during and after colonial rule has cost millions of lives throughout human history. This has taken various guises: commencing from tribal insecurities that relied on attack as the best form of defence, it has morphed over and over again into subjugation of others seen as primitive, religious expansionism and then nationalism. Along the way it has lit a touchpaper for the concept that people who are different are somehow a different 'race' – a deep but wilful misunderstanding of what a biological race is. By treating the *other* as lesser and therefore less entitled, it drove schisms into the human family that some may say were inevitable. Not even powerful ideologies such as religions that insisted all humanity were equal could overcome this idea. Rather, despite the equality preached from positions of religious power, a religion was often viewed by its adherents as a sign of superiority for one set of believers over another. The re-emergence of identity politics with a vengeance in the 21st century is stoking fires of nationalism that form a significant fault line in human societies the world over. It signals a resounding defeat for multiculturalism and pluralism, which had formed a bulwark protecting societies from being overrun by raging forces of nationalism in offering protection to minorities. The rise of majorities appears to be fuelled by their own feelings of insecurity, but this is further underpinned by similar sentiments to those which drove colonialism: an orchestrated greed of some, instrumentalized to inflame the passion of others defined as kin, in order to pursue wealth accumulation by dispossessing others.

The greed that lies at the heart of domination and subjugation projects has been attributed to humans pursuing a Hobbesian view of the world. In that scenario, those with power will inevitably aggrandize and enrich themselves, with the only responsibility of any government being restricted to the maintenance of order while ensuring that 'the market' will automatically regulate the worst of these excesses. The cost of this approach is now experienced widely throughout humanity via the immense environmental destruction, effectively a war against nature, that has re-subjugated human beings, especially those unfamiliar with the dominant system of economic life, to a lesser status. So far so anthropocentric: this analysis does not even begin to take into account the extinctions of other species that have already occurred as a consequence of this human ego-centric approach. It does at times seem impossible to conceptualize how a more peaceful and stable world can emerge from such a scenario, against the looming wildfires, melting icebergs, torrential rain, extinction of species and growing social unrest.

This may seem like another critique of humanity, of which we now have plenty: more vehement critique about human behaviour with scant prospect of concrete proposals emerging that can generate action. Yet this brief treatise seeks to do more. It seeks to articulate an agenda of change that is crucial to recalibrating power and the manner in which it has continued to contribute to devastation that may have seemed subliminal and incremental at the time it occurred but that has, like the rate at which Arctic glaciers are melting, swelled to a torrent. It argues that a specific facet that has contributed to this – colonial crime – needs to be reckoned with, in the belief that urgent social re-engineering is necessary to enhance social cohesion and draw upon the full extent of the human potential that exists when addressing the pressing problems faced.

To do so in a meaningful way, it is important to start by debunking the many myths that are actively called upon to prevent such a reckoning. These are encapsulated in six statements that are often repeated in conversations concerning colonial crime and merit brief consideration. These are:

> *But it was a long time ago*
> *That's life*
> *Just forget it*
> *What's it got to do with me?*
> *It's a nice idea but is impossible to realize*
> *So it's all my fault now?*

But it was a long time ago

This argument is often used to paint those calling for a reckoning of colonial crime as being out to disrupt society and generate claims in the present that would cause new injustices. The *Durban World Conference on Racism* of 2001 sought to generate momentum for reparations regarding colonial crime, but that discussion was not always coherent and was overtaken by events of 11 September of that year, which brought terrorism – experienced as a persistent state of events in many parts of the world – to the forefront of the dominant anglophone Western world. In the midst of the challenging items that pack governmental agendas in that part of the world, colonization is not an electoral issue and could thus be dismissed as being merely another chapter in the annals of human history. And that is among the few States who may admit (under compulsion) it was wrong in the first place. For others, it is still denial that dominates the mindset, with no reason to deviate from this position. Arguably, those that believe colonization was 'too long ago' to merit a reckoning were either relatively untouched by it or have failed to interrogate the extent to which the past continues to affect the present. Another significant factor is that the way in which histories, especially in the former colonial powers, have underplayed these crimes means that many do not realize how significant they were, what precise damage occurred as a consequence and how much of the privilege and wealth they currently enjoy traces directly to these events. For these powers, the plight that may have befallen communities in Africa, Asia, the Pacific and Latin America is dismissed as being probably their own fault, standing in sharp contrast to the perceived intelligence, vision, entrepreneurship and hard work that generated stable societies in their own countries. There is no realization among those who deny the legitimacy of the colonial discussion that their wealth and influence was built on unjust enrichment during colonial rule, which despite the transitions has not led to adequate scrutiny, penalty or return. As a result, they continue unabated in wielding significant power in the present, determining how histories – theirs and those of others – will be told, closing down discussions about the past and denigrating and deliberately obstructing attempts to put this issue on the contemporary political agenda.

That's life

This argument is largely based on the perceived need to 'move on'. It correctly identifies human nature as the cause and driver of such forces, and many linked arguments accurately portray colonization as an integral part of human nature and history. This, they suggest, means that colonial activities including potential crimes do not warrant particular attention. For many who believe this narrative, seeking to address this discussion in the present is dismissed as being unfair and divisive in opening up new wounds. Yet the people who have profited from colonial crime remain close to contemporary sites of power, and it remains in their interest to argue that such unfairness does not warrant any scrutiny. Failing to address these issues has not only contributed to the *strongest wins* mentality; it is also at the heart of the current wealth of a significant portion of the world's most powerful people. In an era that is characterized by a race to the bottom, where disenfranchised communities have been convinced of the need to use electoral systems to further enfranchise those with immense wealth, this has reified the view that 'life is unfair' and that 'nothing can be done about it'.

Just forget it

Unlike the excuse above, this advice is delivered specifically with a view to get the listener to erase the memories of the past that may cause hurt. From the powerful few, the recommendation on this issue is a patronizing 'just forget it', probably followed swiftly by the exhortation to 'get on with life' instead. To the general population in former colonial powers, the implicit and at times explicit message is that if any reparations need to be made, this will likely detract from urgent issues 'at home', leading to current taxpayers being overly burdened in paying for wrongs perpetrated by a previous generation, foisting the unfairness of fathers' sins being paid for by their daughters and sons. This argument needs to be heeded in any discussion about a recalibrating of colonial crime, since passing on a burden of reparations to communities that may already be disenfranchised in 'home countries' would be unfair, as would the transfer of funds that ought to be spent on disrupting entrenched racial discrimination and building stronger and fairer societies at home. The section of this book on designing remedies will return to this argument.

What's it got to do with me?

This question, often framed in response to discussions of colonial crime, goes on to enumerate the many generations that have passed since the alleged crimes, putting distance between the individual concerned and the machinations of high politics conducted ostensibly in their name. The first point has already been addressed in countering the 'but it was a long time ago' argument. The second is an important one and highlights the fact that for many in former colonial countries, the colonial project was conducted by people who had little affinity with the many communities in the country. It is true that asking for individuals from these communities who were already subjugated and dominated by a specific class of people to be held accountable for such actions would be unfair.

So the answer to the question 'What's it got to do with me?' will always likely be 'it depends'. It depends on the extent to which any given individual was linked in some way to the wealth generated from the colonial enterprise. It would also depend on the extent to which the individual belongs to a family or clan that became enriched through the process. It is important for individuals to understand and locate their own colonial footprint, but this is difficult since biased histories have either exonerated entire populations or have failed to even narrate, never mind accurately portray, many aspects of the colonial enterprise. For anyone to understand their own colonial benefit footprint would require the generation of fairer histories.

Irrespective of the existence of an individual's particular colonial footprint, this book seeks to highlight how the persistence of injustice that grew up most recently in colonial rule continues to impinge on the present, and in that sense it implicates a much wider number of people that may at first seem distant from the crime. Supporting a call for a proper reckoning of colonial crimes, including through the generation of a more accurate history, would seem to be a position that any who believe in fairness and justice ought to take.

It's impossible anyway

Complex arguments have been tabled that strongly point to the existence of legal, financial, moral and practical difficulties in achieving a full and fair reckoning of colonial crime. Lawyers trying to advocate for reparations have come up against a host of technical problems, not least the *intertemporal rule of law*, which will be explained below; the question of legitimacy in making a claim (*locus standi*); the argument that the passage of time makes such a reckoning impossible (*statutes of limitation*) and many others. Financial difficulties loom in relation to the challenge of ascertaining the value of loss, determining the price of reparations, understanding whose financial liability is generated and seeking to establish an ordered process through which the claims could be made, heard, financed and disbursed. Those that offer morality as a fetter to this discussion largely focus on the unfairness of making current generations pay for the sins of the past. Then there are the practical difficulties to do with the process of historical verification in the absence of written records, the privileging of witness testimonies that may not meet thresholds of evidence, the significant prospect of fraud in such a reckoning, and the determination of a fair process designed to hear, adjudicate and address the specific crime.

These difficulties should not be underestimated since they encompass significant complexities. In the very few instances where crimes of the past have found a reckoning, in New Zealand through the workings of the *Waitangi Tribunal*, in the context of Nazi war crimes as conducted through the Tokyo, London and Nuremberg Tribunals, or in the various truth and reconciliation processes, such as in South Africa, Ecuador, Kenya and many other locations, the discussions have been complex and have not always yielded a fair outcome. Yet each have shown the power to overcome these difficulties, and in nearly every one of these processes there has been the dispensation of justice and a degree of healing, albeit not perfect.

So it's all my fault now?

This defensive reaction in the face of claims of assertions about colonial crime is natural in view of the scale and complexity of the crimes themselves. However, it is important to understand that it would not be fair to attribute the ills that exist in post-colonial States exclusively to colonial rule even where such crimes created a lasting legacy. The post-colonial State has in most cases of contemporary and persisting human rights violations made an active choice to pursue a particular policy. That they may have inherited the policy from colonial rule, and that it may even have been supported by the colonial ruler through aid and technical cooperation, is not adequate as a reason for exclusive blame on the colonial ruler, nor is it adequate for shifting the primary responsibility, which lies with the post-colonial State. This is discussed below as the first caveat to engaging with questions of colonial crime.

Thus, irrespective of the degree of commission, omission or complicity, the question has a definitive answer in that it is not 'all' the fault of the former colonial State or its citizens then and now. Ascertaining what percentage or element of the persistence of inequality and destitution lies at the feet of the colonial ruler requires a far deeper and more forensic analysis of the violations themselves to be able to determine culpability with any degree of accuracy. This would require tighter classification of the types of crime, as this book tries to achieve, clear collection of evidence trails and the determination of how the crime presents itself in a contemporary context. In any case, in attributing 'fault', crimes of commission are likely to lead to greater attribution of responsibility than crimes of omission or complicity.

Caveats

Preventing the post-colonial State from hiding behind colonial crime

If discussions of colonial crime can be characterized in former colonial powers as attracting a range of reactions from eye-rolling indifference to hostility, they are often met with enthusiasm and passion in former colonies, who use the discussion as a means of avoiding their own liability while asserting an aggressive brand of nationalism. It is true that the legacy of colonial rule, especially in terms of land tenure systems and the establishment of the structures of the State, often trace directly to colonial rule. The legal systems are often a direct and continuing zone of impact, the result of technical cooperation including constitution writing that over decades created permanent frameworks that often do not sit well in terms of dealing with the multitude of questions and needs that arise in the average post-colonial State. Very few States have been able to decolonize their legal system. Singapore[2] and Papua New Guinea[3] stand out as engaging in efforts that actively question and seek to change what they have inherited. Caribbean States have also had this discussion, even if it has mainly focussed on the extent to which the UK's Privy Council should still be part of their system of justice.[4] Fewer have succeeded in having a meaningful discussion about property rights and the return to collective title from the regime of individual title that has become the inherited cornerstone of the law in most countries. While positive decisions on land rights exist in many jurisdictions and the determination to reform land rights has been prominent in the politics of countries like India[5] and Zimbabwe,[6] this has been tailored to win popularity contests and has not resulted in meaningful change to land tenure systems. Another lasting legacy of colonial rule is often the privileging of one group (ethnic, linguistic, religious) over others for the governance function. In many instances, such as in Iraq, Rwanda, Nigeria and India, this has also come about at the end of a concerted policy of 'divide and rule', which sought to maximize societal schisms, exacerbating ancient fault lines in society for the benefit of eliminating a unified threat against the ruler. Independence movements in nearly every post-colonial State where such diversity existed made overt gestures to seek to build that unity, aware of its collective strength in combatting colonial rule. Many of the alliances that emerged were built on dedicated efforts to work across ethno-religious or ethno-social divides, forging alliances under great pressure at a time of transition with plenty at stake. With many post-colonial States entering their eighth decade, these alliances have floundered in the face of development strategies that did not yield the widespread prosperity they

---

[2] Eugene K.B. Tan, 'Law and Values in Governance: The Singapore Way' 30(1) *Hong Kong Law Journal* (2000) 91–119.

[3] John L. Goldring, *The Constitution of Papua New Guinea: A Study in Legal Nationalism* (California: Law Book Company, 1978).

[4] Duke E. Pollard, *The Caribbean Court of Justice: Closing the Circle of Independence* (Kingston: Ian Randle Publishers, 2004).

[5] Varsha Bhagat Ganguly (ed), *Land Rights in India: Policies, Movements and Challenges* (New York: Routledge, 2016).

[6] Alexandre Charles Laurie, *The Land Reform Deception: Political Opportunism in Zimbabwe's Land Seizure Era* (Oxford: Oxford University Press, 2016).

promised. In addition, climate change-oriented scarcities of resources are driving competition with aggressive ethno-religious nationalisms called upon to maintain the hegemony of powerful rulers who operate in a manner not dissimilar to their former colonial masters.

To be able to govern effectively in situations of great need and complexity, post-colonial States that are nearly 70 or 80 years old ought to have found active ways to generate a unified national identity. The decolonization movement often encompassed all communities, but the fragile unity forged in fighting a common enemy appeared to dissipate in the transition from a fight for independence into a government for all within the territory. As for land tenure systems and an overhaul of legal and political systems that may not be suitable in the complexities of the post-colonial State, the newly established ruling classes have often privileged their own positions and sought to solidify their own hegemonies, moving seamlessly into inherited colonial structures, often taking up not only the vacant seats, homesteads and trappings of the former colonial masters but also their attitudes in reinforcing new hierarchies. From this vantage point they have been able to exercise rule that is very similar to that of their colonial masters. Thus, attributing blame solely to those colonial masters abdicates responsibility in pursuing accountability for what are current and still-to-emerge actions.

It is therefore imperative that any claim of colonial liability be articulated as only *one* of the factors contributing to persistent instability, inequality and disquiet within post-colonial States. When calibrating such crimes, it is also important to identify their specific nature, the duration of their persistence and the moment at which colonial liability for an action or phenomenon passes over to the contemporary or past independent governance regime of any given State. If current issues are viewed or portrayed as the sole responsibility and consequence of a colonial past, it exonerates modern States when they clearly bear primary responsibility for current difficulties. Their liability, too, must be understood in terms of crimes of commission, omission or complicity.

Not 'Europeans versus the rest of the world'

Contemporary discussions around colonial crime often target specific European powers. Depending on their geographic spheres of influence, these are usually Great Britain, France, Spain, Portugal, Belgium and, to a lesser extent, Germany, Italy and the Netherlands. This reading and identification is more synonymous of the types of claims made rather than the exclusivity of the colonial club. Other States – Austria, Hungary, Denmark, Sweden, Turkiyë, Mongolia, China, India, Iran, Israel, Poland, Lithuania, the United States of America, Australia, New Zealand and Canada may also have behaved in a manner that is akin to the named colonial rulers but do not tend to face the brunt of calls for accountability, though it is exactly such a discourse that has emerged recently with regards to Israel in the context of the war in Gaza. More generally however, the conversation about colonial crime tends to focus mainly on European States for actions in mainly Africa, Asia and Latin America. Besides ignoring other types of colonial actions that may have caused as much harm but receive less attention, this is also based on two presuppositions: first, that things are deemed 'colonial' when there is a group of individuals from one 'race' that dominates or subjugates another; and second, that the dominant feature of colonization was racial domination and subjugation.

First, the issue of 'race' and colonization. The dominant narrative suggests that European exploitation of distant lands was the first and most egregious form of colonization. The scantiness of the historical record and a tendency to view history from what is most recent make this claim difficult to evidence. Genghis Khan, the thirteenth century Mongolian warrior, captured huge swathes of land and left a trail of decimated communities in his wake. The Chinese experience of Genghis Khan may well lie at the heart of much of the subsequent understanding in China about a fear of being conquered and dominated. Yet Mongolia is not at the heart of any claims for reparation. Similarly, Arab raiders from the 11th century onward conducted raids eastward, including to India, and are attributed in Indian history books as 'stealing' Indian wealth. Contemporary politics has used elements and facets of this story to construct a modern xenophobia and anti-Muslim sentiment, but the States of the Middle East are not targeted in claims of accountability for colonial crime. Rather, it is far more humble Muslim populations who only know India as their home who appear to bear the brunt of that history.

On the flip side, European communities living more remotely from the centres of power in their own States had little power to influence decisions over colonization. In many cases they struggled historically for recognition themselves within their own State and were neglected in national governance agendas. For many populations living in rural areas within the territories of former colonial powers, the colonization of Africa, Latin America and Asia was something that happened beyond their worlds, though they would occasionally benefit from job opportunities that may have come up in the 'new markets'. Politics of that nature was mostly conducted in a distant capital in their name, allegedly for their benefit, with little of that benefit actually trickling down to the community level. To consider these individuals and communities as part of the colonial machinery is effectively the attribution of collective guilt on entire communities of 'white people' on the basis of their 'race' for crimes perpetrated by a few. Against this it would be true to say that the steady inflow of wealth and the growth in the economy did provide benefits across the country; others may have gained downstream benefits beyond employment opportunities, including the chance to migrate and acquire land that had previously been snatched or gained through disingenuous means by those more directly complicit.

Not just about money

Discussions around colonial crime are portrayed in some circles as attempts to claw back money, akin to a 'guilt' tax that does not have its basis in an accurate reading of history. This narrative is laced with a sense in former colonizing countries of these arguments being tiresome: unjust and sometimes unfair attempts to demand restitution for phenomena that are not clearly enough defined and are in any case difficult to quantify and therefore compensate. Some of the perspectives that reflect this view question why a developed country ought to financially compensate developing countries for what many believe are the consequence of their own misgovernance. This view has taken on heightened importance as developed countries themselves struggle with austerity measures that decimated their ability to address key socio-economic rights such as health and education. The idea of a further draw on the exchequer at a time of scarcity is unfathomable.

Yet seeking accountability for colonial crimes goes significantly wider than questions pertaining solely to financial compensation, important as that remains. There are several non-monetary forms of seeking accountability that are neglected in reductive attempts to dismiss the validity of the argument. This includes the need for formal apologies that not only provide solace and legitimation to long-standing accounts of exploitation but go significantly beyond in correcting inaccurate historical narratives that first lead to the dismissal of colonial activity as nothing more than opportunism on the part of some enterprising individuals. The return of stolen and misappropriated artefacts follows closely behind. This may take the form of significantly valuable items, such as the Kohinoor Diamond, or of significant symbolic and actual values, such as Egyptian antiquities including the Nefertiti bust and the Rosetta Stone. Challenging the continued holding for display in colonizing countries, often for profit, of artefacts and objects that were removed through stealth from their places of origin is not merely important for addressing colonial crime; it is fundamental to righting the historical record and building a sense of dignity in the places that were left bereft of these objects and artefacts. Arguments over appropriate levels of care required for these objects are used in discussions around their return, but these remain patronizing and condescending towards countries that have the right to display their own national heritage rather than to have it reduced to caricatures by those who showed little respect for the sense of place that accompanies the objects in the first place.

In the context of discussions taking place over the need for urgent action on climate change, the decision forced by the conservation lobby who pay homage to E.O. Wilson as the founding father of the need to protect biodiversity shows how remote places are objectified. This will be explored in greater detail in the second half of the book in engaging the so-called 30×30 plan and its supposed ability to help regenerate the planet.

Revisionist history

A significant part of the attitude to colonial crime stems from the way in which history is narrated in the home of the former colonial masters. The following is a summary of the history curriculum studied by school leavers (aged 15 or 16) in the United Kingdom:

Paper 1: Understanding the modern world
Section A: Period studies (one of the following options):

- America, 1840–1895: Expansion and consolidation
- Germany, 1890–1945: Democracy and dictatorship
- Russia, 1894–1945: Tsardom and communism
- America, 1920–1973: Opportunity and inequality

Section B: Wider world depth studies (one of the following options):

- Conflict and tension: The First World War, 1894–1918
- Conflict and tension: The inter-war years, 1918–1939
- Conflict and tension between East and West, 1945–1972
- Conflict and tension in Asia, 1950–1975
- Conflict and tension in the Gulf and Afghanistan, 1990–2009

Paper 2: Shaping the nation
Section A: Thematic studies (one of the following options):

- Britain: Health and the people: c1000 to the present day
- Britain: Power and the people: c1170 to the present day
- Britain: Migration, empires and the people: c790 to the present day

Section B: British depth studies including the historic environment (one of the following options):

- Norman England, c1066–c1100
- Medieval England: the reign of Edward I, 1272–1307

- Elizabethan England, c1568–1603
- Restoration England, 1660–1685[7]

There is only *one* option within the 16 themes available across the history curriculum that concerns empire despite Britain's significant impact through this activity in the past 200 years. To be able to formulate a history curriculum without paying significant attention to the activities of the State abroad is either studied ignorance – a continued attitude of superiority of not being interested in what took place beyond these shores – or a deliberate attempt to mislead.

The syllabus for this single unit is described as follows:

> This thematic study will enable students to gain an understanding of how the identity of the people of Britain has been shaped by their interaction with the wider world. It will consider invasions and conquests. It will also study the country's relationship with Europe and the wider world. It will consider the ebb and flow of peoples into and out of Britain and evaluate their motives and achievements. It considers the causes, impact and legacy of Empire upon the ruled and the ruling in the context of Britain's acquisition and retreat from Empire.[8]

Students that chose this option are required to study a range of historical literature deemed to influence Britain's dealings with the wider world, including war, religion, government, economic resources, science and technology, ideas such as imperialism, social Darwinism and civilization and the role of individuals. The accompanying narrative emphasizes the need for students to develop an understanding of how change occurred and to also develop skills in assessing the value of that change while distinguishing between cause and consequence. Somewhat promisingly, this single option is deemed to address five key questions:

1. How has Britain been affected by conquest, settlement and migration?
2. What has motivated migration to and from Britain?
3. Why did Britain gain and lose an empire and with what effects?
4. How have the people of Britain and the wider world responded to, and been influenced by, interaction?
5. What is the significance of key individuals and events in the development of empire and British identity?

---

[7] General Certificate of Secondary Education (UK) *History Curriculum* (AQA Board, UK), available at https://www.aqa.org.uk/subjects/history/gcse/history-8145/specification-at-a-glance.

[8] General Certificate of Secondary Education (UK) *History Curriculum* (AQA Board, UK).

Yet the syllabus shows that the option is itself divided into four further parts, the first of which is internally focussed – addressing the European lineage of the State under the title 'conquered and conquerors' before turning to a theme entitled 'looking west', divided into three sub-themes, only one of which, 'Sugar and the Caribbean', focuses on traditional colonization. The third part, 'expansion and empire', seeks to capture the entirety of British actions in 'India' and 'Africa', emphasizing figures such as Robert Clive and Cecil Rhodes without adequate coverage of the 'subjects' that came under their suzerainty. As in the previous sub-section, the third of three themes that constitute this part is ostensibly reflective of migration into Britain from the phenomena listed. From the syllabus it would seem that coverage is scant about Britain's role in the Opium Wars in China, the Bengal Famine, the Cape to Cairo quest or the takeover of Pacific territories. British 'subjects' such as Gandhi, Nkrumah and Kenyatta do make the syllabus under part four, entitled 'Britain in the 20th century', as one of three sub-themes that constitute this part.

When considered against the backdrop that less than half the student population selects history as one of their optional subjects,[9] the narrowness of the extent to which school leavers understand the impact of their own State's action is immediately put into question even further.

The challenge in other disciplines such as law, charged with the quest of delivering systems that will adequately guarantee the pursuit of justice, is even more acute, as this book aims to demonstrate. The issues contained in this book came into sharper focus after the brutal murder of George Floyd in Minneaoplis on 25 May 2020. He was not the first nor the last victim of police brutality towards African Americans in the United States of America. It is part of a trend, replicated in other countries with far less attention,[10] that bring issues of identity to the fore as scapegoat politics based on an *Us* and a *Them* take root even in settled democracies. The #BlackLivesMatter movement that became re-energized by that killing lit a touchpaper for wider discussions on race and colonization that dominated global headlines for a while, but have, in many ways, dissipated and been relegated to rhetoric, even in more progressive societies that believe in the inherent and equal dignity of all human beings. The energy that led to mass protests, including in UK cities like Bristol with its legacy of slave trading, gradually ebbed as the enormity of the change required to consider past accountability and

---

[9] Matthew Carroll and Tim Gill, Uptake of GCSE Subjects 2017, updated 2019 https://www.cambridgeassessment.org.uk/Images/652041-uptake-of-gcse-subjects-2019.pdf.
[10] See Joshua Castellino, 'Stand Up for Stanislav Tomáš: A Call for Accountability and Structural Change in the Czech Republic', *MRG Blogs,* 24 June 2021, available at https://minorityrights.org/2021/06/24/stanislav-tomas/.

how it informs the broken, polarized present sank in. While the raising of consciousness resulted in a spurt in high-quality academic writing on race, identity, whiteness, white superiority, oppression, gendered intersectional realities and legacies, relatively fewer texts reflected on the role that law ought to play in turning consciousness into a meaningful agenda to stimulate transition. Instead, legal writings and attempts to claim reparations in courts of law for colonial crime flounder on the shores of technicalities such as statutes of limitations. The few exceptions owe more to political acceptance of wrongfulness than claims based in law.

This book is divided into two parts. The first seeks to address this specific lacuna by framing colonial activities into typologies with a view to calibrating them as specific and differentiated crimes. Part I also seeks to demonstrate how the destruction of circular economies, which commenced during colonial times and has become accentuated in the post-colonial phase, constitutes a continuing tort that could be addressed through the construction of imaginative legal tools. This specific facet of the issue makes the engagement of simple blame games – namely, attributing contemporary ills exclusively to colonial powers – a self-defeating task. This is especially true when the wealth of former colonies is currently extracted by privileged domestic elites and any simplistic reparations that may be payable from the coffers of former colonial masters will deplete the public purse at a time of deep scarcity, disproportionately affecting minorities (many of whom are descendants of immigrants from former colonial countries that were forcibly displaced), leaving exponentially growing private wealth untouched while germinating increased xenophobia, racism and social fragmentation.

Part II of this book will commence by addressing contemporary environmental degradation from its point of origin in colonial adventurism, tracing the construction of a vicious circle that has compromised many forms of life on the planet, including our own. It will argue for a five-point plan to arrest the continued damage being caused, seek to mitigate its worst excesses, move towards the system overhaul needed and generate the funds for such a transition through the imaginative use of reparations for the crime of unjust enrichment.

In advancing its central argument as articulated above, the book presents five key ideas:

1. Justification for the contemporary resonance and urgency of discussions about past atrocities by showing their causal links to modernity;
2. Discussion over the nature, scope and impact of UN decolonization, as a process that privatized colonial entities reifying hegemonic trends through dominant male paradigms from other places;
3. Explanations of the role ascribed to identity and its impact in gestating polarized spaces where governments charged with addressing issues

are unable or unwilling to respond to the environmental crisis and the ensuing crises of scarcity, conflict, hatred and migration;
4. Suggestion of a model of cooperation between 17 sub-regions to frame behaviour changes necessary that go beyond exclusive reliance on the sovereign State; and
5. Articulation of the contours of a crime of unjust enrichment to address colonial and environmental crime with the aim of generating funding for urgently needed system overhaul.

PART I

Colonial Crime: Challenges, Classification and Cures

1

Combatting the Challenge of Colonial Crime: Ten Hurdles

The discipline and practice of law treads a fine line between seeking to create an ordered society while attempting to make that order one where justice prevails. Served by these twin objects that do not always coincide, the law – mostly codified in writing – has sought to generate concepts, principles, rules and institutions that work to order society but that can also ensure that justice can prevail through rules that are clearly articulated and well calibrated. A broad reading of the history of laws would reflect how rules have evolved to lean gradually closer to justice.[1] It is not by accident that the progressive bend in the arc of time towards justice has come about through greater participation in the legal project first by women and then by others with lived experiences that are very different from the privileged male for whom law was originally a near exclusive preserve.

On the issue of colonial crime, however, the arc of justice is much farther away from being realized. Each passing year makes the probability and method of achieving such accountability less likely. A number of significant obstacles preclude meaningful discussions around colonial crime, some to do with the hardwiring of law and legal systems, others to do with a common combination of resistance and hegemony, through which incumbents of power seek to prevent aspirants from contesting their hold on power. Prior to the attempt at classifying colonial crime, it is important to identify some of these barriers since they are relevant to how crimes could be classified and to potential route maps for charting how they could be overcome. With this in mind, this chapter addresses some of the conceptual and practical challenges at play. It is premised on the statement that in the quest between order and justice, addressing colonial crime is of significant importance.

---

[1] See Joshua Cohen, *The Arc of the Moral Universe and Other Essays* (Cambridge, MA: Harvard University Press, 2010).

In this context law must serve the project of making justice accessible to all without always compromising it when faced with the challenge of maintaining order. This requires an understanding and interpretation of the barriers that exist and societal thinking, followed by a legislative, administrative and judicial commitment to making the changes necessary for these barriers to be overcome.

The intertemporal rule of law

It is a well-established principle in law that actions can only be measured against the standards of the time in which they were committed.[2] This is of fundamental importance to prevent retroactivity and safeguard legal certainty.[3] In other words, if an individual embarked on an act today that is not proscribed, it would be unfair and unlawful for them to be later held to account for that action if their embarking on that act today was undertaken on the basis that it was lawful. Deviations from this basic principle would create significant uncertainty, in that it would always leave open the possibility that an individual may be prosecuted if later generations decide that their actions were generating a legal wrong at a later period.

While the principle is important and is key to maintaining the efficacy of law itself, it has been offered as a justification to suggest that colonial actions which occurred 'a long time ago' now lie beyond scrutiny on this basis. This argument rests on the suggestion that colonization was widespread and systemic with many participants and that looking at this as a crime today, when standards are more evolved, would fall foul of the principle against the retrospective application of law, also referred to as the intertemporal rule of law. It is effectively a different way of saying that 'in those times, such behaviour was deemed acceptable'. Those making such an argument would usually refer to events, discussions and even legal documents that were agreed to between colonial powers to suggest that they were therefore legal, or in other words part of the 'custom' of the time. For it to meet that threshold, two tests would arguably need to be satisfied. First, that there was no law at that time that they were breaking; second, that they were embarking on these actions in the full certainty that what they were doing was lawful. It needs to be added that even if these two tests were passed, there may still be a moral wrong committed, but perhaps it would be difficult to be able to address and prosecute such a wrong as a crime.

---

[2] Taslim Olawale Elias, 'The Doctrine of Intertemporal Law', 74(2) *American Journal of International Law* (1980) 285–307.

[3] For an interesting take on this principle, see Philip J. Brendese, *Segregated Time* (Oxford: Oxford University Press, 2023).

When the various quests of colonization are scrutinized against the backdrop of the laws existing in each of the colonizing entities, it seems trite to suggest that the actions would fall foul of their own domestic laws. Thus the laws prevailing in the home jurisdictions of Britain, France, Spain, Portugal, Belgium, the Netherlands and others were sufficiently developed to hold clear articulations around themes such as when a contract was valid; how property could be bought, sold or transferred; what constituted just compensation; and the use of fraudulent means to achieve a legal end. In addition, non-interference in the domestic affairs of another sovereign State was key to the entire edifice of Westphalian sovereignty. The jurisdictions also had nascent principles around rules governing discrimination, albeit upon the territories themselves. Yet such laws 'at home' were deemed not to apply 'on the road'. To return to the two-factor test posed above, there is a clear answer to the first test, namely the existence of laws at that time as evidenced in domestic laws and also writings and commentary by courts and jurists.[4] However, those laws were either deemed superfluous or irrelevant to colonial activity. One significant ground for the non-application of domestic law abroad stems directly from racism: the colonizers embarked upon their missions in the belief that they were the only civilized beings and that the populations they came across were not recognizable as human and therefore needed the extended hand of civilized notions of law before they could realize their human potential.

Consequently, the second part of the test – their belief that what they were doing was not illegal – could not be answered with as much certainty as the first. This raises the next question, which is: is it important for both questions be answered affirmatively for the action of colonization to be deemed to be a wrongful act that could constitute a crime? Ignorance of the law is not a justiciable defence against the wrong itself. Thus, the existence of law and the adherence to it by colonizers when at home trumps the argument that they determined it was not relevant in their adventures. International lawyers' attitudes to such activities varied tremendously, among the few that deemed it worth commenting upon.[5] The fact that colonization occurred as a consequence of many simultaneous actions that were launched (literally) from many shores at the same time could not exonerate all such actions on the basis that 'everyone was doing it and therefore it was acceptable'. Even the discussions that took place between colonizers such as at the *Berlin West*

---

[4] For an interesting discussion on emigration and the law of nations, see Vincent Chetail, 'Sovereignty and Migration in the Doctrine of the Laws of Nations: An Intellectual History of Hospitality from Vitoria to Vattel', 27(4) *European Journal of International Law* (2016) 901–22.

[5] See Anthony Anghie, *Vattel's International Law from a XXIst Century Perspective* (Leiden: Brill Nijhoff, 2011).

Africa Conference of 1884,[6] which was sanctified by the presence of High Contracting Parties alongside privateers in the colonial adventure, could not be considered adequate in exonerating the subject of their activity, that is, colonization, from being an international wrong. In that sense it would be inadequate for such activities to be shielded from scrutiny or from the finding that they constituted wrongs at the time of their commitment on the basis of the cloak of protection afforded by the rule governing intertemporality.

Legal personality

A key defence that needs to be explored in any discussion around colonial crime is the implicit, and in some cases explicit, suggestion that native populations were not full legal subjects that merited legal protection. This element is more challenging to address than it might seem at first. It is easy to label colonizers as racist, and indeed it is important that this accusation is levelled at them, since a belief in the superiority of their 'race' and culture over others they encountered is central to why colonization proceeded. The question here, however, seeks to go beyond the mere labelling of such activities as racist to examine what defences ought to be pertinent in what can now be accepted as the *post facto* extension of legal subjecthood to native populations. This issue needs to be placed against the backdrop of wider discussions that are only starting now about the anthropocentricity of the human gaze on the planet. Racism was the way in which a narrow line was drawn between an 'us' and a 'them' at the time of colonization. In other words, European colonizers saw lands that were vacant because they did not believe that those that inhabited them were 'civilized' enough to be considered to have property or other rights in the way that they had. Today that line between the 'us' and 'them' may be drawn slightly wider than being strictly restricted to race to offer protection in a more inclusive way to different ethnic, linguistic, religious, racialized and even gendered groups as humans. But despite such sporadic progress that has not been realized widely, the disregarding of other forms of life on the planet remains a reality.

Here, the amorphous notion of 'progress' may assist in untangling the issue.

The oldest forms of rules were written by men to protect their own interests, even if expressed on behalf of their entire families. There is widespread evidence in several cultures to show that these rules often treated women as objects and not full subjects. In other words, the consent of women was not sought for decisions that may affect them or their wider lives. Men

---

[6] For a colonial account, see Sybil Eyre Crowe, *The Berlin West Africa Conference 1884–1885* (Plymouth: Longmans, Green & Co., 1942). Also see Adekeye Adebajo, *The Curse of Berlin: Africa after the Cold War* (Oxford: Oxford University Press, 2013).

were deemed, and in some cases are still deemed, to be adequately legitimized individuals to make decisions on their own behalf and on behalf of everyone else connected to them. Women were required to obey the authority of the man, even in decisions that may directly and exclusively affect them. Society has slowly been evolving in a direction where the notion of subjecthood could be extended to all human beings on an equal basis between women and men. The gender pay gap, lack of representation, unequal rights access and widespread violence against women show the distance yet to be travelled, but the emergence of such equality as a concept was realized through collective action, not least by women themselves in asserting equal rights. That journey has resulted in greater acceptance of the equality between women and men in law (*de jure* equality), even if the realities on the ground (*de facto* equality) lag behind significantly.[7] A similar process has been undertaken with regards to the many millions of people who fall under the broad and generalized title of 'native populations'. An objective reading of history will show that the treatment of such native populations was significantly below the standards of treatment of others at the time. In seeking to ascribe the word 'crime' to any activity, the existence of law prohibiting such activity at the time is important. It remains equally important to distinguish whether the law was being broken or whether it simply did not exist, which could potentially invalidate such acts from being considered unlawful even if they could still be deemed immoral. Thus, the failure to treat native populations on the basis of equality was merely an episode of the law being broken and not synonymous with a denial of personality to such populations. On the other hand, the wilful seizure of lands and resources which centuries later have not been returned, but also that the very foundations of law discussed in this book have been built around that wrong, suggest something systemic rather than episodic. On this basis, rights accruing to 'native populations' are still becoming recognized more clearly and being better codified in international law. Growing awareness of how racism was a key factor in the robbing of native populations of their subjecthood alongside more explicit evidence of this is a major step forward.[8]

This may suggest that the central argument here is the progressive realization of legal subjecthood. At face value that would fall directly within the legal rule governing intertemporality; in other words, that it would be unfair to judge norms of previous eras that failed to recognize subjecthood against more contemporary evolved standards. Except for one important facet. The *laws of nations* (as international law was traditionally referred to) is

---

[7] bell hooks, *Feminist Theory: From Margin to Center* (London/New York: Routledge, 2015).
[8] Achille Mbembe, *Out of the Dark Night: Essays on Decolonization* (New York: Columbia University Press, 2021).

accepted as applicable across the globe, and not only by the wielders of the most dramatic use of power. Yet under international law there is a premise that all law makers, that is, sovereign States, are equal and have the power to make rules that apply to their jurisdiction. In what is referred to as 'customary international law', the rules that they make, assuming they are for a legitimate purpose, form part of the edifice of modern public international law as a source of that law. Under the legal systems and customs of other places, the populations concerned were very much subjects of their systems. Thus, the failure to recognize native populations as true human subjects of law with attendant rights – recognized in law by colonizers with well-developed systems for such recognition in their home jurisdictions – was already a clear wrong at the time it was committed. The argument that this stemmed from a wilfully ignorant perception of superiority, whether based on race or any other factor, is compelling, making hiding behind the argument of a veil of ignorance invalid. Thus, in the encounter between colonizer and native populations, the failure of the colonizer to extend legal subjecthood to the populations which existed under their own systems constituted a legal wrong in the territories where it occurred, irrespective of whether the people wielding the power claimed to realize or admit it.

Statutes of limitations

Any discussions about remedying legal wrongs inevitably come up against the question of statutes of limitations. These are restrictions, usually codified clearly in law, that seek to foreclose the idea of continually available remedies for events that may have occurred beyond a specified time period. The purpose of such limitations is to safeguard against vexatious complaints while avoiding a situation whereby legal uncertainty persists over an action beyond the set period. One obvious reason for the maintenance of statutes of limitations for all kinds of crimes is the difficulties that the passage of time creates in being able to fully illuminate a specific situation. Thus, time may rob or compromise the memories of victims; victims themselves or perpetrators may no longer be where they were imagined to be, assuming they are still alive; and the crimes themselves may have paled into insignificance compared to other events in such a manner that reopening them would generate new legal or moral wrongs.

Certain types of crimes are already exempt from statutes of limitations. This is not only for crimes of high treason, which can always be assessed, but also include murder and large-scale killings, assuming that suitable evidence can be found despite the passage of time. In any case the continued tort of some of the crimes discussed below is such that a clear remedy would exist for the legal wrong still being experienced, which would invalidate the cloak of statutes of limitations. In a scenario of seeking to adjudicate and determine culpability for crimes that occurred a long time ago, some key general principles of law would need to be relied upon. First, that no one can be the judge of their own situation. Statutes of limitations passed in colonizing countries that prevent scrutiny of their actions could be deemed to fall under this principle. In other words, the passage by one actor of a law that unilaterally declares their actions beyond the reach of law ought not to constrain another actor who is not bound by that law from seeking justice.[9] Second, the general principle of the importance that wrongs have remedies must be drawn upon. In the instance of colonial crime, especially where specific damage can be identified and attributed to an entity, and where it is clear that the entity may be able to provide a remedy, that entity cannot hide behind its own unilaterally declared statutes of limitation.

The right to property

The actual violation of property rights is later discussed in greater detail in relation to the classification of colonial crimes. Here, the issue to be addressed is the potential obstacle to overcome in instances where a property may have been illegally seized but its new incumbent has, through actions deemed lawful, gradually gained the title to that property (adverse possession). In understanding colonial crime, as we shall see, the issue of land and property is fundamental, yet, unlike movable possessions, immovable possessions such as land fall foul of the emergence of new ownership, and the new owners would need to be dispossessed for the restitution to take place. Leases dispensed on ancestral domains of Indigenous peoples have become solidified in law over time, and attempts to overturn them run the risk of perpetrating new injustices against owners who may or may not be implicated in the original crime of dispossession. This presents a significant obstacle to realization of remedies in the context of this specific type of colonial crime. The issue of property restitution has been addressed in many jurisdictions outside the colonial context, for example, with regards to properties occupied during internecine wars including in Yugoslavia or in occupations such as in Northern Cyprus.[10] Domestic courts are also addressing the issue of competing claims to property that emanate from Indigenous peoples whose ancestral properties were inadequately protected in law and where territories were seized and transferred to new owners.[11]

---

[9] Carsten Stahn, 'Reckoning with Colonial Injustice: International Law as Culprit and as Remedy?', 33(4) *Leiden Journal of International Law* (2000) 823–35.
[10] See Hans Van Houtte, Hans Das, Bart Delmartino and Lasson Yi, *Postwar Restoration of Property Rights under International Law* (Cambridge: Cambridge University Press, 2008).
[11] Antonietta Di Blase and Valentina Vadi, *The Inherent Rights of Indigenous Peoples in International Law* (Rome: Roma Tre Press, 2020).

With restitution of land remaining a significant issue in a post-colonial context, not least where the resources on that land have been depleted or continue to be exploited for profit, significant advances will be needed in the law to address the strengths of competing claims, those dispossessed in the past, and those who risk being dispossessed in the present to account for a past violation.[12]

The situation ought to be easier in claims concerning movable properties such as cultural artefacts, but this has proven to be an equally stubborn issue to resolve. Such artefacts, frequently deemed of spiritual and material importance to communities, are often stored in museums of former colonial powers where they have arrived via a process or system that may have been legitimated during colonial rule, though that legitimation process is now hotly contested. Arguments for the return of such properties are growing and will likely continue to grow, depleting museums where they currently sit, with the need for investment in similar museums in former colonized countries.[13]

Validity of contracts

In many instances the text of laws, including preferential treatment of former colonial powers or the undue preference given to specific commercial activities negotiated on the basis of the clear superiority of a departing colonial power over the newly emerging State, could be of dubious value. In some instances, notably Britain, legislation was passed to make all such contracts valid in advance of subsequent claims challenging their legality.[14] Pushing back against such arrangements would be relatively easy in a contemporary context, but seeking to claw back the damage done by them is significantly more difficult. Seeking to invalidate these contracts, whether they were performed through unequal treaties or private contractual agreements instituted through fraud, to gain just recompense is of significant importance. Many such contracts, including around historical oil and drilling concessions, may still be fiercely enforced and protected by a phalanx of lawyers despite their unequal terms.[15]

---

[12] Brenna Bhandar, *Colonial Lives of Property: Law, Land and Racial Regimes of Ownership* (Durham, NC: Duke University Press, 2018).

[13] Nosmot Gbadamosi, 'Stealing Africa: How Britain Looted the Continent's Art', *Unpack the Past Features, Al Jazeera*, 12 October 2021.

[14] See, for example, UK Government, *Colonial Laws Validity Act 1865* (29 June 1865), which is labelled as 'an Act to remove doubts as to the validity of Colonial Laws'.

[15] Everisto Benyera, *Breaking the Colonial Contract: From Oppression to Autonomous Decolonial Futures* (London: Lexington Books, 2021).

Establishing victimhood

A significant difficulty that has emerged in discussions of colonial crime is exactly how victimhood should be established. With many types of colonial crimes, which will be discussed later, it remains important to identify clear parameters regarding those directly impacted by the wrong discussed and those who were indirectly impacted. The passage of time, lack of records, dispersal of communities and intermixing, sometimes between descendants of victims and descendants of their oppressors, makes determining the class of persons who could be deemed victims and who belong to the class difficult to establish.[16] The distance of time and unequal access to potential remedies also make it hard to determine whether the remedy sought will be fairly distributed. Anthropocentricity, even in an approach to colonial crime, will almost inevitably mean that non-human victims, including species made extinct by some of these actions, may be ignored in identifications of victimhood. The extent to which costs could nonetheless be recovered for the protection of other species equally under threat ought to still factor into calculations.

The general versus the specific

The issue of determining the specific instance of crime as distinct from the general critique of colonialism is perhaps the next most significant reason why discussions of colonial crime have been stunted, after the primary reason: the reticence of former colonial powers to admit such discussions.[17] The *Durban World Conference on Racism* attempted to open up the issue on reparations in a general manner, which initially gained traction among the preparatory caucuses in the lead-up to the conference.[18] Yet as these discussions progressed, they revealed that any discourse on reparations for colonialization varied tremendously depending on the region, the colonial power concerned, the community affected and the time period when the worst excesses occurred. This signalled that the discussion itself meant very disparate things to different people, and the points did not always cohere around a theme or remedy. While it remains possible to address the entirety of

---

[16] See, for instance, Mahmood Mamdani, *When Victims Become Killers: Colonialism, Nativism and Genocide in Rwanda* (Princeton, NJ: Princeton University Press, 2001).

[17] For an attempt to provide an insightful history in relation to the Spanish-speaking world (written in English), see Fernando Cervantes, *Conquistadores: A New History* (London: Penguin, 2020). Also see Pascal Bruckner, *The Tyranny of Guilt: An Essay on Western Masochism* (Princeton, NJ: Princeton University Press, 2010).

[18] See Sylvanna M. Falcón, *Power Interrupted: Antiracist and Feminist Activism Inside the United Nations* (Seattle: University of Washington Press, 2016).

colonialism itself as the crime, the seeking of remedies brings key challenges. First, if the quest is to be determinate, it would need to be precise in achieving the pronouncement of specific legal liability, followed by an appropriate form of remedy whether that be restitution, reparation or compensation. The lack of a general framework to think through colonial liability forms an equally difficult barrier to overcome. This work builds the argument that the route to addressing this is through three specific but interrelated strands of work: first, a wider societal acceptance that colonization has contributed to a significant drain of resources through illegitimate means from the global South, which has contributed to scarcity and upheaval there while hardwiring a culture that venerates theft as entrepreneurship; second, the emergence of a deeper understanding of the extent to which that process has created and then actively hastened the climate and migration crises; and third, that such wrongs have to be addressed through remedies designed in such a manner that those most responsible for the damage are entrusted with greatest liability in paying for it. It is also important that the discussion is undertaken with sensitivity and does not paint all citizens of former colonial countries as personally liable for such wrongs. Once a broad acceptance (with adequate room for those who dissent from the idea) is arrived at, the next step would be to think through the specificities of the alleged crime as well as its effects, impacts and potential remedies.

Historical verification

The presentation of history as a linear definitive story is a significant contributor to modern polarization on matters beyond discussions on colonization. When disseminated through an education system, this outlook imposes a set of pre-agreed all-encompassing 'truths' onto a population who subsequently view deviations from that truth as mistruths not to be trusted. Yet history needs to be imagined as an internet page with hyperlinks rather than as a set of printed textbooks, since the events, places and personalities reflected are often based on the choice of the narrator and their proximity to power. The emphasis on male (his)stories are a case in point: they fail to explain that while the men portrayed were going about matters the historian deemed important, women and other men were simultaneously pursuing other objectives that may have been as important or perhaps even more salient, but which were not deemed by the historian to be relevant enough to warrant documentation. By presenting history as a single narrative that occurred in a place, other spaces, perspectives, actors and events are crowded out. The example of the British history mentioned in the Introduction is a case in point.

As diverse ethno-religious, social and linguistic identities that exist within populations come to the fore, newer articulations of history that were previously submerged, eclipsed or deliberately ignored have begun to emerge. In some instances these histories directly contradict events, actors and narratives that have been deeply inserted and respected. Some of these may be verifiably accurate; others may be perspectives coloured by the positionality of the narrator or the critic, to at least the same extent as the originally embedded narrative. Treating alternative histories as 'revisionist' assumes that the single 'original' narrative presented was completely accurate in every forensic detail and did not imbibe conscious or unconscious bias. This attributes values to historians that would make them completely abnormal in relation to the rest of the population at any time in our chequered human histories. It fails to acknowledge that proximity to power is important in being able to tell the story of how power was exercised. Equally, it appears to legitimate a single strand of human existence of a given time, place or event (that is, the official version) as the only valid perspective on that time, place or event. The deeply flawed narratives of events, time, actors, victors, 'losers', civilizations, 'savages', spaces, resources and communities, among other factors, enabled colonial crime to occur in the first place. Any attempt to mitigate its worst impact would at least need to establish that the received and ready-written histories that dominate the archives in colonial and former colonial States are at best inadequate in telling the whole story and are in many instances politically motivated narratives that do not stem from an understanding of the equal and inherent dignity and worth of all human civilizations. In this sense it is instructive to note that Guatemala addressed its immediate past of genocide against Indigenous communities through a historical verification commission, among other remedies.[19]

Calculating colonial tort

The precise value and nature of the reparation sought for colonial crime presents another specific obstacle that detracts from its articulation. As indicated at the start of this chapter, the question is asked as to why the offspring of colonizers ought to bear the burden of making good something they did not do. This argument is augmented by the real sense of scarcity that is prevalent in former colonial countries where poverty and inequality is growing as a factor and underemployment hinders the prospects of the emergence of vibrant socio-economic spaces. Greater privatization has meant that the public purse has shrunk, and the idea that the State should now start making provision for *ex gratia* payments from its narrowing revenues leads to a straightforward denial and closure of the discussion and may even fuel

---

[19] See Victoria Sandford, *Buried Secrets: Truth and Human Rights in Guatemala* (London: Palgrave Macmillan, 2003).

a growing sense of entitlement mixed with xenophobia. Where culpability has been expressed, such as famously by Japan for the actions of the Imperial Japanese army in recruiting Korean 'comfort women',[20] or the Dutch apology in the first part of 2023 for its role in the slave trade,[21] questions immediately follow about the value of the tort being acknowledged, how it may be calculated or dispensed and who the beneficiaries may be.[22]

Discussions around such tort have already featured in law, most successfully in the compensations and other remedies sought and received for war crimes against Jewish communities during World War II.[23] Yet the idea of opening up the discussions to a broader remit of crimes that were committed over the course of a century and a half is daunting.[24] Each of the classes of crime that have been identified is commented upon later in the book, but suffice to say at this stage that damages for some types of colonial crime are easier to ascertain than for others: some are likely to be more arbitrary than others and some are likely to be baseless in terms of any specific reality since they will depend on the nature of the crime, the ability of the victims to press for payment and the decision and ability of the accused to pay or refuse payment. In other words, it is of significant importance to nullify the idea that there could be a simple forensic payment schedule for colonial crime. This may result in outcomes where similar crimes in different locations warrant vastly different payments due to a host of politically important considerations. There are also legitimate questions that may have to be determined on a case-by-case basis as to what proportion of any remedy or payment being made is restorative as opposed to punitive.

Remedies wider than compensation

A final obstacle looms in those instances where restitution or compensation may not to be the end goal of a determination of culpability for colonial

---

[20] Pyong Gap Min, *Korean 'Comfort Women': Military Brothels, Brutality and the Redress Movement* (New Brunswick, NJ: Rutgers University Press, 2021). Also see the translation into English from Japanese, Yoshiaki Yoshimi, *Comfort Women: Sexual Slavery in the Japanese Military During World War II* (New York: Columbia University Press, 2000).

[21] See 'Dutch King Apologizes for the Netherlands' Role in in Slavery, *CNN News*, 1 July 2023, available at https://www.youtube.com/watch?v=aM8I5Z5MYdA. Also see 'Dutch King Willem-Alexander apologies for colonial-era slavery', *Al Jazeera News*, 1 July 2023, available at https://www.aljazeera.com/news/2023/7/1/dutch-king-willem-alexander-apologises-for-colonial-era-slavery.

[22] Olúfẹ́mi Táíwò, *Reconsidering Reparations* (Oxford: Oxford University Press, 2022).

[23] Avi Beker (ed), *The Plunder of Jewish Property during the Holocaust* (Hampshire: Palgrave Macmillan, 2001).

[24] Mwene Mushanga, *Slavery and Colonialism: Man's Inhumanity to Man for which Africans Demand Reparations* (Nairobi: Law Africa Publishing, 2011).

crime. This includes circumstances where the divisions between the former colonial power and the Indigenous population have become blurred through intermarriage, or where the discrimination that has occurred has led to the construction of systemic bias that needs to be addressed in ways other than through the exclusive payment of compensation or the return of artefacts. Such instances may require much deeper societal reckoning that pertains to identities and whether the national identities trumpeted are adequately framed in relation to the dominant history. The example of Aotearoa (New Zealand) comes to mind whereby the genuine attempt at reconciliation between the Māori and Parekha (White European population) also resulted in a reassessment of the national identity of New Zealand as monolingual and European. It involved recognition of New Zealand's rich history that predated the arrival of the White settlers but also the attribution of newly recognized material importance to the Māori language and symbols.[25]

---

[25] Carwyn Jones, *New Treaty, New Tradition: Reconciling New Zealand and Maori Law* (Vancouver: UBC Press, 2016).

2

Classifying Colonial Crime: Seven Deadly Sins

As established in the previous chapter, discussions around colonial crime are the source of much polarization, involving significant sentiments: feelings of loss and theft on the part of those who view themselves as its victims and a range of responses, from guilt to indifference, on the part of those who either stand accused or feel threatened by the discussion. Yet the discussions also vary depending on the claim, based on a range of (non-exhaustive) factors that include location, timeframe, colonizer, contestation of facts and events, victimhood, type of purported event, level of documentation and evidence, and remedies sought. Rather than offer a detailed historical summary, this chapter seeks to construct a typography of colonial crime, with a view to establishing classifications that may assist in determining how they could be thought of, investigated, documented and engaged with in a meaningful manner, whether that be mitigation or repair. The list is neither definitive nor complete. It is possible to frame additional categories and sub-categories, or even to merge some categories. One reason for any discrepancies that may arise lies in the ambition of attempting a classification of this nature. It requires a strong grasp of histories, but many of these remain unwritten while others are incomplete, poorly constructed or biased. The printed word can only be of limited assistance in fully understanding the contours of each crime, whereas going beyond the written word raises questions around the veracity of the information and how it was collected.

The list in this chapter is intended to kick-start conversation, mindful that in the oral histories of colonization that exist in communities, or in the histories that exist in multiple minority and Indigenous languages, there may well be facts, evidence and documentation or validation that either reifies or directly contests or contradicts the portrayals that underpin this classification. With so much of colonization involving the denial of legitimacy to groups, it would be inappropriate and disingenuous to attempt or offer any comprehensive list without the caveat that it is based on understandings from readings of histories that are by definition limited, in terms of the framers' bias, readers' access and the capabilities and training of the writers' interpretation and attribution of meaning to them. Within this significant limitation the rest of this chapter is divided into seven sections, outlining what are proposed as the seven deadly sins of colonial crime. The crimes are identified as occurring during the colonization journey, with the first two committed in the acquisition of sovereignty over the lands themselves and thus deemed systemic, the next category pertaining to behaviours during the maintenance of sovereignty over the territories, and the third set regarding crimes around the extinguishment of sovereignty and subsequent behaviour.

Subjecthood and objecthood

The idea of 'subjecthood' is an important concept in the evolution of laws across jurisdictions. By virtue of this centrally anthropocentric premise, it is assumed that human beings, with their purported inherent dignity and worth codified much later through human rights law, are equal to each other. These principles stem from natural law but are written into the deepest foundations of established legal systems, are omnipresent in religious teachings and are captured in general principles such as equity and fairness. The principle of non-discrimination has also been well established for centuries in customary law and forms an equally strong platform on which the edifice of law it built. The fundamental difference that exists in law and forms a starting point to colonization is the distinction between a subject and an object. Thus, a subject could be distinguished from an object in law in that the subject is bound by the rules created and as a consequence of their deemed human consciousness also would have the right to consent to decisions that are made that impact them. Objects on the other hand are not deemed to be conscious beings and therefore not expected to follow rules that have been established without their consent. The anthropocentricity of such a position has gradually come under scrutiny through growing acceptance of the fact that other non-humans who share the space with us are also conscious beings. Human-made customary laws, traditional laws, formal laws and other rule-creating and rule-giving systems, whatever their origin, have historically distinguished between subjects, offering preferential treatment to some compared to others. Thus, for instance, legal systems still adhere closely to origins in patriarchy in failing to recognize the equal subjecthood of women to men.[1] Similarly, there was also significant differentiation between the rights of citizens as opposed to non-citizens, or in Roman law times between the laws that were applied to the patricians compared to those to which plebians

---

[1] Sylvia Tamale, *Decolonization and Afro-Feminism* (Wakefield QC: Daraja Press, 2020).

were deemed to be subjected.[2] Yet what was uncontested was that human beings by virtue of being human had certain, albeit differentiated, rights.

However, far from recognizing the equality of all human beings as reflected in their own domestic laws and underpinning beliefs, colonialism took place by deliberately obscuring the humanity of populations that were met on colonial adventures.[3] These native communities were often described in the annals of literature as sub-human, and as a consequence a distinction was made in the minds of the colonizers which still has an echo: between the rights of 'civilized nations' and the rights outside that realm. Civilized, in this instance, referred to a specific form of activities that were deemed civilized, with all that failed to acknowledge or respect these, or that deviated in any other way, deemed not to have acquired the rights that were otherwise acknowledged as existing. Consider the text of Article 9 of the *Statute of the International Court of Justice*, still in force today:

> At every election, the electors shall bear in mind not only that the persons to be elected should individually possess the qualifications required, but also that in the body as a whole the representation of the main forms of civilization and of the principal legal systems of the world should be assured.[4]

Formulated in the context of the election of judges to serve on the bench of the highest court in the world, there is a clear suggestion that there are 'main' – and as a consequence 'peripheral' – 'forms of civilization' within the human population; and in addition that there are 'principal legal systems of the world' and as a consequence there are those less worthy of being represented on the global judicial decision-making body. The vast dissemination of Western legal systems through colonization, coupled with the belief within that worldview of it serving as the sole exclusive universal – as opposed to pluralist – system, necessitated the erasure of all other forms of rule-making as 'law' on the lazy and prejudiced assumption that they were not civilized enough to warrant consideration or even recognition. Needless to reiterate, perhaps, but this dismissal was not arrived at after any genuine attempts to engage with the substance of other rule-making regimes. Rather, it was based on pure arrogance and ignorance. A good example of

---

[2] Peter Garnsey, *Social Status and Legal Privilege in the Roman Empire* (London: Clarendon Press, 1970).

[3] Russell L. Barsh, 'Indigenous Peoples in the 1990s: From Object to Subject in International Law?', 7 *Harvard Human Rights Journal* (1994) 33–62.

[4] Article 9, *Statute of the International Court of Justice*, 18 April 1946 (33 UNTS 993, UKTS 67 (1946) Cmd 7015, 3 Bevans 1179, 59 Stat 1055, 145 BSP 832, TS No 993), OXIO 95

this is how China, the culture considered to have the longest documented history was ignored, probably on the primary basis that Mandarin was beyond the reach of European policy makers and historians and thus could not be accessed as easily.

There are several other historical manifestations of discussions concerning the value of native humanity in the historical annals, two of which are shared here as an illustration. The *Valladolid Controversy*, which took place in the 1700s between Bartolomé de las Casas and the Spanish Crown, is a good example to start with.[5] The controversy stems from a context where the world had already been divided into hemispheres by Spain and Portugal to avoid clashing against each other on colonial adventures.[6] Meeting in a place called Tordesillas,[7] the two seafaring powers agreed an actual line on the globe, where one half was deemed to fall under the sphere of influence of the Spanish Crown while the other constituted the Portuguese sphere.[8] It is worth recollecting the Christian origins of European colonization here, which stems from, among other justifications and pursuits, a Papal Bull from the 15th century AD which commanded Portugal and Spain to take on the mantle of making the world a more Christian place.[9] Such a command came at a time when Portuguese naval powers were in the ascendancy and provided a shot in the arm to these activities, enabling them to be justified in the name of Christianity. This, of course, provided the necessary pre-ordained justification for the commercial quest by European States of what they deemed to be uninhabited lands, with a supervening ideology, namely the 'civilization of natives'. During this era native populations were treated in much the same manner as the human population has treated the rest of life on the planet. If today there is understanding of the anthropocentricity of human actions, in the colonial era discussed here, that anthropocentricity did not even include the whole of humanity.

The inhumane treatment of such populations, including brutal massacres, killing, rape, subjugation and domination, raised alarm against some who saw this behaviour as barbaric. But in defending such behaviour, a discussion commenced that has been recorded in history as the Valladolid Controversy. At the heart of the matter was the question of the personhood and 'soul'

---

[5] For a dramatization, see Jean-Claude Carrière and Richard Nelson, *The Controversy of Valladolid* (New York: Dramatists Play Service, Inc., 2005).

[6] See Saliha Belmessous (ed), *Native Claims: Indigenous Law Against Empire 1500–1920* (Oxford: Oxford University Press, 2012).

[7] For a summary in English, see *Encyclopaedia Britannica*, available at https://www.britannica.com/event/Treaty-of-Tordesillas.

[8] Tamar Herzog, *Frontiers of Possession: Spain and Portugal in Europe and the Americas* (Boston: Harvard University Press, 2015).

[9] *Papal Bull Inter Caetera*, AD 1493.

of native populations. The narrative was advanced that such populations sat low in what was presented as a hierarchy where the White European races were at the top, closer in resemblance to the God that they worshipped and therefore construed in their own (male) image and likeness. From this zenith the hierarchy descended via Native Americans (still called Indians after Columbus' misadventure), Africans and then via apes to other animals. The famous racist diagram of purported brain sizes of the different categories of people was offered as a justification for why some native populations were closer to animals than human beings. In advocating for the rights of such populations, Bartolomé de las Casas challenged these ideas, though his position was viewed as being controversial.[10]

The incident is a clear demonstration of how the Portuguese and Spanish Crowns in their acquisition of territory did not believe that the natives they encountered en route needed to be acknowledged any more than the flora and fauna that they confronted along the way, and as a consequence the territories they encountered for the first time were deemed *terra nullius* – open to 'discovery' – which is still how the history of the Americas is narrated. There is also significant evidence of the extent to which their scorched-earth tactics yielded the genesis of the climate crisis that will be explored in greater detail in Part II of this book.[11] The colonization of the Americas proceeded from that point on the basis that there was almost a God-given duty upon humanity to put 'unused' land to cultivation to generate a return rather than leaving it fallow like the native communities that inhabited them. This was subsequently justified in economic theory.[12] In fact the stereotyping and judgement against a fixed set of values went further. Native populations in the Americas were deemed lazy and not very strong in comparison to Africans, who were deemed to be superior in musculature, with this forming a justification for the transatlantic slave trade that has significantly altered the history of the Americas and the world.[13]

Another incident in a very different setting that demonstrates the lack of human personality attributable to native populations occurred in a discussion around the use of *dum-dum* bullets towards the end of the 19th century. The bullets were named after the location of a munitions factory in Calcutta, which the British had deemed would be the capital of their

---

[10] David M. Lantigua, *Infidels and Empire in a New World Order: Early Modern Spanish Contributions to Legal Thought* (Cambridge: Cambridge University Press, 2020).

[11] Emmanuel Kreike, *Scorched Earth: Environmental Warfare as a Crime Against Humanity and Nature* (Princeton, NJ: Princeton University Press, 2022).

[12] Ronald M. Chilcote, *The Political Economy of Imperialism: Critical Appraisals* (New York: Springer Science, 1999). Also see Vincent Barnett (ed), *Routledge Handbook of the History of Global Economic Thought* (Abingdon/New York: Routledge, 2015).

[13] Patrick Manning, *Slave Trades, 1500–1800* (eBook, Routledge, 2015).

colonial acquisitions in India. The bullets were not dissimilar to cluster bombs, except they were fired out of a musket. Rather than emerge as a single shot that could pierce an enemy, these munitions would shatter into shrapnel, creating incredible damage within the range of their trajectory. Progressive individuals among the colonial powers, having witnessed the damage these bullets could do on a battlefield, called for a ban on the use and production of such weapons, with a discussion ensuing in the House of Lords. Writing in the *British Medical Journal*, Surgeon-Major J.B. Hamilton had stated, in relation to a previous Mark II bullet that was the precursor to the dum-dum bullets:

> This bullet was complained of as not having stopping power – that is, it passed through the limbs or body without causing immediate collapse unless some vital part or important bone was struck. In European warfare this was of comparatively little consequence, as civilised man is much more susceptible than savages. As a rule when a 'white man' is wounded he has had enough, and is quite ready to drop out of the ranks and go to the rear; but the savage, like the tiger, is not so impressionable, and will go on fighting even when desperately wounded.[14]

The *dum-dum* bullet itself was developed and deployed by the British Army in India in 1897. But rather than worry about the impact this would have on 'savages', emphasis was placed instead on the efficacy of its ability to destroy. A columnist for the *Daily Telegraph* and later Prime Minister of Britain who is still venerated despite evidence of his persistently racist ideology, wrote:

> The power of the new Lee-Metford rifle with the new Dum-Dum bullet – it is now called, though not officially, the '*ek-dum*' bullet – is tremendous. ... Of the bullet it may be said, that its stopping power is all that could be desired. The Dum-Dum bullet, though not explosive, is expansive. The original Lee-Metford bullet was a pellet of lead covered by a nickel case with an opening at the base. In the improved bullet this outer case has been drawn backward, making the hole in the base a little smaller and leaving the lead at the tip exposed. The result is a wonderful and from the technical point of view a beautiful machine. On striking a bone this causes the bullet to 'set up' or spread out, and it then tears and splinters everything before it, causing wounds which in the body must be generally mortal and in any limb necessitate amputation.[15]

---

[14] J.B. Hamilton, 'The Evolution of the Dum-Dum Bullet', *British Medical Journal* (14 May 1898) 1250–1.
[15] Winston Churchill, *The Story of the Malakand Field Force* (London, 1898) 287–8.

The antidote to such a colonial crime – the principle of equality of *all* human beings – is already written into every global constitution; in that sense it could be argued that in the design phase this colonial crime has already been addressed. Yet the racist legacy perpetrated by individuals who are still venerated rather than even questioned is writ large. Their refusal to extend recognition of the legal personality as configured in their own legal systems on an equal basis is indicative of a deep-seated sense of racial superiority and far from bringing civilization, as their rhetoric may have claimed, it brought inbuilt criminality through means that still haunt legal systems. In contemporary times it is Indigenous peoples, and others including stateless communities, that are denied legal personality, as a consequence of which they are denied basic accesses needed to meaningfully acquire, articulate and claim the rights that ostensibly flow to them by virtue of being human.[16] The cost of such a crime is also visible in the fragmentation that exists within societies where some populations – often distinguished on the basis of their different ethnic lineage or heritage, racialized identity, religion or language – are deprived of equal enjoyment of their rights. The subject–object boundary reveals the clear line drawn between European civilization and natives on the basis of their differentiated perceived value.[17] This manifestation is even clearer in the context of Indigenous peoples who were dispossessed from their lands on the basis that their existence did not constitute adequate recognisable legal personality, as we shall see.

Acquisition of title to territory

Rules on property law are often well established and form a significant bedrock of former colonial powers. The link between property and discrimination is a significant fault line that emerged from European colonization to form a central theme that has generated significant colonial and contemporary crimes. It is worth reflecting that at its very origin even the spirit of democracy, as derived from Ancient Greece, has property bias baked in.[18] This bias has since become a key ingredient to the acquisition, use, possession and claim of territory against all comers.[19]

---

[16] This is often referenced to Arendt's famous questioning of the rights of man as the right to have rights; see Hannah Arendt, *The Origins of Totalitarianism* (New York: Harcourt Brace Jovanovich, 1973).

[17] See Gerrit W. Wong, 'Standards of Civilization Today', in Mehdi Mozaffari (ed), *Globalization and Civilizations* (London: Routledge, 2002) 77–96.

[18] Kurt A. Raaflaub, Josiah Ober and Robert W. Wallace, *Origins of Democracy in Ancient Greece* (Berkeley, CA: University of California Press, 2007).

[19] Brenna Bhandar, *Colonial Lives of Property: Law, Land and Racial Regimes of Ownership* (Durham, NC: Duke University Press, 2018).

Even in the celebrated Ancient Greek democracy it was only 'free men' who owned property that were given voice in the determination of the views of the demos. These individual men, who among their vast properties also held slaves, were given the mandate to create the rules around which their societies would be calibrated. Thus, the earliest forms of representative democracy were premised on a differentiated value attributed to those within the demos. Women could not hold property or vote, neither could slaves or other non-propertied men. This elevated status for men who 'owned' property, and the belief that nature (land, seas, rivers, mountains) could be claimed, acquired and then safeguarded against others while ignoring all other forms of life on that territory stands at the anthropocentric heart of the colonial project, and as this book will argue, it is manifest in the construction of a system that has reified the extractive economic model. In fact, one definition of colonialism could even be articulated as 'a process of territorial acquisition' whereupon the colony becomes a 'sociopolitical organization' while the colonization itself thereby justifies a system of domination. The colonial system thrives while 'an entire society is robbed of its historical line of development, externally manipulated and transformed according to the needs and interests of its colonial rulers'.[20]

At a micro level this involved the designation of land as a factor of production which could simply be claimed by individuals and 'put to use' to 'serve mankind'. The vastness of territories in Africa, Asia and the Americas was used as justification for making them open to acquisition since, as deemed above, the native populations who lived upon them were not accepted as having adequate personality for them to be able to 'possess' the lands. Emmerich Vattel's pronouncement on this is worth reproducing to show how the anthropocentric and Europeanized vision of the world contributed to the building of systems that appropriated property.

> The cultivation of the soil deserves the attention of the government, not only on account of the invaluable advantages that flow from it, but from its being an obligation imposed by nature on mankind. The whole earth is destined to feed its inhabitants; but this it would be incapable of doing if it were uncultivated. Every nation is then obliged by the law of nature to cultivate the land that has fallen to its share; and it has no right to enlarge its boundaries, or have recourse to the assistance of other nations, but in proportion as the land in its possession is incapable of furnishing it with necessaries. Those

---

[20] Jürgen Osterhammel, as cited in Natsu Taylor Saito, *Settler Colonialism, Race and the Law: Why Structural Racism Persists* (New York: New York University Press, 2020) 43.

nations (such as the ancient Germans, and some modern Tartars) who inhabit fertile countries, but disdain to cultivate their lands and choose rather to live by plunder, are wanting to themselves, are injurious to all their neighbors, and deserve to be extirpated as savage and pernicious beasts. There are others, who, to avoid labor, choose to live only by hunting, and their flocks. This might, doubtless, be allowed in the first ages of the world, when the earth, without cultivation, produced more than was sufficient to feed its small number of inhabitants. But at present, when the human race is so greatly multiplied, it could not subsist if all nations were disposed to live in that manner. Those who still pursue this idle mode of life, usurp more extensive territories than, with a reasonable share of labor, they would have occasion for, and have, therefore, no reason to complain, if other nations, more industrious and too closely confined, come to take possession of a part of those lands. Thus, though the conquest of the civilized empires of Peru and Mexico was a notorious usurpation, the establishment of many colonies on the continent of North America might, on their confining themselves within just bounds, be extremely lawful. The people of those extensive tracts rather ranged through than inhabited them.[21]

Vattel, revered as a true visionary of public international law, felt no need to attribute his pronouncements to any scientific basis, nor to reflect even momentarily on what the value of other forms of human existence on the planet might be based upon. It was undoubtedly beyond his limited imagination to be able to understand how anthropocentric his vision was, which probably already departed significantly from many Indigenous communities' more sophisticated belief about the human and natural world's symbiotic interaction. The innate value attributed to land was already clear in Roman times, when all lands that came under the sovereignty of Rome were deemed occupied and thus subjects of Rome, while all non-Roman properties were deemed to be *terra nullius*, that is, blank territories that were open to claimants. Vice President Judge Ammoun drew on Mohammed Bedjaoui in the Western Sahara Case (Advisory Opinion of the International Court of Justice, 1975) to the following effect which captures the essence of the hypocrisy of what constitutes *terra nullius*:

In a bold survey of history from antiquity up to modern times, he distinguishes, with consummate skill, three major epochs:

---

[21] Emmerich de Vattel, *The Law of Nations or the Principles of Natural Law* (1758) Book 1, Chapter 7 'Of the Cultivation of the Soil' para. 81.

(1) Roman antiquity, when any territory which was not Roman was nullius.
(2) The epoch of the great discoveries of the sixteenth and seventeenth centuries, during which any territory not belonging to a Christian sovereign was nullius.
(3) The nineteenth century, during which any territory which did not belong to a so-called civilized State was nullius.

In short, the concept of *terra nullius*, employed at all periods, to the brink of the twentieth century, to justify conquest and colonization, stands condemned. It is well known that in the sixteenth century Francisco de Vittoria protested against the application to the American Indians, in order to deprive them of their lands, of the concept of *res nullius*.[22]

This broad time span was also a period where the rules of international law were basically determined by European States awarding and recognizing each other's sovereignty while determining that all other territories were effectively fair game for being occupied. As Saito puts it:

The logic and law of colonialism were developed by and among those European states that recognized each other as 'civilised'. International law as we now know it evolved from agreements initially entered into between these powers, each interested in minimizing conflicts with others so that its economic and military resources could be put to more profitable ends. The sovereignty of non-European societies was not recognized within this legal framework, and the colonizing states developed what were, in essence, non-complete agreements to respect each other's territories not encompassed within recognized states.[23]

The claim and hold over territory thus lies at the very root of the subsequent sovereignty claimed. Two episodes of the colonial crime with regard to the acquisition of territory that occurred in vastly different settings are worth highlighting. First, the acquisition of land by Cecil Rhodes that he proceeded to name after himself, and second, the European encounter with the Māori as captured in the *Treaty of Waitangi*.

As European competition for African lands heated up in the late 1880s, South Africa had already been claimed as falling under the sovereignty of the

---

[22] Separate Opinion of Vice President Judge Ammoun, *ICJ Reports* (1975) 86.
[23] Natsu Taylor Saito, *Settler Colonialism, Race and the Law: Why Structural Racism Persists* (New York: New York University Press, 2020) 46.

British Crown. Benefitting from this capture of territory far from the lands of the metropolitan State, 'entrepreneurs' such as Cecil Rhodes commenced to seek ways to further grow and consolidate their wealth. A driving element to his greed was the establishment of a Cape to Cairo railway line which, among other benefits he believed would follow, would enable him to request a British charter to proceed to acquire and govern what was the area referred to in historical documents as the Zambezi–Limpopo watershed. The existence of the Ndebele Kingdom under the sovereignty of King Lobengula was an obstacle. Rhodes sought to resolve this by first signing a treaty of friendship between the British and the peoples of Matabeleland in 1888 before dispatching a three-man team known as the Rudd Commission, headed by Charles Rudd, to engage with King Lobengula. The team led by Rudd beat a London-based syndicate who were also seeking to achieve the same aim. The Commission tricked King Lobengula into agreeing mining concessions in October 1888 which, despite being disavowed by the King subsequently, became the basis for a royal charter granted to Rhodes' *British South Africa Company* a year later. This was followed by White occupation of Mashonaland in 1890 and the establishment of administrative rule that eventually led to the declaration of the State of Rhodesia by 1895.

The *Rudd Concession* as a document in international law makes interesting reading in terms of the validity of treaties. Via this document Rhodes supposedly acquired not only the sole rights to mine throughout the jurisdiction under King Lobengula but also the right to use force to defend the concession against all comers. This was considered adequate compensation for a few weapons and a monetary stipend. Despite contestations from Lobengula on the grounds of fraud and deceit by the agents, including as to how the written account – in a language the King was not familiar with – deferred from the oral discussions of the day, the agreement was not only deemed valid and enforceable, it formed the basis for the award of the subsequent grant of the royal charter indicating official approval from the British Crown for these activities. King Lobengula's attempts to invalidate the contract for fraud included the dispatch of emissaries to Queen Victoria, as well as attempts to join forces with a German businessman to regain the lost territory. Instead, Rhodes, after colluding with the rival syndicate and buying off the German businessman, gathered political support that eventually led to the 'award' of his coveted charter. One of the main reasons why his Cape to Cairo railway dream was not realized was because he ran into other European sovereign States on African soil, whose own ill-acquired lands he could not simply claim on the basis of his cunning and deceit.

The encounter between Rhodes and King Lobengula emphasizes exactly how biased the narration of history is and underscores the power of the historian in shaping future perspectives. In European narratives Cecil Rhodes and his agents negotiated with the Ndebele King though he is barely acknowledged as being a sovereign. During the deliberations that led to the *Rudd Commission*, he is claimed to have entered into an agreement to provide concessions on his land in return for a sum of money and some rifles. There are reports of a verbal discussion about the number of White workers who would accompany the mining operation but no reference to any subsequent occupation of the lands.

Despite the contestations and questions that were raised both during and after the *Rudd Concession*, the contract was deemed valid as reflected in the subsequent grant of a royal charter. This indicates a belief that both parties understood the considerations that they were contracting to, that the agreement was reached without any deceit, fraud or coercion and that the subsequent transfer of lands to Rhodes was achieved within the terms of the contract. The European historical narrative goes further to paint Rhodes as a visionary who then commenced the challenging task of taking fallow lands and putting them to cultivation, generating yields and building wealth that would eventually make the emerging State of Rhodesia a thriving economy. The narrative even goes on to suggest that as the economy began to take root, other [European] entrepreneurs arrived and the prosperity within the colony grew steadily. The entire venture is credited with producing work and gainful employment with the construction of quality establishments, ensuring that the population had direct access to education and benefitted from the latest thinking in science and the arts. In keeping with the ostensible Western civilization mission, talented Africans came through the system and benefitted, finding gainful work in the administration of the territories while participating on the basis of near equality with the original European entrepreneurs.

While this history was contested by former Zimbabwean President Robert Mugabe through aggressive dispossession and the encouragement of the occupation of White lands commencing in 2000, in the UK Cecil Rhodes was venerated at the highest levels. It was only in the aftermath of the #BlackLivesMatter movement and the attempt to pull down the Rhodes statue at Oriel College, Oxford, that his legacy came under scrutiny. It provoked the college to set up a commission of inquiry with the mandate to address 'issues associated with memorials to Cecil Rhodes'. The report was published in April 2021 and has some key passages that are worth highlighting. Commission member Professor William Beinart, a White South African who prior to the controversy was *Rhodes Professor of Race Relations* from 2007 to 2015, was mandated to review aspects of Rhodes' career. His findings are summarized as concluding (paragraph 4.11) that:

> Rhodes made a number of important decisions, or supported developments, that intensified racial segregation at the Cape in the late nineteenth century. To a limited degree a pragmatist in Cape

politics, prepared to work with a range of people who would be useful to his interests, Rhodes was a deeply committed British imperialist, convinced about racial superiority.

The report goes on to state:

> He had some power to influence an alternative political direction in the Colony but advocated a racially restrictive franchise, punitive Masters and Servants legislation, a labour tax for African people only, a segregated local government system and segregation in the South African cricket team. He was involved in the beginning of coercive compounds for black workers and other racially restrictive practices as an employer.

The key passage with regard to this particular colonial crime and the fraudulent acquisition, including after the *Rudd Commission*, of the territory is probably best captured in paragraph 4.13:

> In respect of Zimbabwe, 1890–97, Rhodes and his Company were responsible for great violence in attacking the Ndebele kingdom in 1893 and in suppressing resistance to their rule in 1896–7. The Rudd concession concerning mining rights in what is now Zimbabwe was overridden; unbridled use was made of the Maxim gun; cattle were looted by his Company and its agents on a large scale; grain stores, crops and gardens were destroyed over a sustained period during the 1896–7 war; many Ndebele soldiers were shot in flight; supposed rebels were sentenced and hung or shot without due process of law. Over a period of nine months, men (including armed men), women and children sheltering in caves were blown up, when it was clear that many were being killed. Rhodes was aware of these practices, present at times while they were taking place and involved in strategic discussion about the wars.[24]

The use of pieces of paper to justify acquisition of territory is a common and recurring theme across the world. Following the basics of contract law that were well established in the colonial jurisdictions in question, these documents were deemed valid despite the contested interpretations of their considerations, inequality of arms, deliberate attempts to mislead and post-signing subterfuge.

---

[24] Independent Commission, *Report of a Commission of Inquiry Established by Oriel College, Oxford into Issues Associated with the Memorials to Cecil Rhodes* (April 2021).

The *Treaty of Waitangi (Te Tiriti o Waitangi in Māori)* signed on 6 February 1840 in Waitangi, Aotearoa (New Zealand) is worth highlighting as a specific example that predates the Rhodes discussion above. Fresh from adventures in Australia which had successfully led to the claim of a massive occupied landmass as *terra nullius* on the basis that the communities there had no legal personality to make the claim to having occupied it, the Crown authorities arrived in neighbouring Aotearoa keen to expand their remit. They clearly found it difficult to dismiss the better militarily organized and more centralized Māori tribes in the manner that they had treated their counterparts across the Tasman Sea. Instead, the small group of Europeans who descended from the boat adopted what would subsequently become the means of seeking to acquire territory in many other parts of the world, namely, the use of a treaty.

The British arrived in Aotearoa under the banner of the *New Zealand Company* with the aim of establishing a settler colony. The Māori for their part had sought some protection from the British against French interests that were seen as becoming threatening. The *Treaty of Waitangi* was supposed to establish the settler colony with a Governor while recognizing Māori ownership of their lands and forests and extending protection to them as British subjects. The document was then formulated and signed between the consul for the British Crown, Captain Hobson and a group of Māori Chiefs from the North Island, collectively referred to as the *Rangatira*, with the latter believing that this is what the document said. Once translated, the document was then taken around the *Rangatira*, with over 530 signing the Māori version of the document and less than 40 signing an English version.

The short treaty only contained a preamble and three articles. The preamble refers to how the Queen was 'anxious to protect' the just rights and property of the native Chiefs and tribes of New Zealand while seeking to secure them enjoyment of peace and good order. Interestingly, irrespective of any attempt to protect the rights and property of the Chiefs, it refers to 'recognition of Her Majesty's sovereign authority over the whole or any part' of the islands, though this reference is in the Queen's promise to appoint a 'functionary properly authorized to treat' with the communities. The three articles that follow are even more intriguing in the English version. Via the first, not only had the Chiefs who signed the document but also separate and independent Chiefs who had not become members of the Confederation agreed to 'cede to Her Majesty the Queen of England absolute and without reservation all the rights and powers of Sovereignty' which the Confederation either 'exercised or possessed, or were even supposed to exercise or possess over their respective territories' as sole sovereigns. The second separates ownership (*proprietorship*) from the use (*usus*) in a time-tested formula employed throughout the realm of the British Crown, whereby usage is not considered adequate in generating title, effectively relegating former landowners by Indigenous custom, laws and traditions to tenants for no real consideration, as in this case. Thus, in the second article Māori families and individuals are confirmed as having full and exclusive and undisturbed possession of Lands, Estates and Fisheries while yielding exclusive rights to the Crown for pre-emption over the lands, including for disposal or alienation at prices to be agreed. The double blow of the distinction between use and ownership is compounded by the terms of alienation which were then achieved through unequal bargaining powers, deceit and subterfuge. The return that accrued to the Māori for their ceding of sovereignty and the 'right' to acquire the lands is that they would gain the royal protection of the Crown, including 'the rights and privileges of British subjects'. The arrogance of the treaty would be remarkable in and of itself if not for an additional feature – the significant discrepancies between the Māori version that was overwhelmingly signed by the *Rangatira* and the English version discussed above.

The Māori version deviates from the English in some very specific ways. According to the official English translation the text suggests that the Queen would appoint an administrator to protect the Chiefs and 'preserve their chieftainship and their lands' while accepting the Queen's right to establish a government in order to protect her subjects already in the territory and the greater number expected to arrive. The version authorized Captain Hobbs to be the Governor. In light of that preamble the Chiefs, under the first article, ceded governance of the lands to the Queen; in the second they secured agreement from the Queen 'to protect the Chiefs, the subtribes and all the people of New Zealand in the unqualified exercise of their chieftainship over their lands, villages and all their treasures' while conceding the right of the Queen to buy and for Māori owners to sell land at an agreed price. Via the third article the Queen extended protection to ordinary people giving them the same rights and duties of citizenship as the people of England.

The English version in its concluding paragraph sought to preclude later discussions on the Treaty's validity, stating that the Chiefs 'having been made fully to understand the Provisions of the foregoing Treaty, accept and enter into the same in the full spirit and meaning thereof in witness of which we have attached our signatures or marks at the places and the dates respectively specified'.

The marked difference in the English version of the Māori text is compelling: 'So we, the Chiefs of the Confederation and the subtribes of New Zealand meeting here at Waitangi having seen the shape of these words which we accept and agree to record our names and marks thus'.

That text is particularly relevant since the 'shape of the words' that the *Rangatiranga* saw and understood was clearly the Māori version, not that this stopped subsequent agents of the Crown from the acts they engaged in. Even the perspectives recorded by the *Parekha* (settler) emphasize that what happened next was the loss of control over lands by the Māori during the second half of the 19th century. While some of the loss could be attributed to what that history records as legitimate sales, a significant proportion was stolen through unfair deals, forcible occupation by settlers and outright confiscation after a period of armed conflict. The Waitangi Tribunal reports from 1978 to 2023 record these events in significant detail and played an important role in the subsequent restitution but also in setting the record right in terms of these events.[25] The extent to which this history of Aotearoa differs from the more traditional sources of its history is striking and perhaps indicative of the extent to which similar processes elsewhere may reveal equally significant deviations. Despite its unequal terms and duplicitous interpretations, the New Zealand government completely ignored the treaty. By 1877 a White court, set up under the Crown, determined that the treaty was a 'simple nullity' on the basis that it was signed between 'a civilised nation and a group of savages'.[26] The ruling by Chief Justice Prendergast, which drew on earlier Court of Appeal decisions merely fuelled further alienation of Māori land. The mass arrival of Europeans with their guns, germs and steel brought significant disease, which along with the violence perpetrated led to a decimation in the Māori population from 400,000 at the time of the arrival if the settlers in 1840 to 125,000 by 1890.

Episodic colonial crime

While the first two categories of crime identified are systemic and concern the acquisition of the territory and the claim itself to be able to occupy, subjugate and ultimately colonize other territories, this category and the next pertain to behaviours that occurred under the subsequent colonial rule that was imposed. Under episodic colonial crime we consider specific instances or acts that would have been illegal under the laws existing in the colonial State at the time. These are acts deemed punishable by law if they were conducted by anyone (its nationals or others), affected its nationals or occurred on their lands. In addition, in the case of the most severe of these cases, they would most likely also be considered crimes under the broader *law of nations* or international law that existed at the time at which they occurred.

The range of crimes that could fall into this category are most likely to be the broadest of all categories and have warranted significant attention,

---

[25] The reports are available electronically on the dedicated website created for this process. See https://www.waitangitribunal.govt.nz/publications-and-resources/waitangi-tribunal-reports/.

[26] *Wi Parata v. The Bishop of Wellington SC Wellington* [1877] NZ Jurists Report 183; (1877) 3 NZ Jur (NS) 72 (SC); 1 NZLRLC 14 (17 October 1877).

including in official and unofficial bilateral dialogues between the former colonial power and the concerned post-colonial governments. It includes specific instances of ethnic cleansing, crimes against humanity, war crimes and other crimes, some conducted with the specific intention of seeking to destroy communities in whole or part that lived on the lands that came under European sovereignty. In many of these instances such massacres, whether acknowledged or contested, form a significant strand of claims against a sovereign. A second distinct sub-category of episodic crimes involves the theft of movable properties and their expropriation back to the country of the colonial masters. Often falling into the realm of the confiscation of cultural artefacts, frequently though not always under some cloak of legality, such objects have been met with a wide range of treatment: retained in the colonial countries in most cases, damaged in others, carefully maintained or exhibited in for- and not-for-profit museums. Some of these artefacts are cultural products, others are of deep sanctity and historical and emotive value to communities who have no access to them.

Three examples will be used to illustrate the wide range of events that could be considered to fall within this category of crimes. In narrating these it is also important to bear in mind that the depth of the wrongdoing and its continuation into the present means that this category of crimes remains a live issue in contemporary world politics. The first example pertains to the massacre that resulted from the order to fire upon a local demonstration at Jallianwala Bagh, in Amritsar, Punjab, in British India on 13 April 1919. That day General Dyer ordered his troops to fire with live ammunition to disperse a gathering. The sustained firing resulted in 370 deaths according to an official report, though some estimates suggest four times as many when those that succumbed to injuries later are accounted for. The underlying facts and events leading up to this episode are not contested by the British. On the fateful day a gathering of about 10,000 people assembled in a park which only had one exit and was enclosed by walls on other sides. The crowd included men, women and children who had mobilized to protest the extension of emergency legislation by the British which had enabled them to arrest pro-independence activists. These kinds of arrests, which were justified under the legality of emergency actions during the war, were meant to have stopped. According to promises made by the British, they were supposed to be replaced instead by greater local governance in accordance with the *Montagu–Chelmsford Report*, which had been presented to the British Parliament a year earlier. However, rather than ease the repression, the British Government of India passed the *Rowlatt Acts*, which extended repressive measures that had been introduced during wartime, to be used against those agitating for independence. The use of this Act to arrest prominent Indian leaders had already sparked unrest in the city a few days before the protest, leading to an authorization issued to General

Reginald Dyer to restore order including through the adoption of a ban on public gatherings.

The *Encyclopedia Brittannica* describes what happened on 13 April as follows:

> Dyer and his soldiers arrived and sealed off the exit. Without warning, the troops opened fire on the crowd, reportedly shooting hundreds of rounds until they ran out of ammunition. It is not certain how many died in the bloodbath, but, according to one official report, an estimated 379 people were killed, and about 1,200 more were wounded. After they ceased firing, the troops immediately withdrew from the place, leaving behind the dead and wounded.[27]

One of the key elements to this crime that is not recorded in the terse wording above is that aside from the significant loss of life and the callousness with which this was carried out, the shooting eventually stopped because the soldiers ran out of ammunition.[28]

Faced with significant outcry in India as well as at home, the (British) Government of India ordered an investigation into the incident. Sitting as the *Hunter Commission*, the inquiry censured Dyer for his actions and sought his resignation from the military.[29] Appearing before the Commission on 19 November 1919, Dyer confirmed his intent clearly, that he had planned to fire at the crowd, not only to disperse it but to generate a fear that would deter any possibility of a future mutiny. On being pressed on the use of live ammunition, he confirmed that he had planned to use the machine guns as well as the armoured cars he had at his behest. In other words, his actions were impervious to the presence of human life. Rather than holding Dyer accountable in his individual capacity or seeing the implication upon the State in the failure of its duty to protect civilians, the report concluded that Dyer had acted under a misplaced sense of duty and that the order and subsequent firing were justified, though the general ought to have issued a warning first. The report also suggested that the firing ought not to have lasted for the ten minutes it did. It went on to uphold the use of martial law in the region.

In Britain the reaction Dyer received was mixed. While there was criticism of him in the House of Commons for what had happened, the

---

[27] Kenneth Pletcher, 'Jallianwala Bagh Massacre', *Encyclopedia Britannica* (4 December 2023), available at https://www.britannica.com/event/Jallianwala-Bagh-Massacre [Accessed 15 February 2024].

[28] Kim A Wagner, '"Calculated to Strike Terror": The Amritsar Massacre and the Spectre of Colonial Violence', 233 *Past & Present* (November 2016), 185–225.

[29] See *Amritsar: Minutes of Evidence taken before the Hunter Committee* (London: UK Parliament, 1920) Parliamentary Archives, DAV/123.

House of Lords praised Dyer and even awarded him a sword inscribed with the words 'Saviour of the Punjab'. Far from being a pariah excluded from the army, Dyer was celebrated among his supporters, who raised significant money to fund him. He continued to serve in several military missions and retired in July 1920 as Colonel, a title he was allowed to retain. He also continued to write and even justify his actions. In an op-ed he wrote on 21 January 1921 in *The Globe Newspaper*, he stated that India did not really want self-government since 'she does not understand it'. In fact for Dyer self-government would need to be accompanied by a free press and free speech, which was something reserved only for the enlightened. His attitude can be gleaned by his making light of the need in India according to him, for an 11th commandment: Thou shalt not agitate. This attitude was already on full display during the *Hunter Commission* deliberations, where he is recorded as accepting that the crowd could have been dispersed without firing but that they would have returned laughing, making a fool of him. The power of the historian and the inbuilt bias of the written word is revealed in full in that the main source of information on Dyer remains a biography written by a fellow soldier which appears to engage with how Dyer may have felt a deeper contrition about his actions in later life. This account appears to be written to convince those who judged Dyer harshly based on the facts that he may have been better than they gave him credit for. Few written words exist of the impact of the actions on the victims' families, though the issue continues to rankle in independent India's relationship with Britain. There has been no apology for the massacre or any meaningful engagement with this episode of history by the British government.

This stands in sharp contrast to the German government's engagement with its culpability in the Ovaherero (also referred to as Herero) and Nama genocide that occurred between 1904 and 1908 in German Southwest Africa/Namibia. In the first phase of a campaign conducted by General von Trotha, German colonial forces prevented the Herero from leaving the desert, leading to widespread death from starvation and dehydration. As with other colonial crimes, difficulties in compiling the number of dead means that numbers vary significantly – between 24,000 and 100,000 Herero and 10,000 Nama. These actions were also followed by the imprisonment in concentration camps of thousands of members of both communities and the flight of many others into neighbouring countries.[30]

In what is referred to as the Battle of Waterberg, von Trotha ordered that 'within the German boundaries, every Herero … will be shot. I won't

---

[30] Mathias Häussler, *The Herero Genocide: War, Emotion and Extreme Violence in Namibia*, trans. Elizabeth Janikm (New York: Berghahn, 2021).

accommodate women and children any more. I shall drive them back to their people or I shall give the order to shoot at them'.[31]

The decimation of the population as a consequence of this campaign is significant: reports suggest that communities that previously had numbers in excess of 100,000 members were reduced to being less than 20,000, with a significant proportion scattered across the sub-region of southern Africa.[32] The leaders of both communities have been agitating for a considerable period of time for recognition of the events that took place and for their labelling as genocide in keeping with the systematic and widespread attempt by von Trotha to exterminate the community. This included attempted filing of cases against Germany in a range of fora, including US courts and the Permanent Court of Arbitration.[33] The sustained campaign has steadily gained traction not only in official circles but also with cultural institutions in Germany.[34] In 2004 a member of the German government acknowledged that Germany bore a historical political and moral–ethnical responsibility for the events between 1904 and 1908, even acknowledging that the facts showed that it would fall within the modern understanding of the crime of genocide. The official recognition that the events constituted genocide finally came much later in 2016 from the German Federal Government, though it sought to avoid the legal consequences of this admission.

Deliberations have since been ongoing as to what reparations should flow from German acceptance that what occurred was genocide. While a package of measures has notionally been agreed between the German and Namibian governments, the process has been criticized for excluding descendants of the affected populations. The agreement also reads more like a development plan for Namibia, something Germany probably ought to be liable for given the significant extraction of wealth that its occupation and colonization of the country entailed, including through continued land tenure. However, the package falls significantly short in terms of addressing the specific violations that have sustained an agitation amidst the community for over a hundred years. The communities' demands of Germany include remedies that go beyond the payment of compensation, such as the return of artefacts and

---

[31] Mark Levene and Penny Roberts, *The Massacre in History* (New York/Oxford: Berghahn Books, 1999) 211.

[32] David Olusoga and Casper W. Erichsen, *The Kaiser's Holocaust: Germany's Forgotten Genocide and the Colonial Roots of Nazism* (London: Faber & Faber, 2010).

[33] See, for example, *Vekuii Rukoro, David Frederick, The Association of the Ovaherero Genocide in the USA Inc. and Barnabas Veraa Katuuo, v. Federal Republic of Germany*, 1:17-cv-00062 (S.D.N.Y.).

[34] See Allan D Cooper, 'Reparations for the Herero Genocide: Defining the Limits of International Litigation', 106 (422) *African Affairs* (January2007) 113–26.

sacred relics including ancestral skulls which were brought to Germany to be displayed in museums.

This type of colonial crime that resulted in mass loss of lives often remains alive in the memories of the victims' families, where the episodes are narrated in oral histories passed from generation to generation. This is especially true where the events themselves are denied in official narratives and where there is not even a written acknowledgement of their occurring in the languages of the colonial masters. As a consequence, the physical loss and lasting hurt and trauma that occurred are simply dismissed with the lack of its presence in historical annals considered definitive of the events not having transpired at all. The call for accountability for such crimes inevitably starts with a requirement of the admission of guilt and acknowledgement of the events, their severity and impact. Yet re-constructing the narrative is incredibly challenging from among communities that were nearly wiped out and forced to live in subservient roles, often as foreigners in neighbouring countries or mass transferred to somewhere else where they faced discrimination on the basis of their different racial group, ethnic identity or religion.[35] The possibility of a wider range of voices, especially those of women, through art, culture, literature but also presence in research institutions is opening up the possibility that many submerged events of this nature in history will gain greater prominence. The nature of such crimes and their effect puts them beyond any notion of statutes of limitations, but finding a formula that would work will remain a challenge.

The discussion on the return of stolen properties would by contrast seem to be straightforward. Early attempts to claim the return of stolen properties were often met with bewildering responses. While more progressive jurisdictions have stayed silent or sought to engage in dialogues about shared possessions, others have pushed back using claims of a dubious nature. The discussion with India on the Kohinoor Diamond remains in the backdrop to India–UK relations,[36] while the Parthenon Marbles discussion with Greece[37] shows that cultural property was not only appropriated from African and Asian lands. Most recently, the Oba of Benin raised the issue of the Benin Bronzes in a public manner at the coronation of the new King of the United Kingdom. It is worth dwelling briefly on this as a sub-type of episodic crime that will require the design of specific remedies.

---

[35] Olukunle P. Owolabi, *Ruling Emancipated Slaves and Indigenous Subjects: The Divergent Legacies of Forced Settlement and Colonial Occupation in the Global South* (Oxford: Oxford University Press, 2023).

[36] William Dalrymple and Anita Anand, *Kohinoor: The Story of the World's Most Infamous Diamond* (New Delhi: Juggernaut Books, 2016).

[37] Christopher Hitchens, *The Parthenon Marbles: The Case for Reunification* (London: Verso, 2008).

The Benin Bronzes are a group of elaborate sculptures that include plaques, commemorative heads, animal and human figures, items of royal regalia and personal ornaments. Cast in brass and bronze, they were designed and created by guilds attached to the court of the Oba of the Kingdom of Benin, West Africa. The pieces were mostly directed at the governing royalty, with the bronzes used as part of many rituals. They are considered not only to be physical representations of the history of the Kingdom of Benin but also to document the relationships of the Kingdom with neighbouring kingdoms. The cultural tradition of casting objects of this type is recorded as dating back to the medieval period.

Among many things the Benin Bronzes depict, they document the start of contact between the Kingdom and Europeans – mainly by way of trade and diplomatic engagements with the Portuguese, who had begun arriving on the coast around the 15th century. Through processes closely linked to the *Berlin West Africa Conference in 1884–1885* (discussed later in this book), Europeans had begun to overrun local kingdoms as they struggled against each other to gain access to the wealth of the region. The process of the acquisition of territory took similar forms to that described above in terms of the crimes that occurred. In West Africa another dimension accompanied the standard land acquisition and commercial expropriation that drove colonization: the search for slaves. This entailed a process by which individuals could be captured and sold into captivity, mainly to be transferred to the Americas where the Portuguese and Spanish and later the British convinced each other they had discovered 'a new world'. These vast territories had a limited number of people who could be subjugated and put to work to generate wealth through extractive processes that exploited nature, as will be discussed later.

In terms of this genre of colonial crime, however, it is important to note that the Kingdom of Benin came under British sovereignty from 1897. The Kingdom was amalgamated by the British into what it subsequently called the *Oil Rivers State*, which much later through decolonization emerged as part of Nigeria in 1960. Confusingly, Benin City, which was the home of the Oba Court, is today in Edo State in Nigeria. Meanwhile the post-colonial country of Benin, divided from the rest of the territory that became Nigeria through a British–French agreement, came to independence around what was previously the Kingdom of Dahomey. This confusing array of names, places and post-colonial history illustrates the disruptive and disorienting influence of colonization. Today the sovereign State of Benin is geographically not where the Oba Kingdom previously was, but its name draws inspiration from the historical Kingdom of Benin, which is now in neighbouring Nigeria.

British and French interests in the wider sub-region of West Africa were driven by the lucrative profits to be made through the transatlantic slave trade. In fact, the region was commonly referred to by the Portuguese and others as the Slave Coast from the 17th century onward due to the significant dent made by the slave trade in the communities that lived in the region, by the capture of women and men to be sold into servitude for profit. The theft of the Bronzes is closely linked to this period. The British Museum, which still retains over 900 objects from this time, seeks to explain on its website how it came into possession of the objects, stating that 'By the end of the 19th century, the Nigerian coast and its trade were largely dominated by the British. It is in the context of this aggressive expansion of colonial power that the Benin Bronzes came to the British Museum'.

The website also records in very simplistic terms how the Scramble for Africa commenced:

> During the second half of the 19th century, the balance of power between West African kingdoms like Benin and the European nations they traded with shifted towards European control. In the late 19th century, industrialised European nations accompanied by new military technologies began to exert greater power across the African continent. This political and commercial movement developed into the territorial land-grab known as the 'Scramble for Africa'.[38]

British sovereignty over the area began through a military expedition against the Kingdom of Benin, leading to a violent occupation of Benin City in 1897, alongside widespread destruction of heritage and pillage by British forces. Palaces and monuments were deliberately destroyed and defiled, with their stores raided and thousands of objects seized as war spoils and distributed among soldiers. The objects in the British Museum, believed to date back to the 16th and 17th century, were acquired as part of this widespread looting and vandalism. The entire process was justified as a legitimate military action against a 'barbarous' kingdom, and by autumn that year the British Museum began to display the plaques, while others were simply sold into private collections for profit.[39] Over the last few years, also assisted by a rise in consciousness sparked by the #BlackLivesMatter movement, questions have begun to come to greater prominence over the

---

[38] The British Museum, *Benin Bronzes*, available at https://www.britishmuseum.org/about-us/british-museum-story/contested-objects-collection/benin-bronzes [Accessed 22 February 2024].

[39] For some of the attitudes displayed by the British soldiers who returned from the Benin expedition, including their disparaging attitudes towards the populations that were published with approval in mainstream British newspapers, see Barnaby Phillips, *Loot: Britain and the Benin Bronzes* (London: Simon & Schuster, 2021).

return of antiquities. This has been formally requested by the Nigerian Federal Ministry of Information and Culture. Instead of detailing how the objects will be returned, the British Museum website goes into lengthy explanations of the relationships the Museum is building with institutions and people, including His Royal Majesty Oba Ewuare II, the descendant of the rulers of the Kingdom of Benin from where the objects were stolen. In explaining the British Museum's 'position', the following is displayed on its website: 'The Museum is committed to active engagement with Nigerian institutions concerning the Benin Bronzes, including pursuing and supporting new initiatives developed in collaboration with Nigerian partners and colleagues'.[40]

The language used does not in any way indicate a compulsion to return the objects nor to admit in writing the fact that they were wrongfully acquired. Instead, it appears to be satisfactory to the Museum that it is 'committed to dialogue' when a simple remedy would be more appropriate: the return of the objects, plus compensation for their theft and the profits gained from their display.[41] Many other objects taken from many other locations face a similar fate, with discussions over their return encountering similar attitudes towards obfuscation.

Systemic and widespread practices

This category of crimes, which are more difficult to quantify and crystalize, may well be of greater salience to contemporary life due to their persistence in the lexicon and systems of existing regimes. Key among these are the inheritance of land tenure systems that are far from the pre-existing Indigenous, native and customary systems that were prevalent prior to colonization. They also include the imposition of alien religions through missionaries who worked on the basis of the superiority of their belief system over all others, followed by mass conversion of populations,[42] the introduction of legal bias against non-sedentary communities who were painted as primitive,[43] the criminalization of homosexuality based on values derived

---

[40] The British Museum, *Benin Bronzes*, available at https://www.britishmuseum.org/about-us/british-museum-story/contested-objects-collection/benin-bronzes [Accessed 22 February 2024].

[41] For more, see Dan Hicks, *The Brutish Museums: Benin Bronzes, Colonial Violence and Cultural Restitution* (London: Pluto Press, 2021).

[42] Compare the tone of the work by Chima J. Korieh and Raphael Chijioke Njoku (eds) *Missions, States and European Expansion in Africa* (New York: Routledge, 2007) to that of John Theodore Mueller, *Great Missionaries to Africa* (Grand Rapids, MI: Zondervan Publishing House, 1941).

[43] Marco Moretti, *International Law and Nomadic Peoples* (Milton Keynes: AuthorHouse, 2012).

from Abrahamic faiths in British colonies,[44] the determination of crime and punishment,[45] the imposition of school systems and curricula that disrupted cultures on the basis of the superiority of one culture over all others,[46] and the erection of an extractive model of economic growth that, as this work will argue, has contributed significantly to the global climate crisis. Many of these systemic features were achieved through the articulation and framing of laws that have proved difficult to shift post transition. They have also had a fundamental impact on altering the balance and state of values through formal education. Like other colonial crimes, they directly contributed to the climate crisis through the erection of a consumption-based economic model of growth which disrupted circular economies beyond the point from which they can be easily re-engineered.[47] Thinking through an effective set of remedies against such wide-ranging practices that have become ingrained within contemporary systems makes this set of colonial crimes the most challenging to address.

The slave trade easily stands out as the most dramatic example of a widespread and systematic colonial crime.[48] It is worth remembering that the slave trade was not only restricted to European colonization – indicative perhaps of the human nature of dominance.[49] Yet the slave trade under European colonization may have had the widest impact in terms of sustaining the colonial drive, disrupting and dislocating communities and fuelling the push towards unfair economic activities.[50] Its prominence in contemporary writing and a wealth of powerful narratives, including through film, means that it is only identified here rather than discussed in detail. Two other specific systemic crimes are worth dwelling on a little more to show the breadth of this type of crime in creating structures that are hard to unravel. The first is the annihilation of Indigenous and local education systems which,

---

[44] Enze Han and Joseph O'Mahoney, *British Colonization and the Criminalization of Homosexuality: Queens, Crime and Empire* (London: Taylor & Francis, 2019).

[45] Ana Aliverti, Henrique Carvalho, Anastasia Chamberlain and Maximo Sozzo, *Decolonizing the Criminal Question: Colonial Legacies, Contemporary Problems* (Oxford: Oxford University Press, 2023).

[46] Katja Gorbahn, Susanne Grindel and Susanne Popp, *History Education and (Post) Colonialism: International Case Studies* (Berlin: Peter Land, 2019).

[47] Goher Ur-Rehman Mir and Servaas Storm, *Carbon Emissions and Economic Growth: Production-Based versus Consumption-Based Evidence on Decoupling*, Institute for New Economic Thinking Working Paper Series No. 41 (SSRN, 2016).

[48] Olayanju Olajide, *The Complete Concise History of the Slave Trade* (Bloomington, IN: AuthorHouse, 2013).

[49] Charles River (ed), *The East African Slave Trade: The History and Legacy of the Arab Slave Trade and the Indian Ocean Slave Trade* (CreateSpace Independent Publishing Platform, 2017).

[50] Elizabeth Kowaleski Wallace, *The British Slave Trade and Public Memory* (New York: Columbia University Press, 2006).

by their nature, create a blueprint for how society will operate generation after generation. The second pertains to the entrenchment of an extractive economic model deeply reliant on fossil fuels.

Education is often stated as a key benefit that flowed from colonization. The argument, including that articulated by leaders from former colonized countries, is that the import of European education systems brought science and technology within reach. A similar claim is made as to how such education systems contributed to the modernization of countries: creating infrastructure, generating wealth and enabling populations to acquire and live at levels of wealth and luxury that they would never have imagined. The coalescing of educational systems around the world, including through the spread of common languages, has been a contributing factor in the emergence of internationalization and globalization. This has facilitated cross-cultural conversations through enabling mediums such as former colonial languages (English, French, Spanish, Arabic, Turkish, Russian, Hungarian and perhaps even Mandarin).[51]

Yet the internationalization of education has also shaped the world into the image of the former colonizing regimes and enabled a continuation of the salience and hegemony of former colonial powers.[52] For example, the growing emphasis on the use of English has provided its speakers with unrivalled access to an international political system where they continue to dominate decades after the colonial experience, with little awareness or acknowledgement of their inherited legacy. Due to the simultaneously constructed patriarchy, this dominance is heavily biased towards men, primarily those from Britain and other White dominion countries (especially United States of America, Canada and Australia). It has also enabled educational elites from other jurisdictions trained in these values and languages to access such roles, thereby maintaining a standard that has become hardwired.[53] The widespread use of maps which place Europe at the heart of the world – physically in the middle – is such that most people have never seen any other map and assume this is the exclusive way in which to depict geography.[54] The domination of the educational system by elite universities in English-speaking countries have served as beacons

---

[51] Weili Zhao, Thomas S. Popkewitz and Tera Autio, *Epistemic Colonialism and the Transfer of Curriculum Knowledge Across Borders: Applying a Historical Lens to Contest Unilateral Logics* (London: Routledge, 2022).

[52] William Eggington and Helen Wren, *Language Policy: Dominant English, Pluralist Challenges* (Amsterdam: John Benjamin Publishing, 1997).

[53] Rosemary Salomone, *The Rise of English: Global Politics and the Power of Language* (Oxford: Oxford University Press, 2022).

[54] James R. Akerman, *Decolonizing the Map: Cartography from Colony to Nation* (Chicago; University of Chicago Press, 2017).

for talented individuals from other jurisdictions who have then found their newly privileged access to job markets a useful personal benefit, draining resources from the countries from which they emerged.[55]

While the issue of access to education and its consequences must be highlighted as above, the push towards a Western-style curriculum at the cost of other systems of laws and sciences completes the Western hegemony in terms of content production and dissemination.[56] Even in a discipline such as science, which requires wide inquiry in a supposedly continuous quest to gather, distil and further knowledge, the boundaries of the discipline appear not to penetrate cultures and systems that are less familiar to those in the Western world. This has an immediate effect in building new hegemonies where encounters with new 'facts' beyond these worlds are then seized by the 'discoverer' through intellectual property regimes in much the way that Christopher Columbus is meant to have 'discovered' America.[57] These educational systems are sustained and further ingrained into thinking, sometimes even through ostensibly well-meaning plans to combat their legacies, such as through narratives for emancipation which can be drawn upon.

In sharp contrast to crimes that persist through individual action and decision making operating within an ingrained system, the extraction of fossil fuels is a significantly grander meta-frame when viewed against the backdrop of the climate crisis.[58]

The extraction of oil as a resource on a mass scale commenced with British activities in Iran at the start of the twentieth century, eventually turning the Middle East from a mere corridor to India in the eyes of the Western world into a resource hotbed whose future from that point onward would be deeply influenced by orientalist thinking.[59] The first commercial oil wells are believed to have been dug in Azerbaijan (1846), Poland (1853), Romania (1857) and Germany (1859), but these early efforts, the latter in the midst of European populations, paled in comparison to the mass extraction of oil in the Middle East, which treated the entirety of the Arabian desert as a

---

[55] For a work that looks wider than the anglophone world in doing this, see Roland Bloch, Alexander Mitterle, Catherine Paradeise and Tobias Peter (eds), *Universities and the Production of Elites: Discourses, Policies, and Strategies of Excellence and Stratification in Higher Education* (Switzerland: Palgrave Macmillan, 2018).

[56] See, for example, Winniefridah Matsa, *Marginality, Migration and Education: Educational Experiences of Migrants' Children in Zimbabwe* (Switzerland: Springer AG, 2020).

[57] Vandana Shiva, *Protect or Plunder* (London: Bloomsbury Academic, 2001).

[58] Vandana Shiva, *Soil Not Oil: Environmental Justice in an Age of Climate Crisis* (Berkeley, CA: North Atlantic Books, 2015).

[59] Horace Charles Baker, *The Age of Oil: A History of the Petroleum Industry and the Outlook for the Future* (London: Chas A. Stoneham Co., 1917).

store of easy and limitless extractable resources.[60] The impact of these on the world economy was described in the following words in an article written in 2018: 'The establishment of petroleum as a tradable commodity, as well as a natural resource, triggered a paradigm shift in the history of civilization, introducing a new set of values, opportunities and forces, shaping the course of social endeavours as diverse as science, technology, energy production and consumption'.[61]

The last part of that article reads, 'leading to associated improvements in living standards throughout the world'. Labelling it as 'our 160-year-old hydrocarbon-based civilization', the author predicts, in a manner that should strike fear, that 'despite many criticisms and shortcomings, hydrocarbons will continue to be a key component in our lives for decades to come'. The article as a whole shows very well what the effects have been, but in highlighting the rise of living standards throughout the world, it appears to gloss over how that rise can be measured, to whom it primarily accrued and the extent of the loss and damage to the planet itself and other forms of life that populate it with as much right as 'us'. For a publication produced in 2018 its tone is also singularly striking in its anthropocentricity but reflects well how deeply the so-called hydrocarbon-based civilization is enmeshed and how little the author seems aware of the damage it has caused. The breathless celebration later in the piece, under the sub-title 'Pioneering petroleum geologists from Europe', of what is now accepted as a primary cause of the climate crisis also appears to be an anachronism but, sadly, is not. Oil has clearly generated very significant wealth – justified by some as a true sign of how capitalism is key to the economic model. This wealth accrued not only to its producers but to the significant network of industries that rely heavily on it.[62] Its existence continues unabated through the climate crisis, with its leading voices even involved in producing works that have mass appeal, such as the 2018 article referred to earlier, written by the Head of Exploration of the Italian oil giant ENI.[63] The irony is that the title of that work, *The Age of Oil*, is the same as another produced over a hundred years previously in the early years of the expansion of the Middle East oil

---

[60] Jonthan Craig, Francesco Gerali, Fiona MacAulay and Rasoul Sorkhabi, *History of European Oil and Gas Industry* (London: Geological Society, 2018).
[61] Jonthan Craig, Francesco Gerali, Fiona MacAulay and Rasoul Sorkhabi, *History of European Oil and Gas Industry* (London: Geological Society, 2018).
[62] Michael J. Economides, Ronald E. Oligney and Armando Izquierdo, *The Colour of Oil: The History, Money and the Politics of the World's Biggest Business* (Round Oak Publishing Company, 2000), a book that clearly also questions any scientific consensus on climate change.
[63] *Also see* Leonardo Maugeri, *The Age of Oil: The Mythology, History and Future of the World's Most Controversial Resource* (Lyons Press, 2017).

industry, which breathlessly charted what the future of oil would look like. It is almost as if, a century later and with the science that was suppressed about the impact now coming to the fore, it still remains appropriate to talk of how such companies need to modify.

Away from the catastrophic climate damage as oil became central to the emerging global economy, the quest for control over lands and territories that were becoming increasingly uninhabitable due to the polluting impact of the industry grew intense, creating a very different scramble in the Middle East to that which accompanied European incursions into Africa. If the African quest was described as a search for African gold, probably such as that reflected in the shiny Benin Bronzes discussed earlier in this chapter, it was a different mineral that fuelled the chase across the Arabian desert. In this instance too, lines were drawn on maps to delineate one hegemon's territory from that of its European neighbour, with the most famous of these, the *Sykes–Picot* line having stood, dividing peoples, nations and communities for over a hundred years.[64] However, while its impact has been significant on the submergence and emergence of political powers and communities, it is something else that has made this phenomenon a crime that could be considered to fall under the rubric of one that is systemic and widespread. Specifically, this lies in the installation of new hegemons who would continue to be loyal to the extractive industry project, a theme that is addressed more directly under decolonization-related crimes. While significant wealth was transferred out of the region by the extraction of oil and gas under colonial rule, decolonization, as elsewhere, was conducted on the basis of the lines erected by the colonial rulers. Within these lines specific ruling clans were favoured over others and were encouraged through technical cooperation to engage in a process of 'nation building',[65] seeking to turn masses of sometimes autochthonous communities into fully fledged Western-style States.[66] The clans entrusted with the process of leading this transition were closely aligned to maintaining the system of extraction which continued to siphon resources out of the area.[67] A key difference from colonial times, however, was that profit making also now came to

---

[64] James Barr, *A Line in the Sand: Britain, France and the Struggle that Shaped the Middle East* (London: Simon & Schuster, 2011).

[65] Frank Heinlein, *British Government Policy and Decolonisation, 1945–1963* (London: Taylor & Francis, 2013), which seeks to offer insights in scrutinizing the 'official mind'.

[66] Joshua Castellino and Kathleen A. Cavanaugh, *Minorities in the Middle East: A Comparative Legal Analysis* (Oxford: Oxford University Press, 2013).

[67] Gabriele Proglio, *Decolonising the Mediterranean* (Cambridge: Cambridge University Press, 2016).

specific local families who became immensely wealthy as a consequence, deepening their commitment to the practice of extraction.[68]

This example of extraction from the Western Asian region is today a mere microcosm of a wider process that has become systemized and ingrained: namely, an economy based on extractivism that has little or no benefit for the immediate locals, who are often forced to live with the desecration of their home environment and the destruction of their lands.[69] This is compounded by their lack of benefit sharing in the vast profits generated, which mostly flow further up the supply chain to others rather than those from whose territories the resource is extracted.[70] In addition, in the case of fossil fuels their further use has been identified as key to the ongoing tort caused by climate change. In the equation of costs and profits, no accounting enabled a replacement or replenishment of the resource itself, nor were any costs allocated to mitigating the damage caused by its extraction.[71] The lack of attention to biodiversity and other planetary concerns is symptomatic of an avowed anthropocentrism that viewed these endowments as being for the exclusive and limitless use of the human beings who could claim them for themselves without being compelled to accept any restrictions on how they could be used.

If there is to be a single widespread and systemic crime that could be labelled as most significant to the state of the contemporary world, the extractive industries are likely to best fit such a parameter. The persistent attempt by these industries to obstruct the science around their activities implicates former colonial countries, current and past holders of extractive licences, shareholders of the extracting companies and the governments from whose territory the extraction occurs.[72] Even in the midst of the climate crisis and scarcities caused by war that have impacted the supply of such resources, avowed accumulation of profits by such corporations and the States that shield them ought to make them the specific focus of concerted attempts to claw back extracted wealth, seek accountability and pay for persistent planetary and human damage that has made life – widely

---

[68] On Saudi Arabia, for instance, see Madawi Al-Rasheed, *A History of Saudi Arabia* (Cambridge: Cambridge University Press, 2002).

[69] See, for example, Patricia I. Vasquez, *Oil Sparks in the Amazon: Local Conflicts, Indigenous Populations and Natural Resources* (Athens, GA/London: University of Georgia Press, 2014).

[70] Tobias Haller, Annja Blöchlinger, Markus John, Esther Marthaler and Sabine Ziegler (eds), *Fossil Fuels, Oil Companies and Indigenous Peoples* (Berlin: Lit Verlag, 2007).

[71] Marco Grasso, *From Big Oil to Big Green: Holding the Oil Industry to Account for the Climate Crisis* (Cambridge, MA: MIT Press, 2022).

[72] Donald Gutstein, *The Big Stall: How Big Oil and Think Tanks are Blocking Action on Climate Change in Canada* (Toronto: James Lorimer Ltd., 2018).

configured – on the planet significantly more precarious.[73] Instead, the oil industry as a collective is spending millions on attending and disrupting global governance seeking to regulate carbon emissions.[74] The callous granting of hundreds of new oil and gas licences by the UK government in July 2023 in a bid to 'boost British energy independence and grow the economy'[75] shows the extent to which governments are deeply beholden to the fossil fuel industry. This is also reflected in similar calls in India[76] and China.[77]

Decolonization-oriented crimes

The emergence of the United Nations in 1945 heralded an overt focus on the need to maintain peace and security at a global level and to put in place the global cooperation necessary across countries to build a peaceful and prosperous future. The primary need to maintain peace and security was accompanied by significant articulations over the vexed question of colonialism.[78] Fuelled by an emerging East–West divide that continues to date, the imperial countries of the West came under significant pressure to exit from the colonies that they had acquired over the previous century.[79] The treatment of these 'units' as resource hotbeds, the innate racism of the colonial project and the crimes against humanity that were coming to light were determinant factors in spurring the end of colonialism. The concept of self-determination, borrowed from the literature of the colonial powers themselves, was thrust into prominence, not least in the decolonization of the Americas, where the emerging nations most closely resembled the ethno-religious heritage of their colonial masters.[80] Steeped in the only

---

[73] Alex Lawson, 'BP's Profits Labelled 'Heinous' as calls Grow for Windfall Tax', *The Guardian*, 2 May 2023. Also see 'Norway's Wealth Fund Posts $84 Billion Quarterly Profit' *Reuters*, 21 April 2023.

[74] See Global Witness, *636 Fossil Fuel Lobbyists Granted Access to CoP 27*, 10 November 2022, available at https://www.globalwitness.org/en/campaigns/fossil-gas/636-fossil-fuel-lobbyists-granted-access-cop27/.

[75] See Press Release, (UK) Prime Minister's Office and Department of Energy Security and Net Zero, 31 July 2023.

[76] See Nishant Uga, 'India Launches Offshore Licensing Round in Latest Exploration Push', *Upstream: Energy Explored* (12 October 2022).

[77] [Reuters] 'China's CNOOC Discovers Oilfield in Bohai Sea', 1 March 2023.

[78] Yassin El-Ayouty, *The United Nations and Decolonization: The Role of Afro-Asia* (The Hague: Martinus Nijhoff, 1971).

[79] Nicole Eggers, Jessica Lynne Pearson and Aurora Almada e Santos, *The United Nations and Decolonization* (London: Taylor & Francis, 2020).

[80] Jairo Ramos Acevedo, 'El "Uti Possidetis" un principio americano y no europeo', 5(5) *Misión Jurídica* (2012) 145–63.

recognizable formal education of the time, the Creoles, offspring of the colonizers, sought the kind of self-determination that had transferred power in the United States of America and France to argue for their own freedoms from Madrid and Lisbon.[81] They did not consider themselves to be anything other than the legitimate successors to power, and in much the same way that the *US Declaration of Independence* ignored slaves and Indigenous populations as objects and not subjects, the Creole self-determination paid no attention to native populations.[82]

The idea was derived from what was taught and accepted as the ancient *laws of nations*, even though as they evolved these laws paid scant attention to traditions other than those in Europe. Thus, China, with the longest documented history in the world, did not have its systems featured in the articulation of the *laws of nations*.[83] Other less well-inscribed traditions were also dismissed as primitive, but the title of 'international law' was bestowed onto principles on the grounds that it had been contributed to by a range of ostensibly diverse, but mainly European, powers. While the emergence of the 'new world' provided a wider slate for the justification of the tag international, the deep educational ties between the new and old worlds were significant.

In any case, the articulation of self-determination was a norm derived from a right to resist. The 'father of international law', Hugo Grotius, articulated this in the Latin phrase *jus resistendi ac secessionis*, that is, the right to resist oppression including through secession. Defining Spanish and Portuguese rule in the Americas as oppression, the colonizers' offspring sought to control the wealth themselves rather than repatriate it to their original homelands. They called upon this principle inspired by the American and French Revolutions, which lit a touchpaper for freedom among subjugated populations, and the idea found significant echoes among the voices enjoined in leading the vast populations under colonial rule. The result was that the UN Charter featured self-determination as one of its centrepieces, and the United Nations played a significant role in the decolonization process from 1945 onwards.[84] Within emerging and aspirant nations, the educated elite of all hues found these ideas deeply attractive, not only in freeing their territories from the colonial yoke but also in laying their own claim to

---

[81] Simeon E. Baldwin, 'The International Congresses and Conferences of the Last Century as Forces Working towards the Solidarity of the World', 1(3) *American Journal of International Law* (1907) 808–29.

[82] Joshua Simon, *The Ideology of Creole Revolution: Imperialism and Independence in American and Latin American Political Thought* (Cambridge: Cambridge University Press, 2017).

[83] Zhipeng He and Lu Sun, *A Chinese Theory of International Law* (Singapore: Springer Nature, 2020).

[84] Rigo Sureda, *The Evolution of the Right of Self-determination* (Leiden: Sijthoff, 1973).

governance.⁸⁵ The vexed question of contested histories would inevitably come to the fore. Colonization had cut across clans, tribes, communities, nations and people, but these histories were now erased as the unit seeking self-determination was predetermined to be the colonial unit, with elites seeking to unite populations under the flag of nation building.⁸⁶ Thus, the lines drawn upon maps whereby one White hegemon determined his [sic!] sovereign jurisdiction from that of his neighbour now assumed hugely significant import.⁸⁷ Any dissent from the emergence of these independent 'nations' was dismissed by the new rulers and the former colonial masters as uncivilized tribalism that could compromise international peace and security.

As decolonization proceeded, greater emphasis was laid on the transfer of power, with the Trusteeship Council of the United Nations playing a role in developing the concept of how such decolonization could be achieved.⁸⁸ Many of the emerging entities were beset by deep internal divisions that bore scars from the colonial period, including the vaunted policies of divide and rule discussed earlier, through which the previous hegemons segmented local populations and used the division to maintain a hold over power. At the transition there were significant aspirations for what new governance systems may emerge. There were significant options available for the adoption or return to pre-colonial rule,⁸⁹ whether through local community authorities,⁹⁰ *millets* such as those that existed under the Ottoman rule,⁹¹ devolved and diffuse governance,⁹² the maintenance of emirates or respect for wider confederations.⁹³ There were also calls, notably in the Arab world and within Africa, for the emergence of pan-governance regimes that allowed the widest possible configuration of communities to unite and take over the governance of colonial territories. UN decolonization, however, driven

---

85 Jost Düffler and Marc Frey (eds), *Elites and Decolonization in the Twentieth Century* (London: Palgrave Macmillan, 2011).
86 Karl Deutsch and William Folz, *Nation Building* (New York: Atherton Press, 1963).
87 Joshua Castellino and Stephen Allen, *Title to Territory in International Law: A Temporal Analysis* (Dartmouth: Ashgate, 2003).
88 Jan Lüdert, Julius Heise and Maria Ketzmerick, *The United Nations Trusteeship System: Legacies, Continuities, and Change* (London: Taylor & Francis, 2022).
89 Ige F. Dekker and Wouter Werner, *Governance and International Legal Theory* (The Hague: Brill, 2004).
90 Stella Nwokeji, *The Nigerian History: The Pre-colonial Era, Colonial Amalgamation, and Analysis of the Earlier Nigerian Federal Polity* (Independently published, ISBN: 9781696405331, 2019).
91 Heather Sharkey, *A History of Muslims, Christians and Jews in the Middle East* (Cambridge; Cambridge University Press, 2017).
92 Hiroyuki Hino, Arnim Langer, John Lonsdale and Frances Stewart (eds), *From Divided Pasts to Cohesive Futures: Reflections on Africa* (Cambridge; Cambridge University Press, 2019).
93 Colin Newbury, *Patrons, Clients and Empire: Chieftaincy and Over-rule in Asia, Africa and the Pacific* (Oxford; Oxford University Press, 2003).

by the colonial powers and assisted by the support of key Western-trained individuals from within the emerging nations, pushed through a much narrower project: the imposition of the so-called post-colonial nation State as the solely recognizable governing entity.

This decision was justified on a number of bases that appeared reasonable at first sight but that break down when looked at from a greater temporal distance. The most widely circulating statement in favour was the ostensible need to maintain order at a time of transition. This argument was phrased on the basis that engaging complicated identity questions at a time of transition could prove costly and would lead to bloodshed, while maintaining a neat transition along the drawn lines would guard against such eventuality. A second argument advanced was that the proposal had the support of the key independence movements and on that basis had the 'consent of the governed', which was central to the idea of self-determination.[94] Underpinning the discussion was the belief that the new entities were now settled, with an inherited education system and an identity that had crystallized during the colonial period but became even more accentuated in the range of groups that 'united' in opposition to the colonial hegemon. Compelling accounts of 'nation building' featured strongly, encouraging communities to set aside 'narrow historical differences' to unite at the altar of the emergence of an exciting post-colonial future.

History shows that decolonization was not free of violence and that in many significant cases what eventually transpired under the name of the transference of power from the colonial hegemon lay in the empowering of a domestic hegemon who acted in the same manner as the previous masters.[95] The lines drawn on maps privileged certain communities who were then encouraged to adopt a national identity, which they often did on the basis of their particular heritage. Some emerging entities paid lip service to diversity;[96] others sought to impose a supervening nationalism[97] drawn from the literature of its Western masters and superimposed onto native populations,[98] with any dissenters discouraged as traitors seeking to compromise the 'national' project.[99] Kin communities, especially those divided across the now fully

---

[94] Dirdeiry M. Ahmed, *Boundaries and Secession in Africa and International Law: Challenging Uti Possidetis* (Cambridge: Cambridge University Press, 2015).

[95] See, for example, Meredith Terretta, *Nation of Outlaws, State of Violence: Nationalism, Grassfields Tradition, and State Building in Cameroon* (Athens, OH: Ohio University Press, 2014).

[96] Shashi Tharoor, *The Struggle for India's Soul* (London: Hurst & Co., 2021).

[97] Heri Akhmadi, *Breaking the Chains of Oppression of the Indonesian People* (Singapore: Equinox Publishing, 2010, original edn 1981).

[98] R. Mugu Gatheru, *Kenya: From Colonization to Independence 1888–1970* (Jefferson, NC: McFarland Incorporated Publishers, 2005).

[99] Sharika Thiranagama and Tobias Kelly (eds) *Traitors: Suspicion, Intimacy and the Ethics of State Building* (Philadelphia: Penn University Press, 2010).

legitimated 'international' boundaries, faced the hardest situation, forced to conform to aspirations of 'nation' articulated by dominant communities that were not of their community while required to reject cross-border links with their community in order not to be ostracized.[100]

Decolonization in this format achieved three outcomes that are significantly far from the implicit values contained in the doctrine of self-determination. First, it predetermined and enabled new forms of dominance by one community over all others, bestowing a legitimacy upon that community while effectively relegating the future trajectory of other communities, who became subaltern. Second, it reified and extracted significant wealth from new entities that could ill afford it by selling arms, often to the new governing incumbents on both sides of the border, in the name of deterrence. This fuelled an arms race that continues today, with the notable beneficiaries being the arms companies within the former colonial powers and other privateers in various locations who could reap brokerage rewards all to be added to the debt burden facing the new country's exchequer.[101] Third, by favouring specific ethno-religious communities in the competition to emerge into the power vacuum being left behind, it gained the loyalty of the new incumbents, who literally moved into the palaces and institutions that were vacated. A key facet of the arrangement was the continuation of the most prominent economic activities that had been undertaken during colonial rule. This continuation was justified on the basis that these commercial activities were needed as the lifeblood of the new nation and would be expected to generate the funding necessary for the emerging State to embark on a path of development.[102]

Viewed six or seven decades after decolonization, it is suggested here that decolonization effectively signalled the privatization of colonies from (illegitimate) colonial rule to dubiously legitimate private hands dressed up in the garb of speaking for 'the people'. Benefits in a significant number of cases continued to flow to the individuals and clans in governance and to their close associates, as in colonial times, while colonial-era supply chains were maintained. The outflow of capital and investment also continued, but now with a proportion returned to the local jurisdiction, while some was counted as new debt (especially for arms) to be paid for by taxpayers in the emerging country. Foreign investment was encouraged, which justified the continued expansion of colonial-era companies, and the new markets

---

[100] Ramesh Chandra Thakur, Vesselin Popovski and Walter A. Kemp (eds), *Blood and Borders: The Responsibility to Protect and the Problem of the Kin-State* (Tokyo: United Nations University Press, 2011).

[101] Andrew Feinstein, *The Shadow World: Inside the Global Arms Trade* (London: Penguin, 2011).

[102] Adom Getachew, *Worldmaking After Empire: The Rise and Fall of Self-determination* (Princeton, NJ: Princeton University Press, 2020).

were prised forcibly open to ensure that outside firms would continue to be able to undertake gainful economic activity.[103] Key to the argument advanced in the context of this book, discussions around reparations were stalled, submerged or discarded. Instead, the idea grew that development aid could assist these States to emerge from the 'development gap' that they had mysteriously fallen into.[104] Against this backdrop it is suggested that there are a series of acts of omission and commission that fall under this category, including the continuation of certain industries, the process of favouring specific hegemons, the stoking of discontent and the siphoning of resources through arms deals and kickbacks. In some jurisdictions the direct exclusion of certain actors from the transition arrangements, the grant of preferential rights and bias towards some communities and unequal logistics combined to ensure a less than fair fight (where such could even take place) in the process of claiming governance.

Legacy crimes

The colonial powers' legacy of political governance is arguably one of its most significant crimes, not least because it defeated the very purpose of decolonization. Yet this category is distinguished from the previous category by a focus on the trappings of the inherited governance system. At the epicentre of this is the treatment of land rights and the privileging of colonial-era land titles over nearly every other title claim. Post-colonial jurisdictions continue to struggle to fully restore the ancestral domain of its Indigenous peoples that were lost in a flurry of illegal land acquisitions. Instead, the emerging legal system was reified by the sanctity afforded to property rights, which became the basis for what was maintained from the inherited colonial system of law. Indigenous land tenure systems and other elements of pre-existing customary, traditional and tribal laws were mostly dismissed as invalid or primitive, while the formal law derived from publicists of colonial histories accompanied the emerging State's journey into independence. The inherited legal system was validated in its entirety, with new constitutions written that drew heavily from the colonial masters' versions or values, making the transfer of power barely discernible when viewed through the lens of legal principles. Colonial biases towards settled and sedentary populations formed a bedrock, with any deviations from this labelled premodern. Thus, Westernization was sold to the emerging world

---

[103] Nkwazi N. Mhango, *How Africa Developed Europe: Deconstructing the His-Story of Africa, Excavating Untold Truth and What Ought to be Done and Known* (Bamenda: Langaa Research & Publishing CIC, 2018).

[104] Edward Kenneth Hawkins, *The Principles of Development Aid* (London: Penguin, 2007).

as 'modernity', and the continuation of the legal system was deemed crucial in maintaining order and even, in the case of many human rights elements, in underwriting values that protected the equal and inherent dignity and worth of every individual.

The system was locked against change by the determination to apply or impose political systems that favoured incumbent governments or others that were willing to adopt the guise, stature and a significant proportion of the values of the incumbent government. 'Westminster-style democracy' was trumpeted as an ultimate goal; societies were encouraged to accept the need to 'evolve' towards this, with attendant values such as the rule of law and democracy considered integral parts of the accompanying script. It is almost as if the unfolding policy of what was needed was written through the racist lens of General Dyer's comments referred to earlier in describing a specific incident of colonial crime.

There are several types of colonial legacy crimes concerning direct environmental destruction whose impact is still being felt today. The testing of nuclear weapons by France in its colonies and departments, ensuring that the impacts were far from its own population while leaving toxic legacies elsewhere, is merely one example.[105] A specific legacy crime that is worth emphasizing due to its sheer import in a contemporary rather than colonial setting is the notion of Fortress Conservation, a theme that will be returned to in Part II of this book. During the colonial era this modern concept started life as a means by which certain forests, usually rich in biodiversity (though that appeared to be incidental in those more anthropocentric times), could be placed under a special legal regime whereby native populations were barred from entering them. Rather than for the protection of biodiversity, these practices were often in place to privilege the colonial ruling classes' proclivity towards sport hunting.[106] The fact that the native populations may have considered these forests their homes was ignored, and their expulsion resulted not only in the loss of their homes but also their livelihoods and circular economies. The determination to treat such populations as barely different from the biodiversity that existed has been covered under the first type of crime identified in this chapter. The policy remains a legacy crime since it survived the immediate colonial transition, though other justifications were used for its persistence. The maintenance of the areas as 'national parks' for the enjoyment of all was the most common reason, though the enabling of local development, including through tourism, also featured

---

[105] Remus Prăvălie, 'Nuclear Weapons Tests and Environmental Consequences: A Global Perspective', 43(6) *Ambio* (2014) 729–44.

[106] Esme G. Murdock, 'Conserving Dispossession? A Genealogical Account of the Colonial Roots of Western Conservation', 24(3) *Ethics, Policy & Environment* (2021) 235–49.

strongly.[107] In any case, the Indigenous peoples once displaced often stayed displaced and were reduced to subsistence-based existences in unfamiliar peri-urban settings.

Climate change, largely brought on by wanton planetary destruction through exploitation of natural resources and exponential jumps in carbon emissions due to overt use of fossil fuels, has provided a fresh impetus for the reintroduction of this colonial-era practice.[108] The argument is laid out as follows. Man-made activities have brought the planet to the brink of destruction. The extinctions of biodiversity we currently face are key manifestations of this destruction. It is therefore imperative that, in conjunction with other measures, a protective ring is thrown around the biodiversity that remains to safeguard its disappearance. In generating this protective ring, a part of the globe must return to wilderness so that biodiversity can thrive in these areas free from human interference. This will allow the planet to heal and will strengthen these areas as carbon sinks to absorb carbon emissions from elsewhere. Labelled as the '30×30 plan', it envisages that the worst impacts of climate change could be reversed by returning 30 per cent of land and waters to wilderness by 2030.[109]

Like the argument around the need for order at a time of transition described above, this argument seems strong. After all, the climate crisis is biting into planetary viabilities in sustaining life, and radical system change is required. Yet closer scrutiny shows how flawed and colonialist such a strategy is and how its implementation would form a new component of a legacy crime. The counterarguments to it should be understood from the moral, legal and purely pragmatic standpoints. Through a moral lens, the idea that a few selected parts of the globe – the Congo Basin, the Amazon Forest and other tropical forests – should offset vast emissions from urban centres is already deeply flawed.[110] The people in these areas have not contributed to the climate crisis yet risk being evicted, losing their homes, spirituality, identity and livelihoods because of others' decisions taken far from their realm. In this they are treated as objects and not subjects, and the decision to evict them is completely colonial in nature. From a legal standpoint, the

---

[107] David Hulme and Marshall Murphree, *African Wildlife and Livelihoods: The Promise and Performance of Community Conservation* (London: James Currey, 2001).

[108] Dan Brockington, Rosaleen Duffy and Jim Igoe, *Nature Unbound: Conservation, Capitalism and the Future of Protected Areas* (London: Taylor & Francis, 2012).

[109] The Nature Conservancy (2023), *Best Practices in Delivering the 30×30 Target: Protected Areas and Other Effective Area-Based Conservation Measures* (London: A Report for the UK Department for Environment, Food and Rural Affairs, 2nd edn, April 2023).

[110] Lara Domínguez and Colin Luoma, 'Decolonising Conservation Policy: How Colonial Land and Conservation Ideologies Persist and Perpetuate Indigenous Injustices at the Expense of the Environment', 9(3) *Land* (2020) 65.

30×30 plan comprises a non-enforceable standard impossible to contest in a court of law. Thus, this moral imperative is allowing governments and forestry authorities to evict Indigenous peoples while nothing compels the subsequent reservation of these areas as carbon sinks. There are reports that once the eviction takes place, new extractive practices and other exploitative forms of economic activity are being licensed.[111]

Perhaps the most crucial argument against 30×30 is one of pure pragmatism. The reason there is significant overlap between Indigenous peoples' ancestral domains and the areas being selected to fall under the 30 per cent scheme is because these areas are often richest in biodiversity. Crucially, they are richest in biodiversity because the Indigenous communities living in relative harmony with their environments have been able to resist the incursion of the settled States' tentacles into their ancestral domains. Evicting Indigenous peoples from such forests will leave the forests open to exploitation that has deforested other lands around the globe. Thus, at the most pragmatic of levels, strong evidence shows that Indigenous lands are biodiverse *because* of Indigenous peoples' presence and that evicting them will defeat the purpose of the scheme in the first place.[112] The corollary to this is that any determination towards system overhaul and the slowing of emissions will be much more quickly realized by disrupting key urban centres that are among the highest generators of carbon emissions. These locations do not need to be offset; they need to be stopped entirely.

Collusion in the commitment of crime

In attempting to understand and classify crimes, it is important to think through crimes of commission as well as omission. It is equally important, however, to ensure that those who have benefitted through collusion in the crimes that stemmed from colonization are identified and included in any reckoning. This final residual category seeks to capture this group of crimes. As a residual category this classification includes crimes where the principal actor responsible today may well be the post-colonial State or an entity within the post-colonial State that has been enabled through collusion that in some shape or form chimes with the colonial project. The occurrence of the crime in post-colonial settings – like some of the categories explored already – is also a key component to qualifying under this category. However,

---

[111] Hannah Ellis Petersen, 'India Plans to Fell Ancient Forest to Create 40 New Coalfields', *The Guardian*, 8 August 2020.

[112] Victoria Reyes-García, Álvaro Fernández-Llamazares, Yildiz Aumeeruddy-Thomas, Petra Benyei, Rainer W. Bussmann, Sara K. Diamond et al, 'Recognizing Indigenous peoples' and Local Communities' Rights and Agency in the Post-2020 Biodiversity Agenda', 51 *Ambio* (2022) 84–92.

unlike some of the previously identified categories, here the emphasis lies on a supporting cast of actors who would benefit from the crime, whether of commission or omission. This includes former colonial governments who in the name of development and technical cooperation have forced specific avenues upon the State; the retention of preferential trading rights that are framed as benefitting the emerging State but in fact create privileged access to markets; the generation and maintenance of unequal partnerships, especially in benefit sharing from post-colonial commercial activities; and the continued maintenance of preferential financial assets, often for the direct benefit of the colonial rather than the independent State. Included in this list would be the practice that is widely prevalent of maintaining sovereign bases or a military presence that is designed to reflect hegemonic interests but that offers minimal benefit to the hosting territory. Each of these acts or phenomena in and of themselves are the responsibility of the newly independent State. However, in the unequal relationship forged in the aftermath of decolonization and the sheer dependence that many entities were left with, none of these issues could have been fairly negotiated. Instead, the newly independent State was forced into these relationships as a consequence of its inferior bargaining position and has continued in a subdued manner over many of these facets.

The grant of preferential loans for the buying of weapons and armaments is a classical manifestation of this type of crime. In such cases the newly independent State is either persuaded or actively seeks to build up its defence arsenal. It turns to its former colonial master, which in many of the cases under consideration in this book is among the world's most prominent arms dealers. They are then offered a range of weaponry, much of which is beyond the means of the country in question. As in colonial times, these services are provided by private corporations backed by the State. To enable post-colonial States to afford such equipment, preferential loans are offered. This passes the burden of the acquisition of weapons onto the State coffers and creates a guaranteed need for such weapons to be serviced, updated, replenished or replaced. The impact of this activity is twofold. First, it enables the State to prioritize defence over other areas that are perhaps of greater need in serving its governance function. Second, it generates a debt that binds the State into the future. Should there be balance of payment issues, these debts are often rescheduled through additional payments and further commitments to purchase, creating new or renewed dependencies.

3

Curing Cancer: A Five-Point Plan to Address Colonial Crime

It is argued throughout this book that addressing colonial crime is fundamental to achieving long-term peace and security. This would subsume discussions around the sustainability of life on the planet but also address contemporary identity-based fragmentation in the developed multiracial countries that the former colonial powers have become. From the perspective of the intensity of human suffering, the quest to address the persistent problem of underdevelopment remains the most common legacy in the vast majority of countries that have emerged from colonization. Instead of the charity-based agenda driven by global development programmes, a repurposing of finances and the international financial and economic architecture through reparations and other modifications can achieve far more while breaking the neo-colonial reliance promoted by aid dependency. Such a right to a remedy, rather than mere assistance in the aim of achieving global equality, exists in the annals of public international law but has not been systematically implemented.[1]

The viability of any attempted solution to addressing colonial crime will depend on a number of key factors. Significant changes, for instance the decision to abolish the slave trade, were achieved through various means. Perhaps the most important of these was the extent to which power could either be compelled to change or was willing to abdicate or accept the need to do so, whether for pragmatic reasons or in the interest of serving a higher purpose. Whether there will be a reckoning for colonial crime or not, it is clearly unlikely to commence unless serious attempts are made that go beyond critique into systems-related thinking about the mechanics of what

---

[1] See *Basic Principles and Guidelines on the Right to a Remedy and Reparation for Victims of Gross Violations of International Human Rights Law and Serious Violations of International Humanitarian Law*, General Assembly Resolution 60/147 (16 December 2005), UN Doc. A/Res/60/147.

a solution could look like. These processes are already under way and have powerful voices in support of them, such as the inspiring Prime Minister (PM) of Barbados, Mia Mottley.[2] In a powerful message that contained the kernel of the ideas referred to as the *Bridgetown Initiative*, delivered to the 77th session of the United Nations General Assembly (2022), PM Mottley proposed a transformative plan of action for addressing the climate crisis and its underpinning exploitative economic architecture. This statement was made against the backdrop of what is referred to as the polycrisis: global food and energy, debt and the climate emergency, not least the last vestiges of pandemic-related economic sluggishness. As scarcities loom, the global financial architecture once again favours the wealthy countries who could bid up prices for fuel and food while simultaneously cutting aid budgets due to a shrinkage in their economies. Seeking to decarbonize will require expensive system-wide transformations that could plunge developing States further into crisis. The *Bridgetown Initiative* seeks to alleviate pressures by addressing immediate fiscal concerns and building resilience. In the longer term they signal the importance of transforming the international financial architecture. Among the series of measures sought are pressuring the World Bank and other multilateral development banks to better leverage their balance sheet to generate an estimated additional $1 trillion for climate and development funding; the creation of emergency liquidity that is accessible to developing countries through Special Drawing Rights at the International Monetary Fund and development banks; developing a loss and damage mechanism for climate equity that includes a windfall tax on oil and gas profits; establishing a Global Climate Mitigation Trust; and heightened recognition for the climate and development nexus, addressed through innovative financial instruments such as debt for equity swaps, State-contingent debt instruments and regional guarantee platforms. The traction that the proposal has is an important signal of its attraction and salience, though it remains considerably more popular among those looking for system change rather than the incumbents of economic power. As a consequence, it remains a long way from the urgency of the action that PM Mottley so eloquently called for.[3]

PM Mottley is also a key personality who is simultaneously taking significant strides forward in calling for reparations for colonial crime. Alongside the President of Ghana, Nana Addo Dankwa Akufo-Addo, and Columbian Vice President Francia Marquez, PM Mia Mottley is

---

[2] 'PM Mottley Says It's Time for Reparations' (Abu Dhabi, National African-American Reparations Commission), 1 April 2022, available at https://reparationscomm.org/reparations-news/pm-mottley-says-its-time-for-reparations/.

[3] Ronan Palmer and Frank Schroeder, 'The Bridgetown Initiative, A Climate and Development Plan for COP27', 14 November 2022, E3G, available at https://www.e3g.org/news/the-bridgetown-initiative-a-climate-and-development-plan-for-cop27/

likely to build significant consensus among the vast and varied victims of colonial crime. Her attempt to build stronger ties with the African Union is evocative as a response to slavery, which forced so many of her citizens' ancestors from Africa. These overtures are being reciprocated warmly, which will significantly enhance the voices of those calling for reparative justice. The passage of the *Accra Proclamation on Reparations* (2023) under *African Union* auspices is an indicator of growing momentum to these ventures.[4] It galvanizes and builds on ideas that have been expressed by scholars such as Hilary Beckles.[5] Yet for this to move from an idea that is mobilizing powerful voices to its actual implementation will still need significant movement on the part of power. This brief chapter is offered to stimulate conversation in the belief that rather than definitive solutions to specific instances which can only be engineered against a set context, there are some general contours that all such discussion will need to follow.

Acceptance of wrongfulness

The idea that system change of the magnitude required could occur without acceptance of wrongfulness is unimaginable. Yet the corollary to this remains true and is emerging in responses directed at addressing the climate change issue. Steps are being taken to tackle several related and cognate aspects of the climate crisis without acceptance of how wrongful acts were responsible for the causality behind climate change. These need to be lauded since they are changing behaviours and providing victories in terms of seeking compensation and identifying the direction of change. Yet the central thrust required – the drive for a changed system – is unlikely to emerge through this incremental approach to accountability.

Acceptance that colonial crime constitutes a legal wrong that requires a remedy may be among the most challenging of the steps required for mitigation or any of the remedies that may flow from it. With societies, especially former colonizing countries, becoming increasingly polarized around issues of identity, colonial crime may be one of the key fault lines that reignite fragmentation and escalate growing xenophobia and racism. The manner and vehemence with which claims are made is often identified as a reason for why they cannot be addressed. Instead, the argument as a whole is often dismissed as biased and/or coming from a place that makes verification of these narratives difficult, especially where such claims cut

---

[4] *On Building a United Front to Advance the Course of Justice and Reparations to Africans (14–17 November 2023), Accra, Ghana.*

[5] Hilary McD Beckles, *How Britain Underdeveloped the Caribbean: A Reparations Response to Europe's Legacy of Plunder and Poverty* (Kingston: University of West Indies Press, 2021).

across and directly challenge the received wisdoms or 'home truths' that were disseminated through formal education systems and popular culture.

Seeking acceptance of wrongfulness may require several steps, though a start would probably have to be made from a commitment to undertake an investigation into the nature of the allegations themselves. Even were such a commitment forthcoming, it would be imperative that the task is entrusted to a group of committed researchers who have the skills to go beyond the mere existence of literature to probe elements of fact that may be obscured by time. As we have seen from the inquiry conducted by Oriel College, Oxford over its Cecil Rhodes statue[6] and from the ongoing discussions with the British Museum over the Benin Bronzes referred to in the previous chapter, such commissions can be used to delay discussions and create the impression that the claim is being taken seriously.

One of the single biggest challenges across the process of seeking remedies for colonial crimes, commencing from the need for an acceptance of wrongfulness, is access to the process for those communities, who mostly because of the structural discrimination they have faced over generations, are remote from such discussions. It appears common across the world for marginalized communities to focus greater attention to their survival within the system rather than to seek prominence at the forefront of movements to change it, yet increasing contact with such communities is vital in enabling a challenge to the tenor of the framed narratives. Finding techniques to demystify processes, reassure and be reassured about the lack of a backlash and recriminations to create, access and triangulate any metanarratives that may emerge is important in the veracity of any claim. Well-evidenced micro stories, such as those that sit within victims' families as their own legends, could be useful in understanding how personal histories intertwine with the macro political struggles behind colonial crime.

Such techniques have already been tested in the context of transitional justice. Truth and Reconciliation Commissions around the world have paid significant attention to a range of techniques to foster access, which in many cases encouraged testimony that went beyond the published versions of events in official narratives, to unearthing wider truths of other more personal stories which helped triangulate macro claims about wrongdoing. The project of seeking to understand colonial crime would not be dissimilar to such ventures, although the time span of their occurrence may be longer.[7]

---

[6] For a critique of the statue and what it stands for, see Athinangamso Nkopo, Brian Kwoba and Roseanne Chantiluke (eds), *Rhodes Must Fall: The Struggle to Decolonise the Racist Heart of Europe* (London: Bloomsbury Publishing, 2018).

[7] Mia Swart and Karin van Marle (eds), *The Limits of Transition: The South African Truth and Reconciliation Commission 20 Years On* (Leiden/Boston: Brill Nijhoff, 2017).

In any case, whether or not a different narrative emerges, the findings of the verification process must be written in a manner designed to reach a wide audience and actively disseminated with a view to stimulating societal discussion and dialogue. This must allow space for those who dissent, since it would be better for the discussion to be diluted through challenge than ignored. Such a negotiated, perhaps even collective, approach to the documentation of history would stand in sharp contrast to more 'normal' processes of history that are usually compiled by an individual or a group of individuals, often drawn from communities with the benefit of formalistic historical experience and with a degree of access to official narratives. For its veracity to be attested, such a project would need the backing of formal trained historians, not least because they would actively verify the process, but also because such interventions may help to interrogate and actively referee any new biases from entering the narrative. Such a process has already begun, which seeks to view global history through the lens of women's contributions. It unearths figures from the past who were intentionally obscured or deliberately marginalized and enables fresher, more inclusive perspectives on events. In *The Ascent of Woman*, a four-part TV documentary series, Dr Amanda Foreman shows the galvanizing impact of such an approach.[8] The popular film directed by Stephen Williams entitled *Chevalier*, based on the true-life story of composer Joseph Bologne, has a similar galvanizing impact on the narration of history.[9]

The rewiring of the historical narrative should clearly not be an end in itself. Rather, where a wrong has been identified, it is imperative that such a wrong is first acknowledged through acceptance of its veracity, followed to the extent feasible by an apology. As we saw in the discussion around the Benin Bronzes, in many instances of colonial crime the wrongs have been brought to light but little consequence has flowed from that discovery or even the admittance of such a wrong. Instead, the holders of the artefacts appear ready and willing to absorb the criticism while merely engaging in seemingly endless discussions about potential remedies, perhaps stalling it long enough with the hope that the problem or claim will eventually dissipate. Such an attitude, especially if it concerns some of the categories of crimes identified above, will undermine the process of building trust and may worsen the fragmentation in society that had first led to the opening of the issue.

The importance of any acceptance of wrongfulness would lie in the quality of the obligations it ought to create on the party deemed culpable. This could take the form of the acceptance of moral and/or legal

---

[8] See Amanda Foreman (writer), *The Ascent of Woman*, four-part TV series (BBC, 2015).
[9] See Stephen Williams (director) *Chevalier* (Searchlight Films, 2022).

obligations. Some accused of wrongdoing may only have the power and authority to accept wrongdoing at a moral level, without the capacity or capability to address its wrongfulness.[10] This would be especially true where no specific remedy may be appropriate or where it may be impossible to construct an appropriate remedy without causing new injustices. The importance of the assumption of moral obligations could play an important role in marking the wrongdoing and documenting its full extent with a view to it serving as a reminder of the act or omission. Memorials and the adoption of symbols may well fit into this category. Recognition through educational materials would transmit this effectively to future generations while having a validating impact on the present of many communities that are often marginalized.

In other instances where it is possible and appropriate, a finding of wrongfulness must result in the acceptance of a legal obligation towards redress, which could take four broad forms, as will be discussed later. In any case, at minimum it should entail the guarantee of non-repetition and the framing of contemporary policy changes that may be necessary to safeguard against future violations. In the case of *every* type of colonial crime it must be a necessary condition that the new finding of wrongdoing is produced within its own historical narrative to ensure that future generations within that country understand the extent to which their State was implicated in the commitment of an international wrong.

Belgium has been going through an interesting series of processes since 2018 with regard to accountability for its actions during King Leopold II's colonial enterprises in the Congo Basin. After a visit to the country in 2019 the *UN Working Group of Experts on People of African Descent* issued a series of recommendations that read as a good checklist for a country that is early in the process of seeking to accept its role in the perpetration of colonial crime.[11] The visit by the working group arose in response to growing acts of xenophobia in Belgium since the start of this century, so the recommendations sit among a range of measures that are seeking to address the subordinate positions of persons of African descent in modern Belgium. Belgium was called on to:

> Issue an apology for the atrocities committed during colonization. The Working Group recommends reparatory justice, with a view to closing what is a dark chapter in Belgian history and as a means of

---

[10] Japan has had a wide discussion about this issue under significant pressure from its neighbours. See Jane Yamazaki, *Japanese Apologies for World War II: A Rhetorical Study* (London: Routledge, 2012).

[11] UN Doc A/HRC/42/59/Add.1.

reconciliation and healing. The right to reparations for past atrocities is not subject to any statute of limitations.

Among a host of other remedies, the report highlighted need for a truth commission to seek to establish the facts behind Belgian institutions' roles in Congo, Rwanda and Burundi, full access to colonial archives, support for the Royal Museum for Central Africa to transform its portrayal of events seen through a colonial lens to 'enrich its narrative ... thus contributing to a better awareness understanding of the tragic legacies of Belgian colonialism and of the past'. Key, in terms of the wider healing required, is the financial support for a public education campaign, so 'people may learn about and better understand the legacies of Belgian colonialism'.[12] Around a year later in 2020, at the 60th anniversary of the independence of the Democratic Republic of Congo, the King of the Belgians spoke of his 'deepest regrets' over the suffering inflicted upon the peoples of the country during Belgian rule.[13] By the summer of 2020, the Belgian Federal Parliament established a truth and reconciliation commission with a view to assessing the role and structural impact of colonial rule in the Congo Free State (1885–1908), Belgian Congo (1908–1960) and Ruanda-Urundi (1918–1962).[14] While the commission did issue recommendations, these were not endorsed by the parliamentary commission for fear, among some parliamentarians, that:

> the act of expressing apologies would lead to a formal admission of Belgium's international responsibility for injustices committed during its colonial times, thereby opening the floodgates to legal claims for reparations through financial compensation. The impossibility of reaching an agreement on the issuance of formal apologies finally led to the failure of the commission itself to issue recommendations to the Belgian Federal Parliament.[15]

Literature on remedies traditionally identifies specific avenues that could be pursued in the attempt to right a wrong that may have been committed. The right to a remedy in the context of reparations has been described by the *UN High Commissioner of Human Rights* as having the potential of a

---

[12] UN Doc A/HRC/42/59/Add.1, para 75.
[13] King Philippe – Speech at the Esplanade of the Palais du Peuple, Kinshasa (8 June 2022), available at https://www.monarchie.be/en/agenda/speech-by-his-majesty-the-king-esplanade-of-the-palais-du-peuple-kinshasa.
[14] *Parl. St. Kamer* 2019–2020, nr. 1462/001.
[15] Sarah El Amouri and Stefaan Smis, 'Inter-State Apologies for Colonial Injustices from an International State Responsibility Perspective: A Commentary on the Belgian Controversy', 27(4) *American Journal of International Law* (April 2023).

'catalytic power ... on the daily life of victims, families, communities and entire societies'.[16] Reparation measures include restitution, compensation, rehabilitation and satisfaction.[17] In the rest of this chapter the focus will be placed on reparations and how they could be configured in a manner that takes into account the discussions on compensation and satisfaction. The issue of restitution and compensation will, however, be looked at separately in support of the discussion around environmental accountability that is the focus of Part II of the book. Another element could be added to traditional reparative measures, discussed here as solidarity-oriented measures. After a general discussion on reparations, the rest of the chapter will examine these specific forms in greater detail to address how they could be drawn upon in the context of correcting the established wrong of a colonial crime as designated earlier.

Reparations

Clearly, any attempt to repair the damage of a colonial crime would require the addressal of that tort through seeking to reverse the policy that either contributed to or continues to contribute to the elements of the wrong.[18] In many of the types of colonial crimes identified above, it may be necessary to use a series of the remedies identified here. The example of policies concerned with the continuation of the extraction of fossil fuels is a case in point. Thus, while the destruction of the circular economy may have commenced under colonial rule, the continued extraction of fossil fuels is a contemporary wrong that needs to be addressed through a series of reparative measures which must start from the immediate stopping of the wrongful activity in the first place.

In addressing this further, it would be important to identify liability for any specific legal or policy decisions that may have been formulated which contribute to the persistence of the wrong. This includes an assessment of policies and practices concerning recognition of the land rights from where the extraction has taken place but could also feature withdrawal of lawfully granted leases and extractive licences. One of the hardest challenges to confront in such reparations lies in generating a system that will create just

---

[16] Statement by Michelle Bachelet, UN High Commissioner for Human Rights, 16 December 2020, available at https://www.ohchr.org/en/statements/2020/12/15th-anniversary-basic-principles-and-guidelines-right-remedy-and-reparation.

[17] This is listed on the Office of the High Commissioner for Human Rights Fact Sheet on Reparations and Transitional Justice, available at https://www.ohchr.org/en/transitional-justice/reparations.

[18] For a general reading, see Fernne Brennan and John Packer, *Colonialism, Slavery, Reparations and Trade: Remedying the Past?* (London: Routledge, 2012).

and fair processes for the recognition and transfer of such properties to the originally dispossessed populations. In this quest it would be important to factor in others, including leaseholders who may have acquired possession of the territory through means that were deemed lawful at the time of their acquisition.

Previous discussions on reparations have focussed heavily on questions of reconciliatory justice.[19] Thus, amends are designed in the present for violations that occurred in the past with a view to reconciling the offspring of perpetrators and victims. The existence of a historical wrong is a key element for reparations. In his book *Reconsidering Reparations* Olúfẹ́mi Táíwò advocates instead for a constructive view of reparations that draws on the theoretical foundations for the reparations debate from key political thinkers of African descent, such as James Baldwin, Martin Luther King, Jr and Nkechi Taifa.[20]

The *Bridgetown Initiative* referenced earlier also proceeds from the same logic, articulating specific paths that can be followed to unleash the financing necessary to combat change, while referencing the extent to which colonial powers have a duty to address injustice. Caribbean States may well be ahead of the curve in thinking about reparations since the Heads of Caribbean States came together in 2013 under the banner of the Caribbean Community (CARICOM) to establish the *Caricom Reparation Commission* (CRC). Rather than focussing on climate change, it was modelled on the older push for reparations relating to crimes against humanity. Its mandate enables the Commission to formulate a reparations justice programme whereby victims of genocide, slavery, slave trading and racial apartheid (or their families) are able to avail of a legal right to reparatory justice, with those who committed the crimes and 'who have been enriched by the proceeds of these crimes'[21] made answerable. The perpetrators are identified by the CRC as European governments, due to their special role in instituting 'the framework for … developing and sustaining these crimes'. The CRC recognizes these governments as 'the primary agencies through which slave-based enrichment took place, and as national custodians of criminally accumulated wealth'. It makes eight specific assertions against European governments:

1. They were owners and traders of enslaved Africans and instructed genocidal actions upon Indigenous communities.

---

[19] Hilary Beckles, *Britain's Black Debt: Reparations for Caribbean Slavery and Native Genocide* (Kingston: University of West Indies Press, 2013).
[20] Olúfẹ́mi O. Táíwò, *Reconsidering Reparations* (Oxford: Oxford University Press, 2022).
[21] Caricom, *Caricom Ten Point Plan for Reparatory Justice*, available at https://adsdatabase.ohchr.org/IssueLibrary/CARICOM_Ten-Point%20Plan%20for%20Reparatory%20Justice.pdf

2. They created the legal, financial and fiscal policies necessary for the enslavement of Africans.
3. They defined and enforced African enslavement and native genocide as in their 'national interests'.
4. They refused compensation to the enslaved with the ending of their enslavement.
5. They compensated slave owners at emancipation for the loss of legal property rights in enslaved Africans.
6. They imposed a further 100 years of racial apartheid upon the emancipated.
7. They imposed for another 100 years policies designed to perpetuate suffering upon the emancipated and survivors of genocide.
8. They have refused to acknowledge such crimes or to compensate victims and their descendants.[22]

The CRC action plan provides a route map for how reparation may be paid out. The first step is a full official apology that 'accepts responsibility, commits to non-repetition and pledges to repair the harm caused'. 'Statements of regret' offered as a stand-alone component are specifically identified as falling short of the necessary standard of what constitutes an apology. Step two focuses on development programmes for Indigenous peoples. This set of communities is specifically recognized due to the devastating impact of European colonization upon them in the Caribbean, where a population of close to three million in 1700 was decimated to less than 30,000 in 2000 as a result of official actions that brutalized, killed, forcibly displaced and subjugated the communities. With the slave trade link very clear in Caribbean history, the third step is identified as fully funding repatriation to Africa for those who wish to return, including facilitation of issues concerning citizenship and re-integration into the societies from which they were forcibly removed. As a fourth step, the CRC calls for the establishment of cultural institutions and the return of cultural heritage that has been seized. Such a return of heritage would contribute to reversing some of the impact of colonization through a process that would facilitate the population's own understanding of its submerged historical memories.

The fifth point recognizes the legacy of colonization by demanding assistance in remedying the public health crisis that can be traced directly through new medical evidence to a legacy of 400 years of enslavement, manifest through chronic diseases in the form of hypertension and diabetes. The education theme is more directly addressed in the sixth demand, asserting that unwillingness to design a proper education scheme was part

---

[22] Caricom Reparations Commission, available at https://caricomreparations.org/caricom/caricoms-10-point-reparation-plan/.

of a system to maintain an uneducated work force, while where it did exist it created inequalities based on race and class, leaving behind deeply flawed systems and widespread illiteracy. The seventh step addresses the forced acculturation and racist ideologies of inferiority through enhancement of historical and cultural knowledge exchanges to enhance awareness, foster respect and guarantee non-repetition. The eighth step involves psychological rehabilitation from the inherited inter-generational trauma of slavery, while the right to development through the use of technology forms step nine, to overcome the imposed deficit post-colonial countries faced in seeking to rebuild their inherited economies. The final step is one that has been articulated time and again: debt cancellation and monetary compensation. Explaining the fiscal trap that has resulted from addressing the community poverty inherited from slavery and colonialism, the CRC asserts:

> Since correcting the burden of colonialism has fallen on these new States, they are unable to deal with the challenges of development without taking on onerous levels of debt. This debt cycle properly belongs to the governments from the responsible European countries who have made no sustained attempt to deal with debilitating colonial legacies.[23]

And that 'support for the payment of domestic debt, the cancellation of international debt, and direct monetary payments where appropriate, are necessary reparatory actions to correct the harm caused by colonialism'.[24]

This ten-point plan has gained significant traction, and its utility beyond the Caribbean was recognized by the *United Nations Working Group of People of African Descent* in its recommendation 75 (k) (quoted earlier in this chapter) following its visit to Belgium.[25]

In many instances, making the necessary reparations may involve a significant overhaul to legal systems that are based on proprietorship of land that was never unalienated in the first place. With the political and socio-economic system based on the acquisition of wealth through property, unleashing such mechanisms is by far the most challenging part of the debate about reparations for colonial crime. These also expand beyond simplistic assumptions of a colonial power's culpability and the former

---

[23] Caricom Reparations Commission, available at https://caricomreparations.org/caricom/caricoms-10-point-reparation-plan/.
[24] Caricom Reparations Commission, available at https://caricomreparations.org/caricom/caricoms-10-point-reparation-plan/.
[25] For a collection of these points and supplementary arguments, see the special issue dedicated to this theme: 9(5) *Africology: Journal of Pan African Studies* (2016).

colonial peoples' victimhood since they implicate a range of actors across this perceived divide.[26] While the broad thrust of reparations outlined here provides a useful bulwark for broader thinking, restitution, compensation and solidarity-oriented actions provide a more specific and commonly requested form of reparations, to which we shall turn next.

Restitution

While the restitution of land would be a particularly complicated form of reparation, the restitution of movable properties must seem significantly simpler, assuming that such a process is physically feasible. The discussion on the return of cultural artefacts has echoes in many bilateral discussions around the world. With objects like the Kohinoor Diamond or the Benin Bronzes, it is possible to simply extract the items from within the possession of the former colonial power and transfer them to the entity from which they were first removed. Discussions of whether the country seeking the restitution ought to pay a value for the item and for its transportation are contextualized by the process through which the item left the original shores in the first place. Laws governing antiquities, to the extent to which these may have been operable at the time of the extraction, are often not of significant use since the process of colonization often put these jurisdictions beyond the reach of such laws that may have existed and only regulated the treatment of antiquities within 'civilized nations'. Besides, most of the jurisdictions under discussion may not have had formal laws on the books that protected their antiquities, and even in instances where those may have existed, the power of the governing authorities to enforce such measures would be limited. Thus, as we saw with the Benin Bronzes, the racism of the colonial project often placed the simple acquisition of such properties beyond the realm of theft, with arguments used to suggest that the objects would be better 'safeguarded' and maintained as a shared cultural patrimony in the possession of the colonial power. The return of such artefacts in contemporary times may not be a simple process. They may have to be accompanied by suitable investment in the construction of appropriate places for such items to be safeguarded and displayed.

The return of misappropriated financial assets is a far more complicated process than the physical return of artefacts, often because these financial assets may be of significantly different market value in terms of the modern

---

[26] Jacqueline Bhabha, Margareta Matache and Caroline Elkins, *Time for Reparations: A Global Perspective* (Philadelphia, University of Pennsylvania Press, 2021).

world than they were at the time of their extraction. As Shashi Tharoor, author of *Inglorious Empire*, writes in relation to India:

> India was a thriving economy prior to its colonization by Britain, contributing 27% of global GDP in 1700. Post two centuries of exploitation by the British, India's contribution to the global economy drastically reduced to 3%. India was a great exporter of finished cloth, but with the advent of the British, its textile industry was crushed and it became an importer; India's share in the global textile trade went from 25 percent to less than 2 percent.[27]

The Indian economist Utsa Patnaik has calculated that the value of physical assets taken from India over 200 years would amount to $45 trillion, which is around 17 times the size of the current UK economy. This included fraudulent payments made for valuables such as gold. In addition to land and assets stolen and an estimated 35 million who died through either deliberate or negligent efforts by Britain in creating or reacting to famine, Indians also paid tax for the 'privilege' of British occupation, estimated to total approximately $120 million. And all of that is not taking into account the worth of the Kohinoor Diamond, estimated at $400 million. There is another element that needs to be given attention in any discussion on restitution. In the words of William Dalrymple, writing in *The Guardian*:

> We still talk about the British conquering India, but that phrase disguises a more sinister reality. It was not the British government that seized India at the end of the 18th century, but a dangerously unregulated private company headquartered in one small office, five windows wide, in London, and managed in India by an unstable sociopath – [Robert] Clive.[28]

Dalrymple's point about the private corporate nature of the colonizing entity is of fundamental importance in seeking to achieve restitution, but also for the compensation discussed later in this section. It remains important in terms of understanding the nature of the financial gains made over the period of the activity but is equally relevant in terms of being able to ascertain what magnitude of restitution would be possible in seeking the return or joint ownership of non-exhausted natural resources.

---

[27] Shashi Tharoor, 'Saying Sorry to India: Reparation or Atonement?', *Harvard International Law Journal*, available at https://journals.law.harvard.edu/ilj/wp-content/uploads/sites/84/Tharoor-Reparations.pdf.

[28] William Dalrymple, 'The East India Company: The Original Corporate Raiders', *Guardian Newspapers*, 4 March 2015.

One attempt at restitution, albeit a forceable one, was the successful attempt of the government of Iran to nationalize its oil platforms in the 1950s. This was condemned at the time as the unlawful seizure of private assets.[29] As Europe's dependency on oil grew, the opportunity for its commercial exploitation became ever more lucrative. The legal basis for this derives from a story that started with what is referred to as the *Reuters Concession of 1872*, signed between a British banker and Naser al-Din Shah, then Qajar King of Persia.[30] Echoing the discussion that had taken place in Waitangi a few decades previously, the *Reuters Concession* also displayed similar sentiments to those that guided conversations with King Lobengula of Matabeleland. George Curzon's two-volume work *Persia and Persians*, which is essentially a travelogue across the region, has this to say about the concession: 'it was found to contain the most complete and extraordinary surrender of the entire industrial resources of a kingdom into foreign hands that has probably ever been dreamed of, much less accomplished, in history'.[31]

Much like the *Treaty of Waitangi*, which made a wild claim to all the territories concerned, the concession had clauses which gave an absolute monopoly to Baron de Reuter for 70 years, including the exclusive right to operate all Persian mines (except gold, silver and precious stones). The concession also covered a monopoly over all government forests and uncultivated land as well as exclusive rights to contracts for building nearly all the public infrastructure. The consideration in return was a stipulated sum of money to the Shah for the first five years and an additional 60 per cent of the net revenue over the remaining 20 years. The concession was cancelled within a year after a public outcry, including consternation from Russia, which had its own interests in seeking to benefit from Persia. Key to the failure of Reuter compared to the success of Rhodes was that the British government did not support the plan. The agreement regarding oil drilling and exploitation was signed in 1933 between the *Anglo-Iranian Oil Company* and the government of Iran. It came in another period of tension between the governments of Britain and Iran that has been a feature over centuries. The main source of this tension lay in the fact that the British government gained far more from Iranian oil through taxes than Iran gained through the revenues from the sale of oil. With World War II looming greater, more concerted interference was forthcoming from the United States of America and the Soviet Union, as a consequence of which discussions were stalled until the

---

[29] See Rose Marie Proulx, *Iranian Oil Nationalization and International Law* (State College of Washington, 1952) and Mohsen S. Haery, *The Legal Implication of the Dispute over the Iranian Nationalization of the Oil Industry* (Berkeley, CA: University of California Press, 1955).

[30] See Ervand Abrahamian, *Oil Crisis in Iran: From Nationalism to Coup d'Etat* (Cambridge: Cambridge University Press, 2021).

[31] George Curzon, *Persia and the Persians*, Vol. 1 (London: Frank Cass & Co. 1966) 480.

end of the war. The plan to nationalize the industry had been brewing in Iran for a few decades while anger grew at unfair treatment. It was finally achieved through an order passed on 15 March 1951 by Iran's legislative body, the *Majlis*. The order was verified two days later and formed one of the earliest and most forthright pushbacks against exploitative commercial practices perpetrated as normal by Western governments.[32]

Over time, the nationalization of assets such as these may be a means that could be revisited as more legitimate owners of national assets unilaterally claim these from corporations that had acquired them through their presence in the territories as occupiers. The clear downside of such moves is that they serve as a disincentive for future investment in the State; consequently, they are likely to remain exceptions rather than the rule. Those whose assets are effectively confiscated in this manner would, in the same way as the *Anglo-Iranian Oil Company* did, argue that this was theft. There is some justification in this line of argument since it effectively seizes an asset without any payment. To wilfully confuse the nationalization of such properties as the same as the lawful acquisition of private property would be a stretch. To safeguard the reputation of the nationalizing State, it would need to identify specific safeguards to assuage concerns that future investors, whether private or other governments, would have about the safety of their investments. A fair discussion about price for the asset based on market value with an added amount for investment or discovery of the asset may offset the damage to some extent.

Compensation

Discussions around colonial crime are often presented to a wider public in former 'colonizing' countries as ways to extract compensation for wrongs that occurred well beyond most statutes of limitations. Such an attitude seems to assume that the wrongs were a one-off process restricted to a single moment in history. This portrayal suggests that the wrong was akin to a mistake that had been committed which had ceased once its wrongfulness had been established. Yet, as we have seen through the various types of crimes explored in the earlier chapter, they were anything but that. They were mostly wilful activities built on a claimed racial and moral superiority and drawn from a deep sense of anthropocentric entitlement, with a singular pursuit driven by the extraction of wealth. Historical records, even those composed by biased writers who served as its mouthpieces, contain relatively little evidence that the 'Christianization'

---

[32] *The Text of the Prime Minister's Report to Majlis, on the Official Recognition of the Principle of the Nationalization of Oil in Iran by the British Government and the Former Anglo-Iranian Oil Company*, Submitted at the Session of 13 Mordad 1330, 5 August 1951 (Bank Meili Iran Press, 1951).

and 'civilization' were anything other than necessary consequences of the wealth attraction. The idea that one ethno-linguistic group could 'civilize' or somehow change peoples' beliefs on the basis that it is better for them is deeply patronizing and offensive in itself. Yet even those who pursued that agenda with a righteous conviction ultimately merely enabled the unrestricted exploitation of resources to be presented as a greater, more sanitized mission for domestic consumption. Stripped of the questionable rhetoric which ostensibly made it more palatable to European audiences, colonization consisted of straightforward theft: the unlawful seizing of lands and resources in a bid to accumulate wealth. The fact that this was often undertaken by privateers licensed or backed by the State suggests that strict approaches that have dominated the compensation approach, which exclusively target the State, would not be addressed to the places where the wealth truly accumulated.

Acceptance of the harm that colonization caused has been around for a long while, especially in countries that were impacted by it. Yet attempts to generate remedies for this wrong have floundered in nearly every instance, not least because colonization is mostly considered a non-issue in the former colonial powers, who for the large part are yet to grasp its contours. Since compensation cannot be paid unless there is full acceptance by the wrongdoer of the harm their actions caused, attempts at seeking compensation have failed, with a few exceptions. Yet compensation remains the most usual remedy sought for the wrongs committed, sometimes alongside other forms of reparation, including apology or restitution where such an outcome is possible or meaningful. As a stand-alone remedy, compensation builds on the long-standing principle of tort law, whereby damage committed must be assessed, with adequate financial recompense paid for by the perpetrator. The *Chorzów Factory* case in 1928 had already firmly established this as a principle in international law. In that case the Permanent Court of International Justice clarified that a State is liable for damages in the instance where such damage occurred as a consequence of its acts or omissions, including the expropriation of property.[33] The law has developed considerably in terms of issues of compensation, including for human rights violations in domestic courts,[34] with regards to expropriation of assets in international law[35] and

---

[33] *Factory at Chorzów Case* (Germany v. Poland), PCIJ Judgment, 25 May 1926, PCIJ Reports (1926) Series A, No. 7; also see Factory at Chorzów Case (Germany v. Poland), PCIJ Judgment, 13 September 1928, PCIJ Reports (1928) Series A, No. 17.

[34] Ewa Bagińska, *Damages for Violations of Human Rights: A Comparative Study of Domestic Systems* (Cham: Springer International Publishing, 2015).

[35] Sebastian López Escarcena, *Indirect Expropriation in International Law* (Cheltenham: Edward Elgar, 2014).

especially with regards to international investment law.[36] The remedy of compensation for environmental damage is also a fast-developing legal field.[37] However, while there are some moments of success in claiming compensation for colonial crime, these have been sporadic rather than giving rise to any systematic process. The landmark victory for victims of British colonialism in the context of the Mau Mau uprising is a striking example. Five petitioners – Ndiku Mutua, Paulo Nzili, Wambugu Nyingi, Jane Muthoni Mara and Susan Ngondi – brought a suit against the Foreign and Commonwealth Office for:

> action for damages for personal injuries brought by five claimants in respect of alleged torts of assault and battery and negligence, for which it is said the defendant is liable as representing Her Majesty's government in the United Kingdom. The injuries in respect of which the claims are made are said to have been deliberately inflicted on the claimants while they were in detention in Kenya, in varying periods between 1954 and 1959, by officers and soldiers of the Kenya police force, the Home Guard and/or the Kenya Regiment. The particulars of the injuries alleged to have been inflicted speak of physical mistreatment of the most serious kind, including torture, rape, castration and severe beatings …[38]

The case was the first time in British legal history that victims of colonialism had gained a right to claim compensation from the British government for their treatment. The legal action commenced in 2009 with a filing in the High Court in London where victims of the uprising sought compensation for acts that they claimed were known about and sanctioned by the highest levels of the British government. The disingenuous attempt by the British government to pass on its responsibility to the post-colonial State of Kenya as its 'inheritance' at independence reflects the lack of integrity that sits at the heart of some governments' approaches to the subject. That argument was rejected in a ruling in 2011, and the case returned to court the following year. The British government did not dispute the torture that the victims had experienced at the behest of the colonial administration. In keeping with the hurdles identified at the start of this book, their defence was instead focussed on the time element, in other words, that too much time had passed since the acts in 1959 for a fair trial to be conducted into it in 2012. That

---

[36] Irmgard Marboe, *Calculation of Compensation and Damages in International Investment Law* (Oxford: Oxford University Press, 2017).

[37] Jason Rudall, *Compensation for Environmental Damage Under International Law* (London: Taylor & Francis, 2020).

[38] *Ndiku Mutua, Paulo Nzili, Wambugu Nyingi, Jane Muthoni Mara and Susan Ngondi v. The Foreign & Commonwealth Office* [2011] EWHC (1913) QB.

argument, too, was rejected by the court on the basis of the meticulous records that were maintained, which had been rediscovered in a 'missing archive'. The evidence these archives revealed was compelling: policies on interrogation were devised directly by Kenya's colonial Attorney General (AG) in complicity with the Governor of Kenya. A key statement, which probably explains why the archives were hidden rather than 'missing', was the statement by the AG to the Governor, stating 'if we are going to sin, we must sin quietly'.[39] The matter was eventually resolved by a governmental decision to pay £19.9 million in compensation to the 5,000 claimants who had been deemed to have suffered during the rebellion. It also included the unveiling of a memorial in Nairobi that commemorates victims of colonialism. The anticipated spurt in claims after the judgment is yet to materialize over ten years later,[40] though there is clearly no shortage of incidents that fit a similar pattern, even with this type of episodic crime.

The discussion between Germany and Namibia summarized earlier also provides a particularly important inflection into this debate in showing how compensation claims can be developed. They commenced from the widespread acceptance of the veracity of the genocide of the Nama and Ovaherero on the orders of General Von Trotha. The damage done was significant and widespread at the time and may well have implicated other colonial powers including the UK, who the communities claim allowed and even facilitated the hot pursuit and subsequent massacre of community members and other local populations by the Schutztruppen.[41]

In episodic crimes of the nature of the German genocide in Africa or British actions in the Mau Mau uprising, a number of steps had to be undertaken before a compensation claim could be articulated. This included intensive research through colonial archives as well as the wider search, collection, codification and verification of personal narratives of the victims of family members, corroborating and triangulating these against other accounts. The search for compensation would also not have been possible were it not for the testimonies of some soldiers with a conscience and some less biased historians. In the case of Germany, this included testimonies from those who were ashamed of the events that had allowed such a gross human rights violation. Despite discussions on compensation paid for much later crimes committed under the guise of the German State, that is, the Nazis during World War II, it took a considerable amount of time, nearly three

---

[39] See Editorial 'Mau Mau: Sinning Quietly', *The Guardian*, 6 June 2013.
[40] Ian Cobain and Jessica Hatcher, 'UK To Expect More Colonial-Era Compensation Claims', *The Guardian*, 6 June 2013, available at https://www.theguardian.com/politics/2013/jun/06/uk-more-colonial-era-compensation-claims.
[41] Literally translated as 'protection forces', which is what German colonial military forces were referred to as in Africa.

more decades, before the conversation around the Namibian genocide could be addressed. The state of this resolution nearly a century and a quarter after the crimes were committed shows how long-term such a battle can be.[42]

Having managed to get the ear of power to listen to the well-documented testimony, it became important to quantify the nature of the crime's impact. This presented a significant challenge, not least because the policy effectively scattered the populations of the two mainly affected tribes into the neighbouring States and from there into further emigration in search of livelihoods. In this case, the actual compensation that was deemed payable was eventually negotiated, controversially, by the Namibian government, taking a paternalistic attitude to its own populations and edging them out of the discussion. The communities have not recognized the settlement as constituting compensation for the colonial crime of genocide that took place. Instead, it looks and feels like a development plan for Namibia, which may be payable by Germany as the country that benefitted and extracted wealth from that country, in addition to any specific compensation that ought to be payable to victims of family members killed and the wider Ovaherero and Nama communities. The matter remains unresolved to date, with the agreement between the two governments not yet ratified and a case filed and pending in the Namibian Supreme Court on behalf of the communities in Windhoek[43] calling for the court to instruct the government not to ratify the agreement on the basis of the government's failure to adequately seek the participation of the affected communities in the final negotiations.[44]

The attempts to frame these claims for compensation identify a useful checklist of features that could serve as an important guide for conversations in other situations. This includes efforts made by potential victims to kick off the conversation by identifying competing narratives that exist about the specific episode of colonial crime in question. This would need to be followed by a clear determination of the class of individuals who may fall within the category of victims. This process is incredibly complex since many of these episodes involved widespread damage, and the nature of many legal systems means they are not geared towards addressing class compensation claims, even without the added complication of the timeline. Assessing the damage payable is equally tough, especially when it involves loss of human lives and the disappearance

---

[42] Jeremy Sarkin-Hughes, *Germany's Genocide of the Herero: Kaiser Wilhem II, His General, His Settlers, His Soldiers* (Cape Town: University of Cape Town Press, 2011).

[43] *R v. Speaker of the National Assembly, the President of Namibia. The Cabinet and the Attorney General on behalf of Bernadus Swaartboi, the Ovaherero Traditional Authority and 11 Nama Traditional Authorities* (Case number HC-MD-CIV-REV-2023/0023).

[44] See wider developments in Karina Theurer, 'Minimum Legal Standards in Reparation Processes for Colonial Crimes: The Case of Namibia and Germany', *German Law Journal*, forthcoming, posted 26 June 2023 on SSRN.

of entire families and communities as a direct result of the actions. Even once a formula of some kind is arrived at, it remains important to understand how such a tort of malfeasance could be claimed and articulated and who would be deemed the perpetrator(s) of the crime itself. Notwithstanding the judgment in the UK, the state of the art to date involves negotiated settlements between the perpetrators and the potential victims. The loaded nature of such conversations with the inequality of arms on either side often acts as a brake on the compensation payable. Communities that are closer in proximity to power – whether by way of systemic knowledge, their ability to poignantly place their sufferings into the public realm or other means that are effective – have been able to extract a higher price than others without this ability.

Solidarity-oriented remedies

As we have seen in the scattered nature of the examples used in this chapter, in the few instances where an apology, restitution or compensation has been forthcoming in relation to colonial crime, this has rarely translated into a systematic approach for addressing reparations. One reason for this is the extent to which the solutions arrived at to date have been the result of specific campaigns engaged upon by a particular group of individuals of a defined community at a time and place against a former colonial power. Attempts to take a wider, more systemic view of this featured in discussions at the *World Conference against Racism and Intolerance* that took place in Durban in 2001, but these were quickly vanquished as other elements of a problematic agenda took over.[45] That conference was envisaged as a significant event to mark the need for the emergence of a global framework steeped in solidarity that would assist in the dismantling of racial discrimination. It was hoped that the outcome document that emerged from the conference would provide a blueprint of actions that could be taken at a variety of levels and commence the arduous task of offsetting the impact of colonization and slavery while addressing its more modern manifestations in racism, racial discrimination, xenophobia and related intolerances. If the various preparations for the Durban World Conference provided a source of excitement that the time for such an idea had come, its outcomes probably set back the prospect of the discussion for the subsequent two decades. In this period some activity with regards to colonial crime was discernible, but it was back into the bilateral and necessarily unequal negotiations between victims and alleged perpetrators.

The thirst and calls for justice are gaining in strength in contemporary society, not least to combat the internal fragmentation based on identity that is occurring

---

[45] Sylvanna M. Falcón, *Power Interrupted: Antiracist and Feminist Activism Inside the United Nations* (Seattle: University of Washington Press, 2016).

within former colonial powers. Yet for this to be achieved, it is imperative that a systemic and globalized approach is taken to the subject of colonial crime. This would require leadership on the issue by more progressive countries such as the Netherlands, which has recently made an apology for slavery, or Germany, which has negotiated the – albeit flawed – settlement with Namibia over the genocide perpetrated at the commencement of the 20th century.

The more egregious and most widespread perpetrators of colonial crime –, the British, French, Spanish, Portuguese and Belgians – are yet to follow suit. In each country the discussions are alive but have not yet warranted significant movement. In Britain progress has been made by actors below national level – usually universities and some museums – with regard to the return of objects, but the wider discussion with the State has been actively stymied despite several calls emanating from a range of partners. Coming at a time when the government of the day has engaged in active culture wars and polarization, the discussion is also summarily dismissed as an attempt to get Britain to pay for damages while governmental austerity, as a political tool, is depleting its own reserves and transferring wealth from the population to a series of emerging plutocrats.

A first-mover advantage is available for the taking by any of the colonial powers that undertake an honest process and then use that as a basis to advocate for their former colonial adversaries and friends to take similar steps. Yet the agenda for change is significantly wider than an accepted culpability for wrongfulness and the desire to engage in measures of restorative justice. For it to be meaningful, this wider quest would need to feature enhanced participation of civil society organizations and the public at large working with experts and others seeking to change the global financial architecture. The goals of such a union would have to focus first on dismantling the extractive industry-oriented system as an urgent step of climate mitigation. It would need to be accompanied by a concerted push to ensure that necessary changes are made to the multilateral trading systems that continue to treat former colonies as resource hotbeds with minimal financial returns for objects, including primary products that are lawfully extracted. In this process efforts would also be needed to disrupt unfair trading agreements that guarantee full access to such markets for the former powers with no equal recompense that is meaningful. A key part of the discussion ought to also include debt cancellation on the basis that such debt was wrongly awarded as a loan when it ought to have been payable as a punitive charge for the commitment of international wrongs. The *Bridgetown Initiative*, the momentum brewing in the *Caricom Reparations Committee* and the *Accra Proclamation on Reparations* offer some hope in this regard.[46]

---

[46] José Atiles-Osoria, 'Colonial State Crimes and the CARICOM Mobilization for Reparation and Justice', 7(2) *State Crime Journal* (Autumn 2018) 349–68.

PART II

Extraction, Enrichment and Exploitation: Addressing the Tipping Point of Climate Change through Colonial Crime

4

Colonial Crime, Environmental Destruction and Indigenous Peoples: A Roadmap to Accountability and Protection

The contemporary climate emergency can be directly traced to a range of colonial crimes, as listed in Part I of this book. These include the crime of failed recognition of the subjecthood of Indigenous peoples, the illegitimate acquisition of territory and the construction of widespread and systematic practices that have destroyed the environment and desecrated the rights of local communities. These crimes have persisted into the decolonization process, where the dispossession of Indigenous communities was made permanent, assisted by legacy-related crimes which through technical cooperation became entrenched practice within the post-colonial State. Collusion crimes further enabled benefit sharing between colonial, post-colonial and private corporations in a joint criminal enterprise, often undertaken under a cloak of development, based on an extractive economy.

The urgency and scale of change needed to respond to the climate crisis makes this a particularly pertinent area that this book ought to address. It enables a cross-cutting analysis of how systems constructed during the colonial period may make European colonization distinct from all others in driving and maintaining the system of consolidation that has brought humanity to the current environmental brink. It is argued here that confronting the issue of colonial crime must be a central feature in seeking the urgently needed system change to address the climate crisis. In responding to this challenge, the remedies outlined above in a more general sense will now be examined in a specific manner with a view to tackling the scale of the transformation required to unravel the economic architecture that is hastening the planet's approach to its boundaries.

Despite Indigenous peoples' warnings over nearly a century, it took until the Intergovernmental Panel on Climate Change (IPCC) report of

2021 to record the first formal and meaningful acknowledgement from an international body of how colonial activities have contributed directly to the current crisis. These climate-related crimes commenced on territories often populated by Indigenous peoples,[1] then continued and escalated under postcolonial regimes[2] with the active support (material and logistic) of former colonial powers.[3] Several practices contributed to system entrenchment: a stimulated demand for 'products' which drove consumption;[4] the treatment of territories as no more than resource hotbeds;[5] the viewing of nature as bountiful and without limit, breaching of the human rights of Indigenous peoples[6] who were treated as objects rather than subjects of law;[7] ignoring systematic destruction of habitats as only being of interest to botanists;[8] and actively obfuscating the science – including through carefully perpetrated and deliberate curated untruths – around the consequential hastening of the breach of planetary boundaries.[9]

The norms and techniques for framing, articulating, demanding and seeking just satisfaction for these past crimes is yet to be fully developed. It may seem logical to think that such a task needs to be deemed secondary when faced with the pressing need to mitigate climate damage, focus on adaptation and hasten system change. Yet rather than the wholescale redesign of systems, the policy focus appears to lie predominantly in making incremental adjustments that tinker with existing mechanisms, yielding marginal climate-related improvements at best, with some consequences that may even deepen injustices. Some of these solutions continue to commodify nature further, embedding a market-driven anthropocentric vision where

---

[1] Lisa Monchalin, *The Colonial Problem: An Indigenous Perspective on Crime and Injustice in Canada* (Toronto: University of Toronto Press, 2016).

[2] JoAnne Linnerooth-Bayer, Laurens M. Bouwer, Reinhard Mechler, Swenja Surminski and, Thomas Schinko (eds), *Loss and Damage from Climate Change: Concepts, Methods and Policy Options* (Cham: Springer International Publishing, 2018).

[3] See Paul Brenton and Vicky Chemutai, *The Trade and Climate Change Nexus: The Urgency and Opportunities for Developing Countries* (Washington, DC: World Bank Publications, 2021).

[4] For the baked-in nature of colonialism, see, Michael Dietler, *Archaeologies of Colonialism: Consumption, Entanglement and Violence in Ancient Mediterranean France* (Berkeley, CA: University of California Press, 2015).

[5] Jörg Gertel, Richard Rottenburg, and Sandra Calkins, *Disrupting Territories: Land, Commodification & and Conflict in Sudan* (London: James Currey, 2014).

[6] Marianne Nielsen and Linda M. Robyn, *Colonialism Is Crime* (New Brunswick, NJ: Rutgers University Press, 2019).

[7] Russell L. Barsh, 'Indigenous Peoples in the 1990s: From Object to Subject in International Law?', 7 *Harvard Human Rights Journal* (1994) 33–62.

[8] Damian Short and Martin Crook, *The Genocide–Ecocide Nexus* (London: Taylor & Francis, 2022).

[9] See Anders Wijkman and Johan Rockström, *Bankrupting Nature: Denying Our Planetary Boundaries* (London: Taylor & Francis, 2013).

proposed solutions retrace the colonial contours discussed earlier. They are also ineffective.

This chapter returns to one such contemporary climate solution that, it is argued, will merely lengthen the impact of these crimes, being ineffective in solving the problem while delivering marginal change at best, with new victims. This concerns the determination of the climate lobby to tackle biodiversity loss by seeking 'protected areas' that will extinguish native title and, most crucially, remove the environment's traditional guardians from their territories, leaving them in the exclusive possession of sovereign States that have already exacerbated their destruction. The former colonial countries referred to here are directly implicated anew in this bid, which is often already implemented through financial and other support (sometimes including armed force) for protected areas through development funding pledges (0.7 per cent of Gross Domestic Product (GDP)),[10] despite lack of evidence that such a route encompasses environmental protection.[11]

To address these issues, this chapter will commence by reiterating the correlation between historical colonial activities and planetary destruction; it will then emphasize the regimes and techniques used to dispossess Indigenous peoples that replaced them with profit-generating ventures. An assessment will be offered on the push towards protected areas, seeking to demonstrate the causal relationship between this and past colonial practices. The chapter concludes by articulating a rough roadmap to achieve the intertwined goals of environmental planetary protection and protection of Indigenous peoples that live in nature's most precious areas. It will emphasize specific duties and obligations upon international society, commencing with former colonial powers, to achieve this reality, while offering insights into the need for specific legal tools and norms to support this venture.

Colonial crime and environmental degradation

In the *law of nations* developed over centuries, the only territory that could be occupied was blank territory (*terra nullius*). Basic public international textbooks recognized that territory could only be acquired via five possible routes: prescription, accretion, cession, with the remaining two – occupation and annexation – having always been questionable in law. The underlying premise was that the territory in question would have to be *blank* or

---

[10] Robert Flummerfelt, *To Purge the Forest by Force: Organized Violence against Batwa in Kahzui-Bega National Park* (London: MRG Investigations, 2022).

[11] Jonas Geldman, Andrea Manica, Neil D. Burgess and Andrew Balmford, 'A Global-Level Assessment of the Effectiveness of Protected Areas at Resisting Anthropogenic Pressures' 116(46) *PNAS* (2019) 23209–15.

unoccupied, unless it was acquired via the agreement (*acquiescence*) of those who lived there. In times past annexation achieved through the subjugation of inhabitants was a 'normal', if questionable, way in which territories were augmented. Attempts were made to outlaw the use of force through the *Pact of Paris* (1928), but these failed dramatically as the outbreak of World War II shows clearly.[12] In any case the belief in the value of pacifism remained and is emphasized in the UN Charter,) making the acquisition of territory by force illegal. A key element underpinning this decision over past acquisitions, the intertemporal rule of law discussed as one of the hurdles in Chapter 1, remains germane here. Yet, as discussed there and in the subsequent chapter concerning the acquisition of territory, the self-interested interpretation of what constitutes unoccupied territory lies at the root of that crime, and perhaps all colonization.

When the question of what constitutes a test of a blank or unoccupied territory is considered, the Western Sahara Case is worth quoting:

> The expression 'terra nullius' was a legal term of art employed in connection with 'occupation' as one of the accepted legal methods of acquiring sovereignty over territory. 'Occupation' being legally an original means of peaceably acquiring sovereignty over territory otherwise than by cession or succession, it was a cardinal condition of a valid 'occupation' that the territory should be terra nullius – a territory belonging to no-one – at the time of the act alleged to constitute the 'occupation'.[13]

Thus, in interpreting their own rules, European colonial powers determined that it was not a necessary condition for the territory to be physically bereft of people, if any people that inhabited it were not 'socially and politically organized'.[14] This partisan interpretation justified the spread of lawful (though not legitimate) acquisition of territory. This was not even a new justification within international law. Ever since Roman law times the bias existed that enabled power to create and interpret norms to suit itself while insisting they were objective standards, as cited here in the text of the Dissenting Opinion of the Vice President of the Court in the Western Sahara Case.[15] Thus, despite the existence of property rights regimes under Roman law, non-Roman territory could legitimately be acquired by the Roman Empire.[16]

---

[12] David Hunter Miller, *The Peace Pact of Paris: A Study of the Kellogg-Briand Treaty* (New York: GP Putnan & Sons, 1929).
[13] *Western Sahara Advisory Opinion, ICJ Reports* (1975) 39.
[14] *Western Sahara Case* (Advisory Opinion) *ICJ Reports* (1975) 12, para 81.
[15] See Separate Opinion of Vice President Judge Ammoun, *ICJ Reports* (1975) 86.
[16] Joshua Castellino and Steve Allen, *Title to Territory in International Law: An Intertemporal Analysis* (Dartmouth: Ashgate, 2003).

The justification was purely racist: non-Romans were not considered 'human enough' to warrant their presence on territory as 'rights earning', much like the flora and fauna they lived among. This trend paved the way for Spanish and Portuguese occupation of 'the New World', legitimized by Papal Bulls and the *Treaty of Tordesillas*, which sought 'equitable' division of land neither party possessed, as discussed earlier in the book. The example highlighted earlier – the British Crown's acquisition of territories in the Pacific via the *Treaty of Waitangi* – is a standout piece of trickery, even in a playbook littered with downright cheating that remains insufficiently acknowledged to date.

The story of the illegitimate acquisition of land, peoples, resources, wealth and power is mutedly acknowledged today. Consider, for instance, the extent to which the great textbooks of public international law reflect on this in their chapters on title to territory. When entertained at all, quick reference is made to the *intertemporal rule of law* in a bid to foreclose further discussion. While that rule may use contemporary legal tenets of dubious value to eliminate questions of reparations, the failure to discuss the illegality of acquisitions when educating new international lawyers suggests tacit acceptance of wrongdoing.

Yet while awareness of the illegality of acquisition of territory is known, ignored or met with knowing glances of 'Oh, *that* old argument', the nexus between colonial rule and climate change is underexplored. The salience of ignoring this reiterates avoidance of liability ascription for past actions whose tort is experienced acutely in the present. There are at least five specific ways in which colonial regimes contributed and continue to contribute to climate change:

1. Illegal dispossession of climate guardians,
2. Wilful destruction of circular economies,
3. Facilitation of commercial exploitation,
4. The drive for over-consumption, and
5. Sustaining unsustainability.

The starting gun for the current climate crisis fired with the treatment of non-Europeans as objects rather than subjects. 'Europeans' did not invent colonization nor its underlying cruelty, which predate their existence. Global history can be narrated almost exclusively through processes by which one tribe or 'nation' sought to subjugate another by acquiring lands and spreading its power. In instances as different as the Mongol invasions[17] and

---

[17] Nakaba Yamada, *Genkō Kassenki: Battle Records of the Mongol Invasions* (English translation) (Tokyo: Publish Drive, 2019).

the spread of the Ottoman Empire,[18] many lives were lost, with atrocities perpetrated that were similar to those committed later or simultaneously by European powers.

Yet European colonization differed as epitomized by the motto of the 'three Cs': Civilization, Christianity and Commerce. The first two were common factors – many hegemons used their self-perceived cultural superiority as an internal spur to action. This was important in persuading the (mostly) able-bodied men in their populations to abandon their families and ploughshares and pick up swords instead in the name of the defence of their homelands and territories. History shows us that such a call often masked ulterior motives fuelled by greed and territorial aggrandizement which could only be achieved through the subjugation of others. The potential sacrifice required for such a mission meant that the actions often needed to be justified in reference to a higher cause: religion and civilization were useful since they optimized an ostensible need to 'save ignorant human beings from their heathen fates'. This also had the added benefit of arming zealous young men with a shared ideology and belief in the justness of their own cause – a useful motivator when facing adversity in the form of a desperate and often less well-equipped opposition fighting to save their families and livelihoods. Though the religion or ideology of these colonial ventures throughout history may have differed from that of European colonization, it was in the third 'C' that European colonization deviated most dramatically.

While all empire-building processes involve theft, European colonization involved theft on an unprecedented scale, not only in the actual process during the duration of colonization but also in the construction of regimes that would enable a constant drain of wealth from the colonies. Unlike raids from Persia to India in the 12th century that expropriated wealth to the city of Ghazni (today conveniently excoriated by some in India to justify Islamophobhia), European colonization used law as a weapon to establish sovereignty, erecting systems to ensure unfettered access in extracting resources. When Indigenous guardians resisted, they were dispossessed through force, captured as indentured labourers to work on plantations elsewhere, or absorbed and incorporated into new economies as unskilled workers.

This facilitated the second most critical facet that links colonial crime to environmental destruction. The newly acquired lands became 'available' for a new economy. This involved the acquisition of discernible wealth in the occupied territories and its expropriation. When King Leopold II of Belgium viewed the Congo Basin, attributed as the cradle of human

---

[18] Paula S. Fichtner, *Terror and Toleration: The Hapsburg Empire Confronts Islam 1526–1850* (London: Reaktion Books, 2008). See also Alan Mikhail, *Under Osman's Tree: The Ottoman Empire, Egypt and Environmental History* (Chicago: University of Chicago Press, 2017).

civilization, with its super-rich biodiversity and dense forests, he probably managed to look conveniently past the Indigenous forest-dwelling peoples, the *Batwa*, and instead saw vast strands of uncultivated wood that would transform the economic trajectory of the Belgian economy and subsequently European industry.[19] Elsewhere, in an attempt to quell a balance of trade deficit with China due to Britain's increasing demand for Chinese tea, the British saw fit – after the failure to justify the sale of opium to China as free trade – to turn a part of the Himalayas, the world's highest and most precious mountain range in what is now part of modern North-Eastern India, into a large tea garden, destroying the fauna and completely transforming regional lifestyles.[20] That the successor States to Belgian and British colonization – the Democratic Republic of Congo and India, respectively – rely on these activities to sustain their economies shows how enduring the impact of destroying circular economies is. As in colonial rule, it also shows how such exploitation does not generate wealth for the areas: it establishes subsistence-based economies where the extracted resource is not valued until further up the supply chain, where it generates profits for the private shareholders of the corporations that exploit it. The nature of this wealth acquisition, which mostly falls into foreign private hands, also means that the money is drained from a public system where it could instead have contributed to the building of key infrastructure, such as healthcare and education, in both the host and recipient countries. A higher proportion could also have been returned to the workers, which may have mitigated some of the human injustice, though not the environmental damage.

Thus, that supply chain, especially its private-interest beneficiaries, was and is a key component of this exploitation.[21] It is not by accident that a significant part of Britain's global exploitation was achieved by the East India Company.[22] Irrespective of the other two 'Cs', it was the sustained pursuit and accumulation of wealth through systematization that has remained a common thread through European colonization. Despite the racist rhetoric in the dismissal of other forms of social interaction, the 'civilizing' aspect that accompanied the quest for profit included the dissemination of Enlightenment-era ideas concerning the rule of law, democracy and human rights. These more progressive strands that were exported were nonetheless subservient to the profit quest, where private enterprise drove and led the

---

[19] Adam Hochschild, *King Leopold's Ghost: A Story of Greed, Terror and Heroism in Colonial Africa* (Pan Macmillan, 2019).
[20] Seren Charrington-Hollins, *A Dark History of Tea* (Barnsley: Pen & Sword Books, 2020).
[21] See James Thuo Gathii and Tzouvala Ntina, 'Racial Capitalism and International Economic Law: Introduction', 25(2) *Journal of International Economic Law* (2022) 199–206.
[22] William Dalrymple, *The Anarchy: The Relentless Rise of the East India Company* (London: Bloomsbury Publishing, 2020).

mission with a single-minded goal of commandeering the vast resources that remain at the heart of contemporary European wealth and its continued domination of global trade. This encompasses two centuries of uncontested domination, growing multinational firms with extra-long supply chains across every conceivable economic activity and industry, from those manufacturing small-scale household products to heavy engineering, extractive industries, services, entertainment and even sport.

En route to this enrichment, Europe also pioneered the scaling up of a deadly arms industry that dominated wealth generation, creating private–public partnerships that derive from the colonial period. These have enabled maintenance of hegemony while perpetrating injustices and profiting from a distance.[23] In the course of this process, Europe and its ally the United States of America – itself dominated by European immigrants adhering to European values but fuelled by a belief of ever-greater marketization as a source of development – have been central to the erection of an unfair trading system that pays scant attention to the value of raw materials, ensuring that they escalate in value only when they enter jurisdictions of OECD countries, deepening global inequality. At a macro level, post-colonial States had little choice but to participate in this economy to escape the legacy poverty traps they inherited from colonial rule. Within post-colonial States participation in such an economy spurred further alienation and marginalization of Indigenous peoples as State-driven or private entities relying on State patronage profited in place of the former colonial rulers. Meanwhile, Indigenous (and other) territories within the State were methodically stripped of 'tradeable' resources, with species becoming extinct as a consequence of the destruction of their habitats by the new emphasis on extraction of natural resources. The significant competition emerging from China today – and to lesser extents from the other so-called BRICS countries of Brazil, Russia, India and South Africa – may further entrench this model, with Chinese economic ascendancy following similar patterns of external resource domination beyond its borders, though perhaps shorn of the accompanying mission of Civilization and Christianization (or its equivalent).[24] In general terms the attempt to broaden the BRICS club to include Saudi Arabia, Iran, Ethiopia, Egypt, Argentina and the United Arab Emirates is perhaps less alarming to scholars interested in colonial crime than to those who are worried about its impact in challenging Western hegemony. However, the goal of these newly influential economic powerhouses appears aligned to a continuation

---

[23] Paul Holden, *Indefensible: Seven Myths that Sustain the Global Arms Trade* (London: Bloomsbury Publishing, 2017).
[24] Shaomin Li, *The Rise of China Inc.* (Cambridge: Cambridge University Press, 2022).

of the extractive economic model, which at a time of deep climate crisis makes their emergence dangerous.

The fourth factor in this domination cycle is equally critical to the current environmental crisis. The stimulation of demand 'at home' in the colonial country has ensured a steady and at times insatiable thirst for consumption. With the extractive model transferring wealth to home countries, this has meant ever-greater purchasing power with stimulated demand for more. Improvements in technology could have spurred a different growth curve by generating longer-lasting goods, but the technologies instead have veered towards creating products of low durability on a 'use and dispose' model that has stimulated bulk exploitation and manufacturing.[25] At the commencement of the Industrial Revolution in Europe, this brought jobs that spurred economic growth at 'home', spreading wealth beyond immediate investors and contributing towards rises in living standards due to increasing demand and spending stimulation. However, as technology grew and the 'worth' of human capital rose, the manufacturing that dominated European economies sought cheaper production bases. This early proto-globalization was welcomed as a trade and manufacturing boom for developing countries, appearing to establish capacity for their economic growth while seemingly generating momentum towards equalizing the global economy where poorer countries benefitted from external investment attracted to them by the comparative advantages of lower labour and overhead costs. While this continues, two factors hasten its demise: the improvement of technology which makes human labour too expensive compared to machines and a perceived, sometimes xenophobic, resistance to jobs leaving or that may leave the shores of the most developed economies. Nationalistic statements in the countries that home transnational enterprises are thus forced to respond to jingoistic slogans such as Be American Buy American.[26]

In developing countries this trend replicates pre-Industrial Revolution inequalities in Europe, as a class emerges of incredibly rich entrepreneurs who can multiply their wealth without having to account for any return to human labour as a factor of production. These entrepreneurs join an equal-opportunities billionaires club where they are not barred based on their race, gender or any other personal identifier but are rather united with others in their recognized achievement of having generated vast wealth and then profited from its movement and speculation in the new economy. The modern global economy can thus be characterized as automated: movement and reinvestment of capital can create high returns, with no automatic trickle

---

[25] James Sherry, *The Oligarch: Rewriting Machiavelli's* The Prince *for Our Time* (New York: Palgrave Macmillan, 2018).
[26] See for example *Build America Buy America Act* (15 November 2021).

down to employment generation or, where it does generate employment, to fair wages. The consequence is an angry global politics of the disenfranchised, with a sharp distinction emerging between the haves and the have-nots. The former live in a luxurious world of plenty where climate change is at best an inconvenience that is easily mitigated; the latter are beset with the burden of survival amid grinding poverty and faced with the brunt of the climate crisis and its many associated scarcity-driven crises. The communities in the middle are polarized between these. Some aspire to greater wealth themselves and are consequently less sympathetic to the have-nots on the grounds that they ought to help themselves rather than seek handouts and favours. Others may empathize with the poor but are often paralysed by the size and scale of change needed. The significant investment by global oligarchs in media and communication companies enables old-fashioned propaganda control disguised as 'fact',[27] concerted attack on human rights or any instrument that demands accountability, sophisticated and expensively assembled strategies to undermine calls that may arise for system change or fairness, and a pointed quest for political power through candidates selected on the basis of their commitment to maintaining hegemony with accepted nods while gesturing towards system modification to placate the great unrests of the day.[28]

This is the polar opposite of circular Indigenous economies in the past that relied on practices that did not stimulate demand and, in particular, had a respect for natural resources and their ability to regenerate to a level of near spiritual proportions.

The regular refrain against colonial crimes is that they may be barred from scrutiny by statutes of limitations. Yet the tort from these activities continues to this day through structures that prolong the reach of the damage. As the climate justice movement has grown, it has highlighted many facets discussed here. At its heart lie the obvious antidotes: reduce consumption; mothball certain extractive industries; generate solutions at scale to specific environmental issues; and discourage, reduce, ban and tax the quest for unjustifiable profits. The nexus between governance and commerce, so long in the making in European colonization, is now 'decentralized', with nearly every country on the globe harnessing its own domesticized stratum of the wealthy, in nearly every case via wealth gained by the exploitation of Indigenous peoples and their territories. As a consequence of the capture of land and resistance towards system change by these wealth bearers, the collective of modern global environmental governance offers useful

---

[27] Edward S. Herman and Noam Chomsky, *Manufacturing Consent: The Political Economy of the Mass Media* (New York: Knopf Doubleday Publishing Group, 2011).

[28] Aurelien Mondon and Aaron Winter, *Reactionary Democracy: How Racism and the Far Right Became Mainstream* (London: Verso, 2020).

rhetoric, but in nearly every case policies remain fig leaves for what is really needed. The discussions at global level are conducted at the environmental Conference of Parties (CoP), where politics and even the identity of hosting countries is a glaring example of this. Pushed into a corner by civil society about the lack of action, a 'new' drive has emerged which is largely performative. It has its essence in an old colonial practice, shown by the example of the creation of strict targets around protected areas, discussed in the next section.

Law as the enabler of colonization

Martin Luther King, Jr stated that the arc of justice may be long but that it would inevitably bend towards justice. Linked to his belief that a day would come when justice would prevail, his vision has empowered many to struggle for a more peaceful and just world. The emergence of normative standards enshrined in law that are consistently more inclusive points towards the significant impact of international law as a gentle civilizer of nations.[29] The evidence for this seems compelling: the abolition of slavery followed much later by the growth of human rights law, especially over the last century, has yielded greater freedoms; seen increased inclusivity; and eradicated (at least in law, but as the events in Gaza in 2023-2024 show, perhaps not in fact) egregious crimes such as genocide, crimes against humanity, torture and slavery, with punishments as a deterrent. The rule of law has also become a cornerstone of domestic legal systems, and equality and non-discrimination have ascended the hierarchy of norms to take centre stage everywhere, even if its implementation remains distant.

From an Indigenous peoples' perspective, these real and perceived developments never had the same reach. While they paid lip service to accepting some culpability for the destruction of communities, lands and cultures, they seemed in large part – with notable exceptions in some courts and jurisdictions – resistant to calls to redesign methods and recalibrate systems to address historical and present injustices, notably in the economic system.

Legal reification of colonial injustice

The law, legal institutions and structures appear geared towards articulating progressive norms, while taking little responsibility for their implementation and realization. That is attributed as the role of politics and policy making. And at times when politics yields flawed governance, the law seems

---

[29] Martti Koskenniemi, *The Gentle Civilizer of Nations: The Rise and Fall of International Law 1870–1960* (Cambridge: Cambridge University Press, 2004).

relatively impotent. Yet even at a normative level, legal discourses have not meaningfully acknowledged the extent to which the law legitimized colonial enterprises or failed to rein in absolute power abroad. Rather than challenge naked power exercised abroad, the law, legal institutions and the vast majority of venerated jurists that worked within them appear to have worked on the basis of a 'gentleman's agreement' that emphasized values of decency and moderation with no attempt to systematically force answers when political power was seized by those unwilling to conduct themselves within that agreement. This section articulates six key legal themes that heightened the reach and impact of colonial regimes into the climate crisis, ending with a sub-section on protected areas that epitomizes why and how colonization remains a current phenomenon.

1. Impact of the global territorial regimes: As emphasized in Part I of this book, the failure to recognize the personhood of Indigenous peoples lies at the heart of the colonial project. Not only did the violation of the principle of *terra nullius* dispossess swathes of populations outside Europe, it also contributed to the disruption of their legitimacy to exist as autonomous entities in greater harmony with the environment. While the United Nations inspired and sponsored decolonization, this yielded an optically less 'White' world, while the rules, especially *uti possidetis juris*,[30] constrained the process to territorial entities designed in the mind of the colonial ruler. The rule, derived from Roman law, was originally articulated by the Praetor to determine the possession of movable goods contested by rival claimants. Extended to decolonization in Latin America, it sought to foreclose issues of boundary disputes between rival offspring of colonial rulers in a bid to avoid the spiralling of territorial disputes. Even though that decolonization was famed as an extension of Enlightenment-era-oriented principles of consent, it did not factor in the consent of Indigenous peoples, who were treated as chattels handed from one colonial power to another, failing to understand the complexities of their societies, including the role that women had played[31] or the respect they had in living as entities within a wider interconnected biosphere. When scrutinized through the extension of European colonization past Africa towards Asia, the overt racial dimensions appear moderately better respected, but only superficially. To myriads of local populations the quest for decolonization was instigated, voiced and delivered by communities relatively close to the colonial power. These

---

[30] Joshua Castellino, 'Territorial Integrity and the "Right" to Self-determination: An Examination of the Conceptual Tools', 33(2) *Brooklyn Journal of International Law* (2008) 503–68.

[31] Susan Kellogg, *Weaving the Past: A History of Latin America's Indigenous Women From the Prehispanic Period to the Present* (Oxford: Oxford University Press, 2005).

communities – usually dominant (in either numbers or power) ethnic, linguistic or religious groups – claimed to be the legitimate spokespeople for *all* the populations within the emerging territorial entities. In some cases they even made wide outreaches to marginalized communities to support the quest to rid territories of 'White foreigners'. Externally, this legitimized them as new rulers, and they were welcomed into international society as such while often occupying the same palaces and governing seats of the departing rulers. The external rules around the sanctity of borders discouraged adjustments between different colonial entities, and their willing acceptance and acquiescence to notions of sovereignty meant that dissent with regards to their legitimacy could be easily stemmed, usually drawing on externally supplied well-equipped police and armed forces. In more 'successful' post-colonial States (measured in terms of maintenance of order) the superficial adoption of a multiculturalist unified 'national' narrative appeased those with historical claims for resumption of their own sovereignty that had been previously suppressed by the arrival of colonial rule. The promising notion of self-determination, articulated by the United Nations in 1960 was reduced to consisting of, at best, an internal call for autonomy within existing State structures (internal self-determination). This was sold as good for order, highlighted as the best chance for the claimed unity in the colonial struggle to bear real fruits, or simply forcibly imposed against dissenters. The principle of *jus resistendi* (the right to resistance), used as a powerful invective against the White colonial rule was almost dismissed when used against subsequent rulers, a trend that continues to this day alongside the liberal use of powerful anti-terrorism and sedition laws drawn up on the basis of loyalty.

2. Treaty Making: The subterfuge of Cecil Rhodes in hoodwinking King Lobengula and the unscrupulous officials who deliberately misinterpreted the *Waitangi Treaty* English translation are often relegated to mere footnotes in history. But the notion of unequal treaties, unfair at the outset, imposed through power, based on what today would be called fake facts with only a veneer of accountability while being dressed up and celebrated as law worthy of veneration, have remained the norm. Names such as Arthur Balfour, George Picot, Mark Sykes, the Durrands, McMahon – all key boundary makers of modern sovereign States whose cultures they did not feel the need to invest in – sit in the archives of global history with little commentary of their impact on modern statehood or the extent to which they were driven by the need to maintain European hegemony over lands they felt absolutely entitled to.[32] The #BlackLivesMatter

---

[32] This is discussed in significant detail in Joshua Castellino, *International Law & the Reconceptualization of Territorial Boundaries: In Pursuit of Peace* (Routledge, 2025 forthcoming).

movement, as a call to consciousness, ought to have elicited greater scrutiny not only of these individuals and what drove them but of the tacit support and effective silence of the edifice of international law in condoning and even celebrating these dubious achievements. That their estates continue to flourish and thrive while their family names ride high in the annals of history displays the entrenchment of power and maintenance of hegemony.

3. Property Rights: At macro level the principle of self-determination that led to decolonization, especially as driven by the United Nations, was an attempt to redress colonial violations stemming from failures to recognize *terra nullius*. It has been hailed as one of the strongest norms of international law when used to achieve a particular type of decolonization but faced significant restrictions as post-colonial States sought to close down its power of further emancipation, making it, 'a political tenet of uncertain legal value'.[33] In any case, at the root of the principle of self-determination lie two entrenched facets: the legitimacy of the need for people to consent to their fate and the duty in law to create mechanisms to respect and implement that decision. The return of lands and territories seized without the consent of 'the people' is a crucial component in its realization. There are, of course, several potential contradictions in the doctrine of self-determination that have been highlighted in one of the most written-about areas of international law. This includes questions over who are the 'people', the conflict between the norm and territorial sovereignty, the modalities of self-determination, whether it is a continuous right, whether it is a right at all, whether it is politics by other means and whether it ought to be crystallized further or left deliberately amorphous. At the heart of this discussion lies the implicit belief that the self-determination achieved against former colonial States does not extend to discussions of how that incoming power ought to respect and recalibrate the enormity of the property rights that were systematically violated during colonial rule. Discussions about land remain at the heart of the politics of many post-colonial States, with well-represented arguments concerning the return of ancestral domain. Yet the issue of the tort of property rights remains in its infancy despite some stirring jurisprudence from tribunals, which even once passed often awaits favourable winds for implementation.[34]

---

[33] Steve R. Ratner, Drawing a Better Line: Uti Possidetis and the Borders of New States, 90 *American Journal of International Law* (1996) 590.

[34] For a recent development that arrived at the time of the completion of this work, see Zafira Zein and Tim Daubach, 'After a 40-Year Struggle, Indigenous Guardians of Indonesian Forests Gain Rights over Their Lands', *Eco Business,* 8 August 2023, available at https://eco-business.shorthandstories.com/indigenous-group-wins-land-rights/. This

4. 'Free trade': Despite an avowed interest driven by the economic ideology that free trade can create benefits for all,[35] the global trading system does not function on grounds of equity. Raw materials extracted in Indigenous territory still gain a fraction of the return due, with no mitigation of their removal or cost calculations that take into account the opportunity cost of their extraction from the environment. In addition, while there has been development on the free movement of goods and services, this is skewed heavily to benefit richer nations, building their wealth and ensuring that they have the right to both 'invest' in new ventures in Indigenous lands and extract the bulk of the profits that might result from such ventures. There have been successful negotiations protecting certain realms of free trade to benefit strong countries,[36] but there has been no attempt to regulate the spread of harmful goods and services, such as the proliferation of arms (see the following point in this list).[37] Even the attempt to prevent nuclear proliferation is skewed towards countries with such weapons on the basis they will act reasonably. The political motivations of powerful States ensure that the free movement of people, which may result in migration from severely environmentally damaged sub-regions towards the sub-regions that host the wealth from these regions, is severely restricted based on national interest. Meanwhile, the almost unrestricted access to the markets of the developing world – justified as free trade – means that extraction and manufacturing-based exploitation of those sub-regions can continue. The consequences of these actions add to the already significant competitive advantage of corporations from European and allied countries who have been involved in Indigenous territories over centuries, operating for a significant part of their histories as near monopolies in those economies.

5. Tacit and explicit support for armed conflict: The world's former colonial countries are overrepresented in the top five producers and exporters of arms. Their engagement in a bruising battle against each other to manufacture and sell arms has played a significant role in fostering instability and furthering the interests of the former colonial power in maintaining a hegemony over resources in the country of their influence. Decolonization left significant existential threats to the

---

achievement builds on a 2013 case, *Indigenous Peoples' Alliance of the Archipelago (AMAN) et al v. Government of Indonesia & Ors* (2013) Decision number 35/PUU-X/2012.

[35] Arvind Panagariya, *Free Trade and Prosperity: How Openness Helps Developing Countries Grow Richer and Combat Poverty* (Oxford: Oxford University Press, 2019).

[36] Pinelopi Koujianou Goldberg and Greg Larson, *The Unequal Effects of Globalization* (Michigan: MIT Press, 2023).

[37] Sara Kutchesfahani, *Global Nuclear Order* (New York: Routledge, 2019).

fledgling post-independence State, not least because of the failure to pay adequate attention to contestations within the freedom struggles or to be engaged in a meaningful transition of power that would restore the status quo prior to the colonial arrival. Many States were themselves born out of direct colonial actions, including the self-interested carving up of territories dividing peoples and communities, the agglomeration of antagonistic communities within a single administrative unit, the attempt to use divide and rule policies to maintain their hegemony, the failure to achieve decolonization through a wide enough dialogue and the signing of preferential agreements, often with both potential parties to a dispute, to supply weapons to cope with real and imagined foes. Like others discussed, this strategy generated significant wealth in former colonial powers and sowed uncertainties and divisions in the emerging States, often exacerbating a febrile atmosphere with devastating effects in their former colony that continue to this date as a tort. The failure of any emerging regime to tackle the manufacture, sale and proliferation of all kinds of weapons is not only indicative of the kind of 'free trade' aspired to, as typified in the Opium Wars of the 1800s; it lies at the heart of the abdication of responsibility that the United Nations Security Council, responsible for threats to peace, ought to have been mindful of but could not deliver due to the extent to which the permanent members that had negotiating power were deeply implicated in generating the threats to peace.

6. Adjudication of global regimes of law: The emergence of greater accountability and genuinely global participation at international level has been significant since the commencement of the United Nations. Two of the most prominent former colonial players, Britain and France, have retained their pre-eminent role in global regimes of lawmaking as permanent members of the United Nations Security Council, as already discussed. This dominance, despite their waning significance in global affairs, is replicated in key bodies connected with the development and global adjudication of emerging regimes. Thus, the *International Court of Justice* (until the 2017 defeat of the UK representative in an election), the *Green Room* of the *World Trade Organization*, the *World Bank*, the *International Monetary Fund* and other leading international organizations are still driven directly and often blatantly by the interests of former colonial powers and their allies. This has not only squeezed out other potentially more progressive European powers who may be keen to develop more equitable global regimes; it has created an environment where the pursuit of national interest often motivated by greed continues to drive the agenda in the name of the use of expertise, thereby weakening both the quality and the legitimacy of global institutions.

The contemporary case of protected areas

The attempt to protect biodiversity by designating up to 30 per cent of the globe as 'protected areas' is synonymous with the continuing legacy of colonial activities. More alarmingly, it ignores compelling evidence regarding its effectiveness in protecting biodiversity and appears dismissive of or deliberately ignores the damage caused in areas where this policy is already operational.

The ostensible justification that drives the objective is uncontested. The proclivity towards profit making driven by levels of human greed discussed throughout this book has, mainly in the form of logging of forests and extraction of minerals in biodiverse areas, depleted the globe's flora and fauna to a point of no return for some species. Spiralling human population growth has been a significant contributing factor to this demise, with the exponential spread of human settlements into previously untouched areas, creating contact that has proved devastating for biodiversity.

In an attempt to strengthen protection against further loss of biodiversity, some climate scientists in conjunction with large conservation organizations, sometimes supported by sections of civil society, have sought to throw what in their view is a protective ring around the remaining biodiversity to rescue it from further harm.[38] Under this framework, ensuring that some parts of the globe can thrive as wilderness is important in and of itself in protecting species under threat of extinction. In addition to allowing nature to heal itself free from human interference, these areas are viewed as key to off-setting carbon emissions and curbing the widespread destruction that has occurred across the globe from human activity. The proposal is that 30 per cent of the globe will be designated as 'protected areas', a goal to be achieved by 2030, hence references to it as '30×30'. In its goal to undermine anthropocentric domination that assumed that the world's resources should be exclusively available to human consumption, the policy is unquestionably laudable.

Significant problems exist with it, however. First, the areas expected to come under such protection – which are truly rich in biodiversity – are almost exclusively the homes and territories of Indigenous peoples.[39] The policy would require and then justify their eviction, reducing them to penury on the edges of peri-urban areas. Since many of these communities

---

[38] Kate Woolaston *Ecological Vulnerability: The Law and Governance of Human–Wildlife Relationships* (Cambridge: Cambridge University Press, 2022).

[39] Ann M. Mc Cartney, M.A. Head, K.S. Tsosie, J.R. Glas, S. Paez, J Geary and M. Hudson, 'Indigenous Peoples and Local Communities as Partners in the Sequencing of Global Eukaryotic Biodiversity', 2(8) *NPJ Biodiverse* (2023). Also see S.T. Garnett, Neil D. Burgess, Julia E. Fa, Álvaro Fernández-Llamazares, Zsolt Molnár, Cathy J. Robinson et al, 'A Spatial Overview of the Global Importance of Indigenous Lands for Conservation', 1 *Nature Sustainability* (2018) 369–74.

existed in pre-colonial times, their 'ownership' of the lands has often not been documented under any colonial or post-colonial lexicon, and they are thus simply treated as illegal settlers who can, in many legal systems, be evicted without compensation from their lands due to colonial crimes committed in the acquisition of territory. But even this egregious human rights violation is only a small part of the problem.

Indigenous peoples, in their traditions and lifestyles, have often acted as the planet's guardians over millennia.[40] They have not been responsible for biodiversity loss, not least because they were not exploiting nature as a marketable resource but have instead been calling this out regularly over the last century as settled ways of life first visited uninvited, then came to dominate their lands and subsequently sought to extract materials from them, blazing a path of destruction through these ecospheres. The work of artist and activist Imani Jacqueline Brown entitled 'Follow the Oil' displays this through stunning visualizations and geo-mapping techniques in the context of what was known as Cancer Alley but has been renamed Death Alley, in the Louisiana coastal region of the United States of America.[41]

Many Indigenous communities have sought to find ways to continue to live in harmony with nature, including by utilizing the benefits of their environs, in a sustainable manner that promotes regeneration. Thus, the second more critical problem with this strategy, from the perspective of biodiversity protection and the environment, is that it removes from the site of its greatest necessity the traditional knowledge gained from living in close proximity with nature over centuries. The rampaging fires of January 2020 in Aboriginal areas in Australia was a clear manifestation of this. Aboriginal knowledge gained over centuries and passed down orally through generations always acknowledged the importance of using smaller controlled fires to clear the debris from the floor of the forest. Western scientific models instead preached that fires in the forest would create environmental damage and so they were banned by law, with the community implicitly told that their bushfires were (another) sign of their primitiveness and that wider concerns of a global nature (namely, climate change) required that this 'cultural practice' be stopped. When the fire did ignite, common in a dry environment, it drew sustenance from forest debris that had not been cleared through controlled smaller fires as was the previous practice,

---

[40] Victoria Reyes-García, Álvaro Fernández-Llamazares, Yildiz Aumeeruddy-Thomas, Petra Benyei, Rainer W. Bussmann, Sara K. Diamond et al, 'Recognizing Indigenous Peoples' and Local Communities' Rights and Agency in the Post-2020 Biodiversity Agenda', 51 Ambio (2022) 84–92.

[41] Jody Adwoh Pinkrah, 'Imani Jacqueline Brown: What Remains at the Ends of the Earth?', Contemporary And, 18 October 2022, available at https://contemporaryand.com/magazines/imani-jacqueline-brown-what-remains-at-the-ends-of-the-earth/.

growing instead to a massive blaze that spread across Australia, destroying 13 million hectares and 3 billion terrestrial vertebrates.[42] The discarding of local knowledge on the basis of a science that has for the most part been poorly equipped to understand traditional knowledge, and whose doors have often been closed to members of these communities through direct and indirect discrimination, contributed to that devastation. Protected areas schemes, when imposed upon areas that are little understood, regularizes this marginalization in the name of the environment but also at the cost of the environment. At the root of it is the belief that 'we know better', a classic sign that drove colonization through the ages.

A third significant problem looms. Developing countries continue to race each other in seeking growth in the world's extractive economy while coping with the world's unequal trading systems. They are thus likely to rely ever more heavily on 'their' natural resources. With Indigenous peoples removed via 30×30 schemes (where they have remained in situ they have presented formidable obstacles to such 'development' to date), the well-established nexus between the State and corporations whom it can license to generate national growth will move centre stage. Many Indigenous communities have witnessed these phenomena at scale, and while protected areas schemes might create a strong international quasi-legislative backdrop against such practice, the lack of enforcement measures against States that exploit these is likely to be as weak as other global governing regimes. The result is a continuation and reification of a colonial practice. This time the post-colonial State will be in the driving seat; the former colonial economies will be accessories that benefit at a price only slightly higher than in the past. For Indigenous peoples the outcome will be the same as throughout colonial rule. For biodiversity and the planet, it will likely fatally increase current precarities.

Current evidence shows that significant actors with dubious credentials have engaged in and continue to benefit from the protected areas scheme. Chief among these is the World Wildlife Fund (WWF), known across the world for its protection of biodiversity but less known for its links to organized businesses that have profited out of nature.[43] An internal investigation completed in 2021 into the WWF's role in the funding of eco-guards accused of significant violations of human rights, including unlawful

---

[42] Brendan D Cowled, Melanie Bannister-Tyrrell, Mark Doyle, Henry Clutterbuck, Jeff Cave, Alison Hillman et al, 'The Australian 2019/2020 Black Summer Bushfires: Analysis of the Pathology, Treatment Strategies and Decision Making About Burnt Livestock', 9 *Frontiers in Veterinary Science* (2022) 790556, 15 February 2022.

[43] Nowella Anyango-van Zwieten, Machiel Lamers and René van der Duim, 'Funding for Nature Conservation: A Study of Public Finance Networks at World Wide Fund for Nature (WWF)', 28 *Biodiversity Conservation* (2019) 3749–3766.

killings, was damning of its actions,[44] though its subsequent interpretation of the report is far greater cause for worry since it indicates a deeply colonial, business-oriented mindset. The report summary available on the WWF website appears to self-exonerate the organization from these criticisms. This stands in sharp contrast to the content of the report (which is available on the website after some concerted searching). The *Minority Rights Group Briefing* details the level of mischaracterization in the attempt to cover up the findings. The salient findings based on a thorough review of the 160-page report of the Panel found that:

- The WWF had knowledge of alleged human rights abuses in every protected area under review and failed to investigate credible allegations of abuse in half of those protected areas.
- Where the WWF conducted internal investigations into allegations of abuse it did so several years after those allegations came to light and only following pressure from the media and/or civil society organizations (CSOs).
- The WWF consistently failed to take adequate steps to prevent, respond to and remedy alleged human rights abuses in and around protected areas it supports. In particular, the WWF continued to provide funding and material support to eco-guards alleged to have committed human rights abuses despite knowledge of those allegations and without operationalizing its own human rights protocols or the safeguards identified to mitigate the human rights risks uncovered by its internal investigations.
- In the protected areas in which the WWF supported their creation or proposed creation, it failed to ensure the effective participation of affected Indigenous peoples and local communities, and obtain the free, prior and informed consent of those Indigenous peoples in accordance with international human rights norms or its own policies.

This led the *Briefing* authors to conclude that the WWF was operating under a process of 'wilful blindness' which implicated its boards and senior management teams. Rather than being chastened by the scale of findings of human rights abuse across the remit of the parks under its control, the organization 'averted its gaze, sidestepped difficult conversations with the government agencies it partners with on the ground and avoided scrutiny

---

[44] Independent Panel, *Embedding Human Rights in Nature: From Intent to Conservation*. Report of the Independent Panel of Experts of the Independent Review of Allegations Raised in the Media Concerning Human Rights Violations in the Context of WWF's Conservation Work (17 November 2020) available at: https://wwfint.awsassets.panda.org/downloads/independent_review___independent_panel_of_experts__final_report_24_nov_2020.pdf.

from donors about the coercive conservation model it has promoted'.[45] The unmasking of these egregious violations appears to have had little impact on the durability and funding of the WWF as a corporate actor in the guise of a CSO despite a US Congress hearing which emphasized and upheld the veracity of the report.[46] In fact, global development agencies of powerful countries – some of whom are also historically colonial countries – may also be implicated in these crimes as they have used their 0.7 per cent of GDP in support of such ventures that are now evidenced as being fatal for both nature and Indigenous communities.

It needs to be stressed that protected areas per se are not the problem. Such areas may be significant to planetary regeneration, especially if envisaged as safeguarding areas from commercial exploitation and illegal settlement while creating zones where flora and fauna may once again flourish. The major flaw lies in seeking to create these without Indigenous peoples at their core, which amounts to no more than dereliction of territories in the hope that damaged nature will be able to heal itself. Many far more progressive and potentially more effective options exist: to have Indigenous peoples work hand in hand with conservationists, with the latter learning from the former; to create conditionalities for Indigenous habitation within protected areas; and to articulate responsibilities upon Indigenous tenure holders to regenerate the environment while providing them with the means and resources necessary to achieve these aims. These tenets are inadequately framed and underexplored in the current protected areas policy.[47] The supreme irony in terms of this book lies in the fact that protected areas were first constructed by colonial rulers to ensure exclusive zones where they could carry out their pastime of hunting unmolested. At that time the Indigenous peoples were deemed a nuisance that got in the way of 'fun'. The shooting and maiming of animals for pleasure or for the acquisition of trophies was a spectacle that was deeply traumatizing for most Indigenous communities, whose cultures were not as anthropocentric. Those practices over time depleted resources

---

[45] Lara Domínguez and Colin Luoma, *Violent Conservation: WWF's Failure to Prevent, Respond to and Remedy Human Rights Abuses Committed on Its Watch* (London: MRG Briefings, 17 December 2020), available at https://minorityrights.org/publications/violent-conservation/.

[46] For a reaction from Professor John Knox, former UN Special Rapporteur and member of the three-person Independent Panel, see https://www.youtube.com/watch?v=1fhCnpHBshE. The hearing also featured former UN Special Rapporteur on the Rights of Indigenous Peoples Victoria Tauli-Corpuz.

[47] See, for example, Aditi Vajpeyi, 'India Needs Community-Centred Governance, Not '30 by 30' Gatekeeping', *Mongabay*, 15 December 2022, available at https://india.mongabay.com/2022/12/commentary-india-needs-community-centred-conservation-governance-not-30-by-30-gatekeeping/.

and dismantled communities. That global politics may choose to stumble towards this as a solution today reflects a deep collective failure of humanity to understand and appreciate human diversity and lived experience. It also shows how objects in the rearview mirror if not acknowledged and understood can prove fatal, in this case to continued human inhabitation within the environment.

Conclusion

Indigenous peoples have been victimized twice by colonization in the past two centuries. First, at the often-deadly moment of the arrival of colonial rulers in many parts of the world. Second, in the abrupt manner of their departure, which usually encompassed a legacy of systems that proved harmful to the natural environment, leaving behind quasi-colonial rulers trained in the system of continued exploitation and domination over natural resources, with ready-made markets and supply chains. This victimization sits in addition to the fact that life under occupation was a constant struggle as ancestral lands were appropriated and physically destroyed, cultures were systematically destroyed in the name of civilization, living beings within the biosphere were treated with disdain and people were extracted and mutilated.

Today, on the ledge of the climate change precipice, it is abundantly clear that lifestyles fuelled by aggressive anthropocentric domination, encompassing a belief that all of nature was an exclusive human legacy to be expended without limit, are the root cause of the crisis. The dominant worldview nonetheless remains one where profit making is viewed as heroic, which justifies flows of 'rewards' by way of enormous profits to such 'enterprise'. For many parts of the world that view came centre stage with the arrival and subsequent departure of European colonial rulers, the solid global supply chain and the political economy they constructed and left behind. Like their predecessors, post-colonial States are equally, and in many cases even more, culpable today in maintaining hegemonies over peoples and resources, and they are equally at fault for their continued domination and subjugation of Indigenous peoples. As awareness of these continuing destructive pathways becomes clear, there are a number of solutions that suggest themselves as ways forward. This chapter ends by articulating six of these.

First, full recognition of the personhood of Indigenous peoples and complete recognition and return of all ancestral territories. Courts of law across the world have already been showing the way on this issue, but ensuring that this is systemic and widespread rather than achieved against a recalcitrant State through complex legal processes remains key to a more sustainable future.

Second, the installation and equipping of Indigenous peoples with the knowhow gained from modern technology in environmental regeneration.

This may still involve throwing a protective ring around certain territories but would restore traditional Indigenous knowledge alongside modern science and technology as drivers of environmental regeneration.

Third, the continued regulation and eventual phasing out of reliance on any 'natural asset' that is exploited without adequate opportunity for regeneration. Indigenous communities have lived for centuries within their environment. This has involved benefitting from nature in a manner that pays adequate attention to its regeneration.

Fourth, returning to the debate around reparations, but this time seeking out corporations rather than former colonial States that have historically benefitted from the exploitation of nature and whose current operations continue to deplete it. This goes beyond the 'polluter pays' principle to understanding the importance of legacy firms with hundreds of years of history that have profited from unfettered access to resources but made negligible returns for them, generating vast profit edifices. This idea is fleshed out in greater detail in the last substantive chapter of this book. It is where the missing trillions of climate finance sit, misappropriated and currently serving lavish consumption of the few who accessed it unjustly.

Fifth, to pay significantly more attention to ensuring that product supply chains see monetary value distributed more evenly across the process. These supply chains need to also include replacement costs for natural assets removed and monetary compensation for the owners of the territory from which it may emanate.

Sixth, concerted action to implementing a list of economic activities that should be proscribed completely. Fossil fuels would be top of such a list, but equal consideration should be given to restricting the extent to which other products are sourced, produced, manufactured, sold and disposed of. Curbing current consumption cycles is vital in taking steps towards a more secure future.

If done right, this set of activities could unmask the profiteers and those who served them in governance in due course, including many international lawyers that are currently venerated. Rather than celebrating these men as pioneers and placing them on pedestals, an honest reckoning of their wanton exploitation and self-serving interests will present them in the light in which Indigenous peoples view them: as brutal armed thieves who came in the dark, connived their way to profit, devastated the people and planet and, despite expressing Enlightenment-era ideas about justice and fairness, will not take responsibility for their actions unless compelled to do so.

5

Financing System Change: A Recovery-Based International Law Response to Colonial Crime

Even discussions around colonial crime that are most advanced flounder at the final hurdle of understanding how the wrongdoing can be costed, where the finances could be generated for the reparation whether via compensation or other means, and how any such remedies could be devolved to the victims and their families. An equally crucial decision is needed to understand whether the compensation being sought is restorative or punitive. In short there are enough questions of a sufficiently complicated nature that signal that even when the most significant step of acceptance of the culpability of colonial wrongdoing is articulated, the remedies that flow would be slow to be designed and even slower to be realized. As the issues disappear into a maze of legal complexities they get further away from the victims and the public squares where change is demanded, retreating instead into boardrooms far removed from the original realities. There they often fester with the occasional breakthroughs suggesting that the quest still has a pulse, albeit a weak one. While the emergence to the centre stage of the climate crisis has focussed the minds of the more progressive elements of society, few are willing to accept the link between this and the origin of the crisis. For many of those working hard to generate financing for climate change, planetary survival is *exclusively* the central challenge of the day. For many working to seek the transition towards environmental sustainability, the issue of colonial crime – even assuming there was willingness to accept it as a systemic violation rather than *ad hoc* events that gave us the climate crisis – would need to wait its turn while the literal and metaphorical fires of climate change rage. This is portrayed as a pragmatic view discerning what is urgent from what may be necessary.

The issue of structural discrimination came storming back into the public imagination after the brutal killing of George Floyd which captured on film and disseminated widely, sparked a strong sense of outrage around the globe in 2020.¹ The impunity and arrogance of the officer was clearly visible in his disregard for the human life that was lost in his grasp. The event, simply another in a string of killings of a very similar nature where protest had been suppressed, led to other mobilizations and eventually stirred a deeper sense of injustice in many disenfranchised and fair-minded populations around the world. Moving beyond police forces as institutions of oppression, the call grew for wider soul-searching of what structural discrimination fully entailed. The photograph of a white man in the uniform of those charged with safeguarding societies by upholding law and order in society, kneeling confidently on the neck of a black man as first his protests and then his life ebbed away proved evocative of so much history of oppression. As previous killings of this nature had shown in the United States of America this was not an exception but an all too common occurrence.

Many institutions and organizations in the United States of America and beyond were forced to reckon with questions from their employees, customers, service providers and shareholders. In the United States of America, besides attempts to seek remedies through the justice system, the movement also encompassed greater awareness of the need for Diversity, Equality and Inclusivity as segments of society sought to acknowledge and change or in nearly equal measures, deflect and defend their own attitudes towards questions of race and oppression.

While the call for the unravelling of what is now accepted as entrenched ossified structural discrimination has been widespread, the actual task of achieving meaningful change remains obscure.

It is impossible to address the climate crisis without a thorough overhaul of a system that was built during colonialism assisted by the perpetration of various types of crimes, and one that is still alive and implicates many actors who continue strangling the environment for their own benefit.² These actors form a significant majority within the equal opportunities *Billionaire Club* referred to earlier, from where they seek to assert direct control over the State, former colonial, post-colonial and other, in a bid to acquire profit they see as legitimate and no more than adequate reward for their enterprise.

The need for wholesale system change has perhaps never been as obvious in human history as it is now. After much prevarication, sponsored mistruths and cunning subterfuge, it is now finally accepted

---

[1] Joshua Castellino, 'In the Name of George', *Minority Rights Group Blog*, 4 June 2020.
[2] Also see David Whyte, *Ecocide: Kill the Corporation Before It Kills Us* (Manchester: Manchester University Press, 2020).

that environmental destruction based on an anthropocentric worldview has driven humanity face to face with planetary boundaries that sustain life on earth. To many this is no more than the inevitable consequence of the sharp rise in the risk and consequences for the climate which commenced during European colonizers' exploitation of territories and seas well beyond their own jurisdictions.[3] These actions have become super-charged in the past few decades as the post-colonial State flexed its own muscle in a bid to boost its living standards. The ballast thus comes from the race for development in an extractive economic system. As former colonies have sought to catch up and deliver the lifestyles widely advertised and coveted, this extractive economy has been pushed to exponential proportions by post-colonial governments keen to prove their mettle in generating the highly coveted economic growth that will sustain them at the helm of power.[4]

Meanwhile, discussion on colonial reparations mainly levied at the State appeared to have had their heyday in compensation paid to victims of the Holocaust.[5] Further attempts to extend this to other episodic and systemic crimes merited polite agreement but little action.[6] Successes in seeking accountability for any kinds of past crimes have been sporadic and individual, rather than consistent and systemic. As a consequence accountability has only been achieved when assisted by a level of privilege in access to processes and remedies, rather than any ability to reimagine and achieve systemic change that can right wrongs.

The most recent attempt to codify the crime of ecocide may prove an exception to the trend of talk without action.[7] In pushing for the incorporation of ecocide as a crime, its sponsors are taking an important step towards ensuring that someone could be made accountable for the wanton destruction of Earth's environment. This destruction generated immense profit – labelled for much of human history as 'progress', despite its destruction of circular economies and displacement of Indigenous and local communities. Like all other codification missions and potential

---

[3] Martin Crook, Damian Short and Nigel South, 'Ecocide, Genocide, Capitalism and Colonialism: Consequences for Indigenous Peoples and Glocal Ecosystems Environments', 22(3) *Theoretical Criminology* (2018) 298–317.

[4] Carole Ammann, *African Cities and the Development Conundrum* (Leiden: Brill, 2018).

[5] Carla Ferstman, Mariana Goetz and Alan Stephens (eds), *Reparations for Victims of Genocide, War Crimes and Crimes Against Humanity: Systems in Place and Systems in the Making* (Leiden: Brill, 2009).

[6] Rhoda E. Howard-Hassmann, *Reparations to Africa* (Philadelphia: University of Pennsylvania Press, 2008).

[7] Darryl Robinson, 'Ecocide – Puzzles and Possibilities', 20(2) *Journal of International Criminal Justice* (2022) 313–47.

remedies, including human rights itself, naming the crime can only be a starting point. Without adequate attention paid to its implementation across situations it could remain an impressive moral standard that fails to yield change or remedies to its victims. Thus even assuming implementation is possible, the codification of the crime of ecocide within international criminal law may still fall short in: (i) ensuring that perpetrators of the environmental destruction are not granted impunity; and (ii) returning the wealth necessary to rejuvenate efforts towards climate justice. Standard statutes of limitation may also hinder its application to the most egregious of activities that lie at the core of the ecocide witnessed today.

This chapter originated as a policy brief on the issue of colonial crime directed at international criminal law practitioners. It seeks to combine the approach of remedies for colonial crime with other gaps that lie in the vast space between the articulation of a potential colonial crime, its acceptance as a driver of environmental destruction and the push towards system change. It does so by drawing attention to two central elements: the nature of the tort of environmental destruction; and a wider call for inter-generational justice and accountability through codification of a new international crime of unjust enrichment.

To achieve these aims the chapter is divided into three sections. It commences by outlining a commentary on the genesis of the contemporary environmental crisis, linking it back to the discussion so far, exploring its nature and showing how it derives directly from colonial activities that destroyed communities and economies in the name of progress. The opening section seeks to attribute responsibility for such crime, identifies potential victims beyond the Anthropocene, and briefly highlights why discussions around resolution of this issue stalls regularly. The second section then develops the fourth point identified in the conclusion to the previous chapter viz. the corporation as a key actor in reparations, advancing the case for a conceptualization of a crime of 'unjust enrichment' suggesting this as a potential way forward to overcome the difficulties encountered in seeking accountability and generating the financial means to tackle system change. The section goes on to outline what a crime of unjust enrichment could look like, drawing the concept from its private law origins and seeking to extrapolate it to the present situation. The third section shows that the idea itself already exists in the annals of public international law, albeit buried in obscurity. This section seeks to explore its legal application in responding to the imperative of achieving inter-generational justice that is mindful of the tort of environmental crime, while generating levels of finance necessary to address the ecological, structural and human damage. The chapter ends with a few tentative conclusions in a bid to stimulate further discussion.

Drawing on science to understand the nature, impact, victimhood and responsibility for environmental crime

Mired in the depth of the environmental crisis, the *Intergovernmental Panel on Climate Change's* (IPCC) clearcut identification in 2022 of the link between colonial activities and climate change[8] barely stirred significant interest within the community of public international lawyers or the wider public. The polarized world into which any such report lands these days is probably one of the reasons for this. Those who agree with its findings have been seeking such a validation for a very long time based on what they see as irrefutable and widespread evidence collected over decades. For them this statement is merely overdue recognition of the multifaceted impacts of the global colonial adventures of European superpowers that gained momentum commencing in the eighteenth century. Scholarship outside the mainstream have focussed significant attention to this for a long time with many facets of post-colonial and Indigenous Peoples oriented studies making this point often.[9] At the other end of the spectrum, Anglosphere-centric[10] and anthropocentric thinking tolerated these narratives in the same way that 'subaltern' perspectives were received: as points to be noted in preambular introductory phrases to classical disciplines, before continuing substantive discussions in the same way as they had always done, referencing the same great masters who must be held culpable at the least for not adequately contesting or effectively challenging the blatant disregard for the law they were supposedly custodians of.[11] Instead, cursory nods are generally proffered to acknowledge the existence of 'alternative' thinking, usually restricted to overtly succinct commentaries on feminist, Marxist and third

---

[8] Intergovernmental Panel on Climate Change ('IPCC'), *Climate Change 2022: Impacts, Adaptation and Vulnerability* (Cambridge: Cambridge University Press, 2022) 3056.

[9] See, for example, Richard Grove, *Ecology, Climate and Empire: Colonialism and Global Environmental History, 1400–1940* (Cambs: White Horse Press, 1997) or Pallavi Das, *Colonialism, Development and the Environment: Railways and Deforestation in British India 1860–1884* (Springer, 2016). The many statements of Indigenous leaders decrying 'development' for its impact on the planet were often ignored as non-scientific and anti-progress.

[10] With acknowledgement to Morten Bergsmo for his comments and the suggestion of this term to capture the widespread domination of the 'mainstream' beyond Eurocentricism and American influence. The term is envisaged to capture the colonial domination of the Americas (north and south) and Australia by European thinking which displaced Indigenous populations and facilitated population transfers through slavery and indentured labour.

[11] See also Rohit Gupta, 'Voicing and Addressing Colonial Grievances under International Law', Policy Brief Series No. 134 (TOAEP, Brussels, 2022), available at https://www.legal-tools.org/doc/5bhfr7/.

world 'perspectives' in standard social science and legal textbooks, before the time-honed views of the discipline are disgorged to eager audiences of aspiring social scientists and lawyers.

As for its reception in the public square amidst the general population, two additional factors in addition to deep polarization can be identified as part of specific tactics designed to elicit muted responses, not just to this, but any news deemed unpalatable. The first lay in how public response is engineered through careful monitoring and sharing of the news, in a bid to play down the significance of the findings (assuming it was aired at all). In a short film, *The Guardian* columnist George Monbiot captures how antisocial elements aligned to the dirtiest industries have captured modern governments like that of the United Kingdom by presenting their policies as in favour of disenfranchised masses while actively discrediting social movements seeking to draw attention to the urgency of climate realities.[12] The contrast between the substantive elements and the press release of the independent report into WWF violations of human rights, as highlighted in the previous chapter, are an exemplar of how such messaging works. Essentially the driver is the need to counter how deeply implicated those in power may be held to be in the findings. A second equally effective strategy that has become common place is to emphasize other problems and manage the news cycle in ways that ensure other issues are pulled into centre stage in a way that deflects attention from adverse news or findings.[13]

It could have been imagined that a finding that directly implicated colonial powers in the environmental damage would have generated a significant response from developing countries. After all the report was issued shortly after heated discussions over 'loss and damage' that have dominated environmental politics in recent times, galvanizing developing countries to seek greater accountability. However such a widescale response was not forthcoming with a significant number of large former colonial countries: India, Pakistan, Nigeria, staying relatively silent to the news. The fact is that the leadership of the vast majority of developing countries are deeply connected with the wealth generating machinery and thus abandoning the system requires levels of altruism they have not yet displayed in any form. Second, in terms of the popular imagination which drives modern politics, there are always less uncomfortable stories that can be

---

[12] See George Monbiot short film on corruption, available at https://twitter.com/George Monbiot/status/1700795324325917072.

[13] Yochai Benkler, Robert Faris and Hal Roberts, *Network Propaganda: Manipulation, Disinformation and Radicalization in American Politics* (Oxford: Oxford University Press, 2018).

pushed instead, as the politics of distraction creates the necessary foil against a real impetus towards system change.

It does help system preservation significantly that any discussions on colonial adventures – especially the actual genesis and formation of modern States themselves – are often deemed beyond the realms of every disciplinary boundary. Historians in the States that emerged from colonization highlight the powerful sentimental forces that led to the overthrow of colonial powers, while the documented histories in the former colonial powers barely mention their colonial adventures. International law and international relations scholars validate the post-colonial State as an improvement on the colonial State, without seeking to understand how they came about or why they may be deeply implicated in system preservation. Scholars of politics immediately get down to the task of understanding how power can be regulated within the new unit, while sociologists and anthropologists seek to chart how relations between communities may or may not gel together within the emerging social fabric. Meanwhile economists appear to have placed greater emphasis on understanding how growth can be generated rather than how wealth has accumulated in few hands. In assessing costs they have paid scant attention to replenishment costs or the true costs of the extractivism of nature that forms the backbone to the modern economy. Thematic engagement with colonial crime is therefore completely ignored or deemed beyond the remit of various disciplines.

In law the primary justification offered is the existence of the intertemporal rule of law – which dictates that a crime needs to be looked at in the context of whether it existed as a crime at the time of its commission, and not through a *post facto* lens. Meanwhile structural discrimination, with its emphasis on the constitutional architecture of established and emerging States, is relegated to the study of human rights; and explorations of environmental justice mainly focus on the construction of institutional architecture towards addressing this as an 'emerging' issue.

Substantive discussions around 'third world approaches to international law', are relegated to a niche specialist audience while the rest are never made to confront the fact that the 'third world' even by conservative estimates, constitutes and generates over two-thirds of customary international law practice, not that this is reflected in any way in the authors, the commentaries or the legal texts. As a starkly visible and visual reminder the continued and widespread use of the dated world map with Europe at the centre of a world of five continents that remains the central geographic tool in use despite its obvious limitations, emphasizes how grand the task of system change is. That one of these 'continents', Asia, accounts for 60 per cent of the global population[14] with rising influence is not (yet) deemed significant – analogous

---

[14] See United Nations Population Fund, *Asia and the Pacific: Population Trends*, October 2022.

to living in the basement of a house and referring to the rest of it as 'the non-basement'.[15] Feminist worldviews emphasizing power dynamics of the 1 per cent patriarchy while mostly excluding 50 per cent of the population did not warrant change either. The 'defeat' of communism meant that previous lip service paid to 'Marxist views' could be conveniently mothballed since capitalism had 'won' over other forms of organizing the economy, and the West had triumphed over the rest.[16]

Despite wider awareness of criticisms of the nature offered in this book, significant justification remains mobilized with clear preferences for the continued maintenance of the status quo hegemonic world vision of public international law. Two specific facets support its dominance: post-colonial sovereign States as modern power brokers in a system dominated by themselves support the current structure of international society which views them as the only legitimate government of their inherited territories. Second, this provides new sovereigns with exclusive beneficiary rights from the extractive economic system in place, often enabling escalation of exploitation ostensibly to generate wealth to aid State building. That much of the wealth exploited and monetary benefits generated do not accrue to communities facing loss and damage is not featured in discussions over accountability. Nor is the need to cater for replenishment costs or clean-up costs from such economic activity deemed relevant. Other species of life impacted simply do not feature.

As a consequence of the neat vesting of interests between the outgoing colonial power and the incoming post-colonial administration, the destruction of circular economies that came with colonization has become hard-wired into an international political economy based on such extractivism, that is now systemic. This extractive model relies heavily on the premise of the existence of an 'economic good' whose benefits are considered to legitimately flow to those with the means to extract, refine, generate demand, market and invest in its exploitation. Two stakeholders are immediately relegated to being objects and not subjects with the right for the seeking of their consent: first, the natural environment, its flora and fauna, that are deemed mere playthings within the anthropocentric system. Nature is acknowledged as existing, but no provision is made to factor the laws governing natural replenishment and sustainability into any commercial equation.[17] But it was not simply a lack of awareness about nature that has played a role. The

---

[15] An analogy that must be ascribed to Carl Söderbergh, Chief Editor, Minority Rights Group, London.

[16] Francis Fukuyama, *The End of History and the Last Man* (Penguin, 2020, original edn 1992).

[17] Clive Hamilton, François Gemenne and Christophe Bonneuil (eds), *The Anthropocene and the Global Environmental Crisis: Rethinking Modernity in a New Epoch* (New York: Routledge, 2015).

second constituency ignored commencing from the colonial period and into the present were the human communities that lived directly within the coveted environment: Indigenous communities who, due to an intense and deep-seated racism were merely considered factors of production (including as slave labour) that warranted minimal return until other technologies were found to achieve the same outcome more efficiently in terms of cost and therefore profit. The entire operation was wrapped into a rhetoric that promoted the pursuit of 'economic growth and prosperity' as an inherent and necessary good. To solidify the entrenchment of the current system further, its founders were actually venerated as visionaries and progressives whose actions were hailed by historians as great leaps forward for humanity's quest to tame nature's natural breaks on human dominance of the environment. Virtue signalling system adjustments (for example, abolition of slavery) were celebrated from victims' perspectives as self-congratulatory markers of civilization, while perpetrators and the exploitative economic system itself were left unmolested. The continuation of slavery in a contemporary format highlights the dangers of such system adjustment rather than deep overhaul.[18]

As highlighted above the entrenchment of systems has many explicit and implicit allies who were directly and indirectly enlisted in perpetrating myths of its widespread benefits. This included historians who were commissioned to sing praises of adventurers and produce singular male-oriented entrepreneurship narratives; economists who could justify exploitation of resources as furthering 'growth and development' without paying adequate attention to the deepening of inequality; lawyers and jurists who conveniently deemed established fundamental principles of title to territory in perpetrators' home States as irrelevant elsewhere while consistently failing the challenge of delivering justice; adventurers and profiteers who used free trade and finders' principle arguments to seize what they determined to be theirs by their own rules; and leaders who constructed patriarchal societies and an international economic system with fairness as no more than guiding rhetoric.

Meanwhile for the two entities that were ignored in the construction of the system, the costs incurred are monumental and have, in many instances already proved fatal. In fact it is only because the climate crisis has now begun to affect the wider masses with some echo for the super privileged that the issues about environmental destruction have even become a political issue. Failures to account for the value of 'raw material' meant that only acquisition costs were recognized with no attention to replenishment costs since nature, bereft of legal personality, was not deemed compensable. The resulting damage to biodiversity from extractive activities were accentuated

---

[18] *Report of the United Nations Special Rapporteur on Contemporary Forms of Slavery, Including its Causes and Consequences*, UN Doc. A/77/163, 14 July 2022.

by post-production emission impacts, including not just in the destruction that the fossil fuel industries have contributed, but also in instances such as the ignominy of sport hunting which became an acceptable even lauded pastime – something the busy hard-working entrepreneurs occupied themselves with while 'resting' from their 'contributions for the good of humanity'. Other more contemporary leisure activities include the acquisition of vast capital and assets, fuelled by patterns of wanton consumption, wealth acquisition and the construing of appropriately safeguarded tax havens where the wealth acquired could be placed with discretion far from scrutiny and challenge.

While the IPCC report makes sobering reading for some, persistent objection to environmental destruction from the extractive economic model has been voiced by indigenous leaders via every platform to which they have had access and through intensive physical resistance over centuries. Where successful, this resistance has had a dramatic impact on biodiversity preservation in stark contrast to places where the resistance was broken through a combination of guns, germs, steel[19] and the kind of subterfuge discussed throughout this book. Highlighting how the colonial-era mindset is not relegated to history books, the attempt to frame a global 30×30 protected areas initiative 'to preserve biodiversity'[20] as discussed, shows how one voiceless constituency, the environment, is instrumentalized against the second constituency, that is, Indigenous populations. That Indigenous communities with net zero climate footprints living in symbiosis with their environment while protecting global biodiversity against all comers,[21] should now be considered collateral to a manufactured 'global' desire to protect an environment destroyed by wanton quests for profits that have accrued to very few, is not just morally dubious. It is in addition, deeply ineffective, as emerging scientific consensus shows beyond doubt.[22] Its persistence as a policy imperative heightens injustice, deepens structural discrimination and is potentially disastrous for climate mitigation. Greater environmental impact could be achieved in transitioning any one of the world's megacities to sustainable energy sources over the next decade. The ability to bully one

---

[19] Jared Diamond, *Guns, Germs and Steel: A Short History of Everybody for the Last 13,000 Years* (London: Vintage, 1998).
[20] Joshua Castellino, 'A Four-Fold Path to Mitigating the Environmental Crisis', *Minority Rights Group Blog*, 11 June 2021.
[21] ICCA Consortium, *Territories of Life: 2021 Report*, September 2021.
[22] Christopher J. O'Bryan, Stephen T. Garnett, Julia E. Fa, Ian Leiper, Jose A. Rehbein, Álvaro Fernández-Llamazares et al, 'The Importance of Indigenous Peoples' Lands for the Conservation of Terrestrial Mammals', 35(3) *Conservation Biology* (2021) 1002–8; Kira M. Hoffman, Emma L. Davis, Sara B. Wickham, Kyle Schang, Alexandra Johnson, Taylor Larking et al, 'Conservation of Earth's Biodiversity is Embedded in Indigenous Fire Stewardship', 118(32) *PNAS* (2021) 1–6.

category of the population with the inbuilt guarantee of ingrained impunity in contrast to tackling those that control levers of power gives rise to this so-called 'green solution'.

Another key facet concerns the specific nature of the tort perpetrated, who has perpetrated it and who its victims are. This is vital if a remedy could be designed that is targeted enough to avoid those who have been made vulnerable from now also being forced to mitigate its damage. At least since the *Durban World Conference on Racism*,[23] debates on reparations have focussed on former colonial powers.[24] These discussions have at best, received polite hearings with little action. The potential exception, the German discussion over the Nama and Ovaherero genocide, commenced as a reparation claim, but the marginalization of the communities and the 'takeover' of proceedings by the Namibian government, instead yielded what is more recognizable as a national development plan. While such a plan may be appropriate and necessary, the lack of engagement with the communities means that the genocide itself remains unaccounted for. Other reparation claims, whether concerning the return of artefacts, the generation of vast wealth on former colonial territories, the loss and damage at sites of colonial activity or the continued influence in maintaining an extractive system skewed towards European and American dominance have been muted at best. Critics emphasize the 'unworkable' nature of such quests: who will pay, what would they pay and who should such money flow to.[25] These albeit legitimate questions restrict reparations discussions to rhetoric and emotion, with even symbolic victories gained in 'de-plinthing' statues of oppressors[26] not widely tolerated in societies where this has occurred.[27] As a consequence it seems clear that the legal tools that exist are unable to tackle one of the most central elements towards garnering system change. The next section advances a call for the design of what may appear a new legal framework, but one that has actually existed on statute books though never applied to this specific problem. That is the crime of unjust enrichment.

---

[23] Ulrika Sundberg, 'Durban: The Third World Conference against Racism, Racial Discrimination, Xenophobia and Related Intolerance', 73 *Revue Internationale de Droit Pénal* (2002) 301.

[24] See Pablo de Greiff (ed), *The Handbook of Reparations* (Oxford: Oxford University Press, 2006).

[25] As discussed by Katrina Forrester, 'Reparations, History and Global Justice', in Duncan Bell (ed), *Empire, Race and Global Justice* (Cambridge: Cambridge University Press, 2019).

[26] See Kaitlin M. Murphy, 'Fear and Loathing in Monuments: Rethinking the Politics and Practice of Monumentality and Monumentalization', 14(6) *Memory Studies* (2021) 1143–58.

[27] 'Edward Colston Statue: Boris Johnson Says We "Cannot Seek to Change Our History"', *ITV News*, 6 January 2022.

Sharpening legal tools to address accountability and remedy structural discrimination

According to Webster's Dictionary, the legal definition of '*unjust enrichment*' is:

> 1: the retaining of a benefit (as money) conferred by another when principles of equity and justice call for restitution to the other party. Also: the retaining of property acquired especially by fraud from another in circumstances that demand the judicial imposition of a constructive trust on behalf of those who in equity ought to receive it. [...]
> 2: a doctrine that requires an equitable remedy on behalf of one who has been injured by the unjust enrichment of another.

Lionel Smith explains the concept of unjust enrichment in the following terms:

> In a wide range of situations, the law requires that a defendant who has been enriched at the expense of a plaintiff make restitution to that plaintiff, either by returning the very substance of the enrichment, or, more often, by repaying its monetary value. But only if the enrichment is unjust, or unjustified: a gift, for example, is justified enrichment.[28]

Smith refers exclusively to private law, though his explanation ends ominously by stating, 'this generic description of the scope of the subject can hardly give an inkling of the range of situations in which it plays a role'. According to Peter Birks, often credited in the anglophone world as the leading authority on the subject, rules governing unjust enrichment form the 'indispensable foundation of private law'.[29] Even though it has manifestations in several jurisdictions and is notably better developed in civil law jurisdictions, at the beginning of the twenty-first century, unjust enrichment remained unfamiliar to common lawyers, playing 'no independent part in their intellectual formation'.[30] A 'gain-based recovery', distinguished from 'loss-based compensation', its evolution in common law traces back to attempts in the United States in the 1930s to address problems concerning misrepresentation and misdescription of products, which resulted in the American Law Institute's *Restatement of the Law of Restitution*.[31]

---

[28] Lionel Smith, 'Unjust Enrichment', in 66(1) *McGill Law Journal* (2020) 165–8.
[29] Peter Birks, *Unjust Enrichment*, 2nd edn (Oxford: Clarendon Law Series, 2005).
[30] Brice Dickson, 'Unjust Enrichment Claims: A Comparative Overview', 54 *Cambridge Law Journal* (1995) 100–26.
[31] American Law Institute, *Restatement of the Law of Restitution* (St. Paul, MN, 1937). Also see Andrew Kull, *Restatement (Third) of Restitution and Unjust Enrichment* (St. Paul, MN: American Law Institute Publishers, 2011).

From the purpose of this discussion, unjust enrichment should be acknowledged as an accepted private law remedy that seeks to substantiate and address corrective injustices that have arisen due to a liability emanating from defective transfers of value in the context of a business relationship. Drawing on its underpinning theoretical foundations, Ernest Weinrib describes this as:

> [...] the law can recognize a claim involving an unjust transfer of value even though the defendant's right to the thing of value is not in question. A transfer of value ('enrichment at another's expense') occurs when one transfers a thing of value without the reciprocal receipt of a thing of equivalent value. The question then arises whether such a transfer is 'unjust', that is, whether circumstances are present that create an obligation to retransfer the value. This obligation arises if the transferor has given the value without donative intent and if the value has been accepted by the transferee as non-donatively given; the transferee cannot keep for free what was given and received non-gratuitously.[32]

Further,

> [...] unjust enrichment situates the parties correlatively as transferor and transferee of what was not transferred gratuitously, thereby conforming to corrective justice. In accordance with Kant's conception of an *in personam* right as a right to the causality of another's will, the claimant's right is not to the value as such, but to having the value retransferred. This is the right to which the defendant's duty to make restitution is correlative.[33]

An immediate question that arises is to whether a private law remedy developed within a specific set of circumstances could be applied to public law in the manner being argued in this chapter. Loughlin identifies the involvement of politics in the public law as a key differentiating factor from private law. According to him,

> The challenge for politics, and therefore for public law, is to find ways to ensure, as a prudential matter, that the sovereign power of the state can

---

[32] Ernest J. Weinrib, 'Correctively Unjust Enrichment', in Robert Chambers, Charles Mitchell and James Penner (eds), *Philosophical Foundations of the Law of Unjust Enrichment* (Oxford: Oxford University Press, 2009).

[33] Ernest J. Weinrib, 'Correctively Unjust Enrichment', in Robert Chambers, Charles Mitchell and James Penner (eds), *Philosophical Foundations of the Law of Unjust Enrichment* (Oxford: Oxford University Press, 2009).

be deployed in order to improve public well-being, practically rather than theoretically speaking, even in the presence of such disagreement. This is a matter of wisdom, judgement, or statecraft rather than selection of a particular normative theory.[34]

This would support extension of the concept and attendant norms of unjust enrichment to the public sphere through legislative change. Emphasizing how colonial crime reified structural discrimination amidst the continuing tort of environmental damage makes it logical that focus shifts to those that gained from the harms rather than those who suffered loss and damage. In any case as the next section delves into further, there has already been acknowledgement that unjust enrichment applies not only in a public law, but specifically in the public international law sphere.

What an international crime of unjust enrichment could look like

From an international legal perspective, the crime of unjust enrichment could be described as a general principle of law stemming from Pomponius' grand adage: *Jure naturae aequum est neminem cum alterius detrimento et iniuria fieri locupletiorem,* a facet of natural law that 'no one should be enriched by the loss or injury of another'. In enunciating its use in the *Lena Goldfield Award*,[35] the principle was already deemed by Friedman as a 'general principle of international law' in 1938. In that arbitration, the Tribunal granted monetary compensation against the Russian government for the value of the benefits of which the company had been wrongfully deprived, 'applying the principle of unjust enrichment as one of international law'.[36] Its usage in customary international law may be significantly wider, drawing on the *Chorzów Factory Arbitration* discussed earlier,[37] but also other cases such as *ADC v. Hungary*,[38] and the *Iran-United States Claims*

---

[34] Charles Mitchell and Peter Oliver, 'Unjust Enrichment and the Idea of Public Law', in Robert Chambers, Charles Mitchell and James Penner (eds), *Philosophical Foundations of the Law of Unjust Enrichment* (Oxford: Oxford University Press, 2009) 406.
[35] *Lena Goldfield Arbitration Award, in* The Times (London), 3 September 1930, p 13, col. 2.
[36] W. Friedman, 'The Principle of Unjust Enrichment in English Law', 16 *Canadian Bar Review* (1938) 384.
[37] Permanent Court of International Justice, *Factory at Chorzów (Germany v. Poland),* Jurisdiction, Judgment, PCIJ Series A No. 9, ICGJ 247, 26 July 1927.
[38] International Centre for Settlement of Investment Disputes, *ADC Affiliate Limited and ADC & ADMC Management Limited v. The Republic of Hungary,* Award, ICSID Case No. ARB/03/16, 2 October 2006.

Tribunal[39] between 1983 and 1987.[40] Its existence in a number of jurisdictions is well developed: on statute books in France,[41] the Netherlands,[42] Italy[43] and Germany.[44] This led Dickson to state that in civil law unjust enrichment is merely a residual category from the law of obligations which comes into play when other categories have been exhausted.[45]

Just as the original principle evolved to eliminate the accountability gap in restitution law when tort, property and contract law failed, the preconditions now exist for its extension to address contemporary environmental tort that commenced under colonial rule. The *intertemporal rule of law* incorrectly indemnifies past actions. Historical exploitations of resources have been made irrecoverable by a web of laws, not least statutes of limitations. The intricate mixing of populations makes inter-generational liability difficult to gauge, while holding a post-colonial State solely responsible for reparations is simplistic when the gains have long been usurped by private actors. The difficulties around 'costing' compensation for loss and damage are overstated

---

[39] For more, see John R. Crook, 'Applicable Law in International Arbitration: The Iran—U.S. Claims Tribunal Experience', 83(2) *American Journal of International Law* (1989) 292–3.

[40] See Charles Manga Fombad, 'The Principle of Unjust Enrichment in International Law', 30(2) *Comparative & International Law Journal of South Africa* (1997) 120–30; Emily Sherwin, 'Restitution and Equity: An Analysis of the Principle of Unjust Enrichment', 79 *Texas Law Review* (2001) 2083–104.

[41] An ordinance from 10 February 2016 created Article 1303.1-4, framed as 'l'enrichissement sans cause' (unjust enrichment), now entitled 'enrichissement injustifié'. Prior to this, the principle was reflected in jurisprudence (see France, Court of Cassation, Civil Chamber 1, Judgment, 4 April 2001, 98-13.285, and France, Court of Cassation, Civil Chamber 1, Judgment, 25 June 2013, 12-12.341). See also Wouter Veraat, 'Two Rounds of Postwar Restitution and Dignity Restoration in the Netherlands and France', 41(4) *Law and Social Inquiry* (2016) 956–72.

[42] For a discussion of the revised Dutch Civil Code in 1992 and the changes to restitution, see B. Wessels, 'Civil Code Revision in the Netherlands: System, Contents and Future', 41 *Netherlands International Law Review* (1994) 163, and E.J.H. Schrage, 'Restitution in the new Dutch Civil Code', in P.W.L. Russell (ed), *Unjustified Enrichment: A Comparative Study of the Law of Restitution* (Vrije Universiteit, 1996) 10–53.

[43] See G. Criscuoli and D. Pugsley, *Italian Law of Contract* (Jovene, 1991) 194. See also Paolo Gallo, 'Unjust Enrichment: A Comparative Analysis', 40 *American Journal of Comparative Law* (1992) 431.

[44] It appears that in Germany most commentators refer to two main categories of unjust enrichment claim – those based on unlawful interference (*Eingriffskondiktionen*) and those derived from a performance (*Leistungskondiktioneri*). For more, see Michael Martinek and Dieter Reuter, *Ungerechtfertigte Bereicherung* (1983). Also see Berthold Kupisch, 'Ungerechtfertigte Bereicherung', in E.J.H. Schrage (ed), *Unjust Enrichment: The Comparative Legal History of the Law of Restitution*, Vol. 15, 2nd edn (Duncker and Humblot GmbH, 1999) 237–74.

[45] Brice Dickson, 'Unjust Enrichment Claims: A Comparative Overview', in 54 *Cambridge Law Journal* (1995) 100–26.

in a bid to reduce conversations around colonial crime to diatribes of limited consequence.

A change in focus from victims' loss and damage to victors' gain and enrichment could alter this trajectory. Rather than focus on understanding what the dimensions of the loss are and how they can be costed we must turn our attention instead to who gained and by how much. Rather than the exclusive emphasis on former colonial States whose financial gains from colonial crime are difficult to track, attention must shift to long-standing corporations and famous individuals and their estates who benefitted in ways that remain traceable, not least in the contemporary opulence on open display. The wealth extracted through legal wrongs is provable beyond doubt. The IPCC report makes this clear at a macro-level and there is now a considerable body of scientific evidence in conjunction with attempts to obscure this by key corporations and sectors. Similarly the accumulation of wealth within key estates and corporations, its shareholders and proprietors, not least within extractive industries, is also traceable through forensic accounting and long-standing financial records that track declared profits over a century at the very least in many cases.

Greater emphasis needs to be placed on the relationship between the colonial State and the private entity that acted in its name. The latter generated significant profits that stayed in private hands, enabling ever greater investment in resource exploitation which commenced the process of exponential destruction of natural resources. The emphasis on seeking reparations from the colonial State has meant that these entities have generally avoided scrutiny in terms of their past actions and wealth accumulation. Many of the corporations from colonial times exist in a form not far from their original guise. Some may have splintered into other profitable ventures, still with significant shareholders in the former colonial State while many may have transferred ownership to more local hands. It is argued here that much of the wealth that dissipated from Africa, Asia and Latin America either sits within corporate bodies' assets or has been disseminated through a manner than can be tracked to its shareholders over time. Tracing such wealth acquisition would be challenging in scale, but it is not difficult to imagine how this may be possible, especially to forensic fraud investigators and those equipped in investigating white collar crime, who have developed significant tools for such a task.

The task could equally be commenced from investigations into the wealth acquisition process of the most significant companies or the wealthiest individuals, including royal families, who presided and gained from the process. At the very least the profits generated by way of interest or other gains that accrued as a consequence of the criminal acquisition of capital ought to be taxable. Knowing and proving where the wealth sits may be easier that seeking an acknowledgement of the tort committed. This would therefore need to be strictly established through the construction of clear causal chains that show how the resulting environmental damage at macro (global) or micro (local) level stem as a consequence of the tort inflicted. Once this has been established it would seem easier to link the identity of the direct beneficiaries in monetary terms of the economic activity, especially in tandem with the results from the investigation conducted into wealth acquisition. Such a series of events would bring the problem and remedy in closer proximity.

Over the last 75 years discussions around colonial crime have been centred around seeking to gain an admission of some form of culpability from the colonizing State. This is understandable since from the perspective of the victims the remedy being sought was to address the loss and damage to their community. Inevitably such ventures have then also sought compensation from the former colonial State for that loss and damage. The reparations made to the Jewish community by Germany in the aftermath of the Holocaust reaffirmed the utility of this model. However a different point of inflection is needed when the issue of colonial crime is twined with the current environmental crisis. Here the issue needs to focus more heavily on seeking a form of justice that also results in system transformation while generating the financing for such a transformation. The former colonial State is a clear beneficiary of the system, is directly associated with its construction and is deeply implicated in its preservation. The profits generated by the systematic exploitation of natural resources has not historically accrued as much wealth that flowed into the coffers of the former colonial State as into private hands. Thus while seeking to make that State solely responsible is acceptable at a moral level, it will likely fail in being able to extract the means to be engineered in the righting of colonial-era wrongs. Even seeking a remedy such as non-repetition would likely be relatively meaningless since the former colonial State is not as likely to be in a position to engage in colonization in the same form as in previous centuries, though newer economic powers may well be able to carry on that mantle with their tacit backing.

In addition the make-up of the modern former colonial State has changed radically through its colonial activities. Far right politicians and even mainstream parties in power who win majorities on the basis of a supposed 'national identity' under threat, seek to influence politics towards their agendas while pretending colonization never occurred. These States today have a mix of populations that include members of the former colonies as tax payers. Due to structural discrimination these communities are often in subservient roles within the State today. The nature of wealth acquisition from colonial activities meant that such wealth was not spread equally in their home countries. The colonial countries also sought, acquired and attracted what was euphemistically known as 'unskilled labour' effectively serfs who could build the gleaming infrastructure of the modern State for wages that enabled subsistence but only very rarely the acquisition of significant wealth. As a consequence on average in the inter-generational wealth acquisition game, persons from the 'former colonies' living in the former colonial power find themselves at the bottom of the socio-economic structure – a point made very well in the report that followed the visit of the *UN Working Group of African Descent* to Belgium.[46] The few who break through are held up as being particularly skilful or virtuous when often they were also major beneficiaries of luck. They are used as examples to emphasize the existence of a meritocracy. This then further justifies stigma against those who 'do not make it' but are forced to live overtly reliant on the public services they have often physically built or contributed a significantly greater percentage of their income than anyone else. Austerity measures disguised as privatization of public services which concentrate wealth in fewer hands within these countries have decimated the overall public facing financial purse, resulting in the growth of in-country poverty. The stark reality is that in countries such as Britain – the master colonizer with the greatest geographical reach – colonial-era tools traditionally used elsewhere are now deployed more overtly at home. In such an ambience even assuming a transfer of monies as compensation for colonial crime could be compelled, this may provide mere short-term relief, but would likely come at a cost of increased xenophobia, paid for disproportionately by people who are multiply victimized. The situation with addressing environmental injustices as proposed here overcomes key elements of this difficulty.

The attempt to seek reparations for activities that have damaged the environment during colonial rule and brought us to the brink of planetary boundaries necessitates a significantly different approach from one that gleans moral acceptances of culpability from the former colonial State. First, the nature of the crime is that it relates to a specific tort which may have originated during colonial rule, but which could be said to continue into the present, overcoming the intertemporal rule. Second the wealth gained from the tort itself has accrued in the developed world to specific corporations who can be named, whose balance sheets are audited on an annual basis, and where it will be possible to detect both the volume and scale of wealth accumulation on a geographic basis as well as its dissemination into private hands. Third, in most cases the wealth accrued in this manner still resides either on the books, within the assets of these corporations, or in the private hands of directors, shareholders and their families, often shielded from scrutiny in tax havens and protected by a barrage of lawyers. Fourth, science shows that, at least in the case of extractive industries the

---

[46] Report of the Visit of the *Working Group on African Descent* to Belgium, UN Doc A/HRC/42/59/Add.1.

only feasible remedy to mitigate climate damage is for these entities to cease operations entirely. Rather than this resulting in wind-ups with dividends paid to shareholders for the alleged risk they may have taken, it could be used to unlock the necessary finance for the mitigation, clean-up and transition costs that are required. A wider net could simultaneously be cast to address the accrued wealth of shareholders, not necessarily in a punitive manner, but in line with the private law remedy of unjust enrichment, to restore the original equilibrium that was lost in business practices that were either deliberately fraudulent or based on a proscribed ground: racial superiority.

For any of this to be feasible it would require a commitment to wholescale systemic change. The multiple crises currently brewing, not least over the environment, in conjunction with existing knowledge of its damage, needs better recovery mechanisms than the ones that are presently configured. Innovative and committed climate lawyers are constantly making breakthroughs in how environmental tort can be calculated and how damages can be claimed from perpetrators. Defenders of Indigenous peoples' rights have also found success in forcing the law to contend with both the loss and damage to their territories, as well as the importance for the recognition of their ancestral domains. This body of law has two established approaches at accountability – land rights claims and tort litigation against multinational corporations – both of which have made significant inroads into corrective justice.[47] On land rights the struggle has yielded long-awaited legal recognition of ownership over ancestral domains from States that have superimposed others' laws onto existing custom without consent.[48] In terms of multinational corporations the litigations have yielded payment of compensation and modification of practices, won against a phalanx of well-oiled corporate lawyers.[49] The key difference in the approach identified

---

[47] David N. Fagan, 'Achieving Restitution: The Potential Unjust Enrichment Claims of Indigenous Peoples Against Multinational Corporations', 76 *New York University Law Review* (2001) 626.

[48] Notable among these are the Ogiek case, African Court of Human and People's Rights, *African Commission of Human and Peoples' Rights v. Kenya*, Judgment, 17 May 2017, Application No. 006/2012, and its subsequent reparations judgment on 23 June 2022.

[49] See, for example, United States of America, Court of Appeals, Second Circuit, *Jota v. Texaco, Inc.*, Judgment, 5 October 1998, 157 F.3d 153 (2d Cir. 1998); United States of America, District Court for the Central District of California, *National Coalition Government of Burma v. Unocal, Inc.*, Judgment, 5 November 1997, 176 F.R.D. 329 (C.D. Cal. 1997); United States of America, District Court for the Eastern District of Louisiana, *Beanal v. Freeport-McMoRan, Inc.*, Judgment, 10 April 1997, 969 F. Supp. 362 (E.D. La. 1997); United States of America, District Court for the Central District of California, *Doe v. Unocal Corp.*, Judgment, 25 March 1997, 963 F. Supp. 880 (C.D. Cal. 1997); and United States of America, District Court for the Southern District of Texas, *Sequihua v. Texaco, Inc.*, Judgment, 27 January 1994, 847 F. Supp. 61 (S.D. Tex. 1994), among many others in United States' jurisdictions.

here is that rather than focussing on contemporary quantifications of loss and damage, greater emphasis needs to be placed on forensic tracing of wealth extracted and its multiplication. The Ogoni experience in Nigeria makes this explicit. The community's successes in litigating against *Shell Oil* based on loss and damage yielded compensatory settlements that have neither restored the Niger Delta environment nor significantly assisted the fishing communities that relied on it. The loss and damage approach allows corporations to build compensation payments into their economic model and continue wrongful action with impunity.[50] Further tactics include the passing-off of responsibility to local subsidiaries to avoid claims, or declarations of bankruptcy to avoid clean-up and restoration. In any case an approach that relies on hugely expensive litigation on a case-by-case basis, while inspiring and a source of hope to others in similar positions, will not necessarily yield widespread systemic change that is required, at the pace at which it is required, not least due to the inequality of access to law.

Conclusion

The well-articulated need for structural change has struck a chord among populations in the midst of the climate emergency, the cost-of-living crisis and the Covid-19 pandemic. A palpable growth in inequality has emerged accompanied by a decimation of public services through austerity measures that transferred wealth into private hands as the State disinvested in providing essential services. Meanwhile scarcities caused by climate change and war have polarized societies feeding a simmering anger. This has been simulated by those with deep pockets who have also sought control over social media companies. These corporate interests clearly benefit from the 'new' economy and are vested in its maintenance at all costs, especially against the real threat of climate mitigating closures of polluting industries. In this febrile 'must-win' scenario, scapegoat politics has emerged as a reliable force that can be ratcheted up along existing schisms in the human family, playing on insecurities to engineer artificial majorities capable of sweeping populists to power through elections.[51] Often orchestrated at the instigation of the super-wealthy who have seized control of media and messaging, this politics aims to rile populations into frenzy to distract from the continued over-exploitation of resources, while detracting and seeking to eliminate dissent

---

[50] See EarthRights International, *Wiwa v. Royal Dutch Shell: Getting Away with Murder: Shell's Complicity with Crimes Against Humanity in Nigeria*, https://earthrights.org/case/wiwa-v-royal-dutch-shell/

[51] Joshua Castellino, 'The Rise of Majorities and& Emerging Existential Threats to India and China', 8 *Chinese Journal of Comparative Law* (December 2020) 538-77.

over the current trajectory of societies accompanied by unwillingness to embark on urgent structural change. Identity politics' incursion into the mainstream has fragmented societies at a time when societal unity and a calm focus on climate adaptation and mitigation ought to be uppermost on every policy agenda. The Green Plans set out with fanfare in a bid to placate opposition, merely tinker with systems, specifically avoiding the overhaul climate scientists and civil society, especially the youth, demand. Students of colonial history must note the close nexus between modern governments and the big businesses that profit under their patronage, especially in the realm of extractive industries, which are a key driver for the maintenance of the current extraction-based international economic system. For many of these players, system overhaul would necessitate their complete exit from it. It is thus unsurprising that the evidence emanating is of long-term policies of distraction and denial not least by support for dubious science and active lobbying against change.[52]

It is of central importance to those seeking accountability to scrutinize the corporations at the forefront of the bid for system preservation since they may also be among those that were the biggest beneficiaries of colonial crime. Focussing on the genesis of that wealth, tracing its accumulation and subsequent flight from sites, its dispersal to think tanks, academies and political parties while emphasizing its role in the continued contemporary tort driving climate change would be a fundamental blow to strike in favour of system change. The stances political parties take over engaging, confronting, framing and accepting responsibility will be indicative of their willingness to act for system overhaul over sombre sounding sound-bytes.

---

[52] See the BBC TV series *Big Oil vs the World*, which narrates the 40-year story of how the oil industry delayed action on climate change (2022).

6

From Vicious Cycle to Virtuous Circle

One illogical but often offered answer to the question, '…what is the quickest route is to get to where we need to go on system overhaul?', is '…to avoid starting from where we are'. Yet the extractive economic model is entrenched in our midst and as predicted by many elders of Indigenous communities around the world for nearly a century, it has brought with it the inevitable descent towards the current challenges we now face. The discussions in this book have focussed so far on why it is important to tackle colonial crime and how the link with the past is so crucial to the present, especially to the climate crisis. It has sought to emphasize how its nature is directly linked to and impossible to address without a simultaneous effort to address colonial crime. The first part attempted to draw on a wide range of activities undertaken around the world in the last century and a half, a significant proportion of which correspond to the exponential rise in the Earth's temperature. A decade ago attempts to make this link were dismissed, but the IPCC support for this argument shows that those calling for urgent change over the full range of colonial activities were prescient in recommending the caution they articulated. In addressing this interlinkage the book argues that a wilful profit-making agenda extended out of greed and manifested in domination, subjugation, annihilation, fraud and mass scale theft drove the imposition of the current system with all of the consequential colonial crimes attendant to it.

Despite well celebrated attempts to construct just and fair societies based on law, such activities have occurred relatively uncontested over at least two centuries. The most recent failure to acknowledge and address colonial crime in the transition that occurred in the UN era since 1945 has meant that many other achievements are relegated to the will of authorities motivated more by greed than a commitment to building sustainable and peaceful societies. This has dissipated the efforts of the many individuals and institutions that sought to create strong rules that would guarantee order, ensure the rule of law and seek to move societies to the avowed values of justice. One central reason for this could be that law, lawyers, lawmakers, legal commentators and the institutions charged with upholding the project for a just and fair world were themselves consciously or unconsciously implicated in the profit making and greed. They failed to challenge the manner in which their discourse could be framed to circumvent criticism based on a deep but untested conviction in their own moral, religious and eventually racial superiority. This strand of thinking which has dominated empire-building in nearly every part of the globe for probably the length of human inhabitation on the planet, was however different in the most recent colonial domination in terms of its scale and impact. A largely anthropocentric venture, like the most common governance ventures through history, it painted other systems that were less anthropocentric as primitive and by dismissing them gave themselves licences and free rein to embark on a sustained campaign that not only depleted earth's resources for profit but also spawned a system for its continued maintenance into the future, with other beneficiaries, this time also drawn from the originally subjugated classes. With the terms for the global economic race now set to these parameters, it is inevitable that planetary exploitation is the norm, with all governance mechanisms serving this pursuit rather than any other. The idea that system change may come driven primarily by institutions such as the governments of sovereign States who are so closely linked for their own survival to its maintenance requires the suspension of disbelief to an illogical level.

The evidence for this is clearly demonstrated in the incremental systemic adjustments that global environmental governance has been able to achieve. Each of these come with a continued growth imperative which will continue to reap profits – albeit in a modified form, for the same people who benefitted from the exploitative system. Further, despite the unquestionable damage there is no attempt being made within emerging international environmental governance systems to hold perpetrators to account despite the long-standing polluter pay principle. Many of these worst perpetrators driving the climate emergency sit at, dominate and even host such discussions with impunity. Most crucially perhaps the wealth that has been acquired from the pursuit of the fraud is protected with impunity while the quest for finance is transferred to others whose contribution to the crisis is minimal.

In seeking to identify the broad contours for the system overhaul needed, this book is based on the principle that every wrong must have a right to remedy, but also that the right must be framed in a manner that equips society to address the consequences of that wrong. In order to articulate how this could be achieved it is important to agree some characteristics of the current global architecture that supports the extractive economic model that has been referenced widely throughout this work. This could be characterized as supported by ten specific elements:

1. Nature has been determined to have a value of zero and exists solely to benefit human beings.
2. Economic activity and wealth can be generated by a process where goods are extracted from nature, 'value' is added to them and they are sold, generating profit far from the site of their original extraction.
3. Labour has a quantifiable price tag and is considered merely a factor of production, like land and finance.
4. Value and wealth is generated by trading related services far removed from the extractive and manufacturing process.
5. Rising levels of consumption are mandatory for the continued generation of wealth and results in steadily growing production rates and demand stimulation.
6. There is no restriction on profit generation while taxation is deliberately limited in the name of rewarding enterprise, leading to mass accumulation of private wealth.
7. Wealth can be taken out of the economic system easily through flight which rewards its placement in tax havens where it can grow in value through speculative processes with a high risk that generate lucrative returns.
8. Extraction from nature without replenishment or mitigation generates scarcity disrupting nature and hastening the arrival of finite planetary boundaries.
9. Scarcity leads to conflict and polarization which can be tailored to detract from an urgent system change agenda towards the interests of system preservation.
10. Wealth determines governance that favours system preservation.

Against this characterization the level of system change required could be subsumed under two simultaneous strands of work. The first with a view to disrupting the cycle described above, the second with ensuring the governance mechanisms that could override those that effectively block the system overhaul by suggesting incremental changes geared towards maintaining hegemonies and access to levers to power.

Disrupting the cycle

In seeking to disrupt the vicious cycle described above, every element of the chain must be revisited. Thus, it is imperative that the economic model *vis-à-vis* nature is reconfigured entirely, with nature placed at the centre of the process rather than the human need to benefit or profit from or tame it. To start with there is an urgent need to stop exploitation, replenish or enable the replenishment of certain parts of nature, clean and address the damage caused to certain areas and understand the levels of extraction that could be tolerated assuming this may still be necessary in certain sectors.

In any instance where extraction is undertaken – for instance in the case of water – it is imperative that this is done with a view to ensuring replenishment or mitigation of the extraction. In every case where extraction feeds into a commercial economic activity the cost of such replenishment and a notional cost to the environment must be factored into the business model and reinvested for that purpose. Where the extraction process uses human labour the financial compensation for this work must be based on the payment of a fair living wage in full recognition of the need to better distribute value across the supply chain and not only to privileged usually urbanized marketeers, financiers or entrepreneurs that feel entitled to exponentially higher returns from the activity generated by labour further down the supply chain. The profit made must be taxed fairly to ensure an adequate return that can be reinvested in the provision of services that will be available for all.

Inevitably the significantly higher production costs would lead to a rise of prices. To offset this, consumption patterns must be curtailed, while goods that are produced must be of higher quality measured through enhanced durability and lifecycles. The use and throw away element of the extractive economic cycle is a significant contributor in terms of using more resources in production, generating greater demand and growing mountains of resulting waste.

While all of these elements and changes to the vicious extractive economic model would make a dent in the vast change necessary for adaptation and or mitigation, it would still take significantly more to generate the system overhaul needed. Such a system overhaul will only occur if the wealth accumulated in the hands of a few through activities that stem from or continue to stem from the exploitative model is brought back into the system to finance the transition. It is thus at points (f) and (g) (i) and (j) that the most significant system overhaul can be achieved.

The accumulation of wealth is celebrated in significant parts of the world as a victory for brilliant entrepreneurs over the mundane or mediocre. It is justified in folklore as a necessary and justifiable return that is mostly fairly accrued by individuals who can innovate, create, problem-solve, dare, take on risk, mobilize, lead, generate economic growth or strike out new pathways and directions. If it is true that human survival has traditionally been based on human innovation, we ought to justifiably be proud of those at its forefront and perhaps not be too slow in recognizing their achievements or rewarding them for their endeavours.

Yet the accumulation of wealth to the extent we see, especially the kinds of boundless wealth that seems to exist within the billionaires club is mostly based on a flawed version and valuation of human innovation. Aided by the creation of tax havens this wealth is generating more wealth while being siphoned away in tax havens or climate costly luxury goods beyond the reach of the rest of society at a time of significant scarcity. Finding a way to address the questions of accountability that ought to be answered in its accumulation and proliferation is extremely important, but perhaps most urgently it is imperative that the messaging on wanton and extravagant consumption is reigned in at a level where it can make a striking difference, rather than the current direction of attention solely at the level of individual households. With a vast proportion of the wealth having been accumulated through processes that are documented throughout this book, it is of fundamental importance that efforts are mobilized to unlock the potential that exists in this resource to addressing the deep-lying needs that stem from the push towards system overhaul. Yet rather than a mere revolution that simply seizes assets as being ill-gotten which would go against the grains of natural justice, the crime of unjust enrichment, carefully configured, can be drawn upon forensically to identify the specific parts of wealth acquisition that need to be addressed. For such a system to be durable it is inevitable that the principle of retroactivity will need to be addressed. The extent to which this may be feasible is perhaps a greater indication of how urgent the crisis is felt to be, rather than a reliance on amorphous terms of justice which were conveniently overrun when the vicious cycle described above was in its ascendancy. It is also important to acknowledge that while two wrongs to not make a right, treating wrongs that are unequal as equal in order to seek protection under such an adage may itself constitute the bigger wrong. To be willing to sacrifice a significant proportion of the world's flora and fauna, including a large chunk of the world's most vulnerable population as acceptable collateral to preserve some principle, indicates a likelihood that the principle has been accorded with an inflated sense of its own value.

Undermining global and national governance

The arguments above are not new and have been articulated in whole or part by many different segments of population across the world for many decades if not centuries. They have spurred calls for revolution and have yielded significant political change. Even the drive towards decolonization, flawed as it was in its outcomes, was calibrated on grounds not too dissimilar from those above. There have been many points in history when those in governance have been too implicated to provide the spark necessary for system change, when their arguments of system evolution, if framed in that context at all, were deemed inadequate and not proportional to the scale of change that was needed. The urgency behind the need to create a system overhaul to address climate change is thus only new in the specificities of the context, which differs from others. When *Fridays for Future*, *Extinction Rebellion* and *Just Stop Oil* among many other movements make statements and take direct action drawing attention to the harms being visited upon the planet, they fall into a hugely relevant and mostly progressive set of movements including women's movements globally and decolonization movements across the world. Among these there have been some seeking to overthrow power who have resorted to violent means, some even felt justified *post facto* in this avenue by their rehabilitation as statesmen and stateswomen after the 'successful' use of violence in achieving system change. Many if not all of these movements faced or have been being labelled as anti-State, terrorist, anarchists and other labels too many and too varied to recount here. History also records many movements seeking systems change that failed and floundered, swallowed and destroyed by powerful adversaries who ratcheted up or continued their subjugation and dominance. There are many Indigenous peoples' movements among these alongside a host of many others, some of which may not even had aims and objectives that are in line with what we could loosely refer to as the attempt to create a just and fair world based on the inherent dignity and worth of all. With this in mind it is important to turn to why global and national governance may be inadequate, ill-equipped and insufficiently motivated to address the climate crisis.

According to public international law, the sovereign State is the primary actor in world politics and law. Blessed with exclusive jurisdiction within its territory, it is omni-powerful in determining the systems, mechanisms, activities, rules, customs, institutions and even ethos of those (people) who live within its territorial boundaries. How such States are governed is usually a matter to be determined exclusively by the people who live or in some cases have alliances to those within that State. By virtue of this perceived legitimacy the State is then metaphorically welcomed to the banquet of international politics where it sits with other such States to determine how global society can be organized. This includes joint responsibility for determining systems, mechanisms, activities, rules, customs, institutions and – to a lesser extent than the domestic State perhaps – the ethos of the global population. At that international political banquet there is a notional equality between all members as mandated by the UN Charter. Yet it is not difficult to see through this theoretical equality even in the metaphorical quality of the attire and trappings attendant to each State. It is also noticeable as to which guests in the room capture an audience, influence a crowd and have the ability to make allegiances and friendships, some relying on long-standing ethno-political and kinship links. Much of what truly transpires at this banquet actually takes place in secret rooms where only some are invited, and where advisers, sponsors, lobbyists and others jostle for attention and favour.

The Conference of Parties (CoP) convened in the name of creating an effective plan of action in the face of the climate crisis is perhaps the best manifestation of this metaphor. Key among the sponsors of some of the guests, are significant interests including in the case of CoP, representatives of Big Oil who are keen to ensure that their interests are protected. Some of these extractive industries masquerade as post-colonial States based on lines that were drawn to ensure Western hegemony over 'their' decolonized resources. The strength of oil as a resource for the extractive economic model means that States with the oil have been able to mobilize to protect their own interests from being unfairly expropriated, notably through the *Organization of Petroleum Exporting Countries* (OPEC). Their supposed unity raises concern but is also mixed with older attitudes that appear to stem from the long-standing pre-colonial belief in them being primitive or backward. Yet many of the same mainly Western States that pretend such dislike nonetheless stand in alliance alongside these States on the basis of their shared interests in system maintenance. The most hallowed of guests at the banquet are the former colonial powers who made their fortunes and continue to consolidate these in a steady alliance with these other oil producing States some of who are now part of the G20. The issue of colonial crime is clearly visible even in this setting where some of the former colonial powers played an active role in determining the territorial jurisdictions, boundaries and installation of the hegemonic system of political governance, hence their alliance is based on the bias attendant to their creation. In fact many of the former colonial powers, the traditional hosts of the banquet who determine the rules and admit other guests, have been directly responsible for the ascendancy to power of the governments, a relationship they have maintained since decolonization through the sale of arms, which acts as a further return from the vast profits made in the extractive economy. In other words, the space for any impetus to act for system change is restricted based on the deep implication of the guests in maintenance of the status quo.

Previous banquets of this nature have had success in constructing an edifice of global governance, including mechanisms that govern world trade, regulate global order and seek to unite world populations on values such as peace, development and human rights. The banquets have never been willing to address the issue of colonial crime which is deemed much too divisive a topic and not one fit to be raised in erudite surroundings. Thus former victims sit as the notional equal of former perpetrators on the grounds that bygones must be bygones, drawing on the need to forgive, forget and move on, but also keen to ensure that they benefit from the obvious wealth extraction that gave the original perpetrators their hallowed place at the table. Irrespective of the agenda of previous banquets, these most recent convenings are organized in the name of finding means to mitigate, adapt and respond to climate change.

The direct nexus between those interested in system preservation and governance is very clear. The ceremonial passage of incremental Green Plans, an unwillingness to tackle the mothballing of certain extractive industries, the well-entrenched concept of passing the burden of climate adaptation onto individuals within the population rather than engaging in system change and the easy 'willingness' to treat Indigenous peoples as collateral whose ancestral domains can act as climate sinks to activities elsewhere are all manifestations of this. Tackling emissions at an emergency level could be achieved through the shut down and transfer of populations of about five of the world's biggest cities, and the complete ceasing of activities by the world's five biggest polluting industries. Instead we are being convinced that we all need to do 'our part' in sharing the burden of the problem, with the poor and marginalized most disproportionately shouldering this burden, while those with finances in tax havens and lavish consumption will not be unduly inconvenienced.

Three conclusions can be drawn from this. First, that the current governance structures at national and global levels are unlikely and/or unwilling to provide the leadership and drive to tackle the scale of the problem because they are deeply implicated in its maintenance. Second, that the issue of climate change cannot be addressed at the level of the State since the sovereign boundaries are irrelevant in terms of the cross-border transnational nature of the problem. Third, that the governance agenda of systemic tinkering continues due to the tacit support of the world's populations who are either convinced that the correct path is being chosen, misled into believing the actions being taken will address the problem when scientists tell us it will not, or are completely agnostic and ignorant of how this path may affect them (or they are so convinced we are doomed it is no point doing anything).

Rather than revolution it is a deep-seated and committed collaboration between those convinced of the need for system change that is needed. This necessarily involves looking beyond national boundaries towards sub-regions facing common problems to cooperate in seeking more local adaptation and mitigation plans that are meaningful. Such cross-border linkages between communities with historical lineage to each other prior to the random line-drawing of colonial boundaries can foster unity but also act to undermine the divisive fragmented politics being foisted upon States to maintain artificial majorities designed to win elections. Cross-border cooperation between communities, scientists, interested businesses, and other stakeholders irrespective of the flag of their governance could also create the necessary political pressure needed to make sure that the finances that are sitting locked away beyond scrutiny are made available to offset the adaptation and mitigation burdens that will fall upon frontline communities. Such an approach would also address the colonial crime attendant to decolonization which divided the world into resource hotbeds that could be controlled. It could foster an understanding that the world needs to be viewed as more than the sovereign States that have been drawn onto maps, many who are artificial entities constructed by colonial powers to maintain their hegemony over resources through installed domestic hegemons. Such functional cooperation would be based on common approaches to the ravages of climate change which are shared across borders and unlikely to stall based on the adoption of national level policies. One suggestion for such a regional approach would be to view the world as consisting of 17 sub-regions, one of which – the polar regions are largely inhabited, but the remaining 16 of which have a historical coherence that was, in most cases either deliberately disrupted by colonial crime or forced into newer relationships as a consequence of it. The rationale for the 17 sub-regions is explored elsewhere, but the regions can be identified as: The Polar Regions, The Pacific, East Asia, Southeast Asia, South Asia, Central Asia, West Asia, East Africa and the Horn, Central Africa, North Africa, West Africa, Southern Africa, Central and Eastern Europe, Western & Northern Europe, South America, Central America & the Caribbean and North America.[1] It is of great importance in this quest that alliance is sought with the many businesses who are committed to the need for serious change in contrast to many who appear to merely pay lip service to it while continuing business as usual, or making cosmetic changes to appear like system change but are in effect business as usual.

In the final analysis, our ability to mobilize and act will depend on how acutely we experience the climate crisis and/or how much empathy we can muster for those who experience it most severely. Human greed was the single most dominant element that drove all colonial activities including the more recent episodes that form part of European colonization. This greed was based on a constructed form of superiority and entitlement. It stemmed from the entrenched anthropocentric belief discussed throughout this book that the world was created for and for the exclusive benefit of the fittest and smartest, which by our own account, were ourselves. The systems that were constructed were maintained by these self-assuredly smart people who set to task in engineering mechanisms by which their greed could continue to be fuelled though they enlisted others to ensure that the joint enterprise would be successful. The successes gleaned have been several and many of them were glittering. But they benefitted one species at the cost of all others, and within that species they only benefitted a very small, almost marginal proportion with a disproportionate gender bias, though this was justified by the narrative that it created and fuelled economic growth around the world. Even if that was true, this form of development clearly failed to understand its impact on the habitability of the planet for its own and other species.

The antidote to such ingrained greed must be empathy. Not only towards the most marginalized and vulnerable in the context of the climate crisis,

---

[1] Joshua Castellino, *International Law & the Reconceptualization of Territorial Boundaries: In Pursuit of Perpetual Peace* (Routledge, 2025 forthcoming). The Annex attached to this book identifies how the current countries and territories are attributed to each sub-region.

but also a wider empathy to the nature that has been destroyed in the quest to enrich the very few in the name of humanity. The scale and enormity of the crisis demands urgent and decisive moves towards system overhaul. This refrain is heard in louder voices than before but emphasis is still being placed in seeking to mitigate these voices, soothed by powers still driven by greed, unwilling to accept their culpability in the crisis and only marginally willing to make the changes necessary. The challenge of the here and now is to collaborate in making the collective empathy that is a significant part of the make-up of human characters, to focus on mitigating its own worst excesses in the drive for greed. In short, we have to clear up our own mess. Do we have the appetite for it?

Bibliography

Civil society reports and commentaries
The Nature Conservancy, *Best Practices in Delivering the 30×30 Target: Protected Areas and Other Effective Area-Based Conservation Measures* (London: A report for the UK Department for Environment, Food and Rural Affairs, 2nd edn, April 2023).
Domínguez, Lara and Luoma, Colin, *Violent Conservation: WWF's Failure to Prevent, Respond to and Remedy Human Rights Abuses Committed on Its Watch* (London: MRG Briefings, 17 December 2020).
EarthRights International, *Wiwa v. Royal Dutch Shell: Getting Away with Murder: Shell's Complicity with Crimes Against Humanity in Nigeria* (nd), https://earthrights.org/case/wiwa-v-royal-dutch-shell/
Flummerfelt, Robert, *To Purge the Forest by Force: Organized Violence against Batwa in Kahzui-Bega National Park* (London: MRG Investigations, 2022).
Global Witness, *636 Fossil Fuel Lobbyists Granted Access to CoP 27* (10 November 2022), https://www.globalwitness.org/en/campaigns/fossil-gas/636-fossil-fuel-lobbyists-granted-access-cop27/
Gupta, Rohit, 'Voicing and Addressing Colonial Grievances under International Law', Policy Brief Series No. 134 (Florence: TOAEP, 2022).
ICCA Consortium, *Territories of Life: 2021 Report* (September 2021).
Independent Commission, *Report of a Commission of Inquiry Established by Oriel College, Oxford into Issues Associated with the Memorials to Cecil Rhodes* (April 2021).
Independent Panel, *Embedding Human Rights in Nature: From Intent to Conservation*. Report of the Independent Panel of Experts of the Independent Review of Allegations Raised in the Media Concerning Human Rights Violations in the Context of WWF's Conservation Work (17 November 2020) https://wwfint.awsassets.panda.org/downloads/independent_review___independent_panel_of_experts__final_report_24_nov_2020.pdf
Ur-Rehman Mir, Goher and Storm, Servaas, *Carbon Emissions and Economic Growth: Production-Based versus Consumption-Based Evidence on Decoupling*, Institute for New Economic Thinking Working Paper Series No. 41 (SSRN, 2016).

Media articles and statements

[Editorial] 'China's CNOOC Discovers Oilfield in Bohai Sea', *Reuters*, 1 March 2023.

[Editorial] 'Dutch King Apologizes for the Netherlands' Role in in Slavery', *CNN News*, 1 July 2023.

[Editorial] 'Dutch King Willem-Alexander Apologises for Colonial-Era Slavery', *Al Jazeera News*, 1 July 2023.

[Editorial] 'Edward Coulston Statute: Boris Johnson Says We "Cannot Seek to Change Our History"', *ITV News*, 6 January 2022.

[Editorial] 'Mau Mau: Sinning Quietly', *The Guardian Newspaper*, 6 June 2013.

[Editorial] 'Norway's Wealth Fund Posts $84 Billion Quarterly Profit', *Reuters*, 21 April 2023.

[Editorial] 'PM Mottley Says It's Time for Reparations' (Abu Dhabi: National African-American Reparations Commission), 1 April 2022.

Adwoa Pinkrah, Jody, 'Imani Jacqueline Brown: What Remains at the Ends of the Earth?', *Contemporary And*, 18 October 2022.

Bachelet, Michelle, *Statement by the UN High Commissioner for Human Rights*, 16 December 2020, available at https://www.ohchr.org/en/statements/2020/12/15th-anniversary-basic-principles-and-guidelines-right-remedy-and-reparation.

BBC, 'Big Oil vs the World Tells the 40 Year Story of How the Oil Industry Delayed Action on Climate Change', 21 July 2022.

Castellino, Joshua, 'In the Name of George', *Minority Rights Group Blog*, 4 June 2020.

Castellino, Joshua, 'A Four-Fold Path to Mitigating the Environmental Crisis', *Minority Rights Group Blog*, 11 June 2021.

Castellino, Joshua, 'Stand Up for Stanislav Tomáš: A Call for Accountability and Structural Change in the Czech Republic', *Minority Rights Group Blog*, 24 June 2021.

Cobain, Ian and Hatcher, Jessica, 'UK to Expect More Colonial-Era Compensation Claims', *The Guardian*, 6 June 2013.

Dalrymple, William, 'The East India Company: The Original Corporate Raiders', *Guardian Newspapers*, 4 March 2015.

Gbadamosi, Nosmot, 'Stealing Africa: How Britain Looted the Continent's Art', *Unpack the Past Features, Al Jazeera*, 12 October 2021.

King Philippe – Speech at the Esplanade of the Palais du Peuple, Kinshasa, 8 June 2022, available at https://www.monarchie.be/en/agenda/speech-by-his-majesty-the-king-esplanade-of-the-palais-du-peuple-kinshasa.

Lawson, Alex, 'BP's Profits Labelled 'Heinous' as Calls Grow for Windfall Tax', *The Guardian*, 2 May 2023.

Palmer, Ronan and Schroeder, Frank, 'The Bridgetown Initiative, A Climate and Development Plan for COP27', *E3G*, 14 November 2022.

Petersen, Hannah Ellis, 'India Plans to Fell Ancient Forest to Create 40 New Coalfields', *The Guardian*, 8 August 2020.

Pletcher, Kenneth, 'Jallianwala Bagh Massacre', *Encyclopedia Britannica*, 4 December 2023, available at https://www.britannica.com/event/Jallianwala-Bagh-Massacre [Accessed 15 February 2024].

The Text of the Prime Minister's Report to Majlis, on the Official Recognition of the Principle of the Nationalization of Oil in Iran by the British Government and the Former Anglo-Iranian Oil Company, submitted at the Session of 13 Mordad 1330, 5 August 1951 (Bank Meili Iran Press).

Vajpeyi, Aditi, 'India Needs Community-Centred Governance, Not "30 by 30" Gatekeeping', *Mongabay*, 15 December 2022.

Zein, Zafira and Daubach, Tim, 'After a 40-Year Struggle, Indigenous Guardians of Indonesian Forests Gain Rights over Their Lands', *Eco Business*, 8 August 2023.

Film and TV

Foreman, Amanda (writer), *The Ascent of Woman*, four-part documentary series (BBC, 2015).

Monbiot, George, Short Film on Corruption, https://twitter.com/GeorgeMonbiot/status/1700795324325917072

Williams, Stephen (director), *Chevalier* (Searchlight Films, 2022).

Books

Abrahamian, Ervand, *Oil Crisis in Iran: From Nationalism to Coup d'Etat* (Cambridge: Cambridge University Press, 2021).

Adebajo, Adekeye, *The Curse of Berlin: Africa after the Cold War* (Oxford: Oxford University Press, 2013).

Akerman, James R., *Decolonizing the Map: Cartography from Colony to Nation* (Chicago: University of Chicago Press, 2017).

Akhmadi, Heri, *Breaking the Chains of Oppression of the Indonesian People* (Singapore: Equinox Publishing, 2010, original edn 1981).

Al-Rasheed, Madawi, *A History of Saudi Arabia* (Cambridge: Cambridge University Press, 2002).

Aliverti, Ana, Carvalho, Henrique, Chamberlain, Anastasia and Sozzo, Máximo (eds), *Decolonizing the Criminal Question: Colonial Legacies, Contemporary Problems* (Oxford: Oxford University Press, 2023).

Ammann, Carole and Förster, Till, *African Cities and the Development Conundrum* (Leiden: Brill, 2018).

Anghie, Anthony, *Vattel's International Law from a XXIst Century Perspective* (Leiden: Brill Nijhoff, 2011).

Arendt, Hannah, *The Origins of Totalitarianism* (New York: Harcourt Brace Jovanovich, 1973).

Bagińska, Ewa, *Damages for Violations of Human Rights: A Comparative Study of Domestic Systems* (Cham: Springer International Publishing, 2015).

Baker, Horace Charles, *The Age of Oil: A History of the Petroleum Industry and the Outlook for the Future* (London: Chas A. Stoneham Co., 1917).

Barnett, Vincent (ed), *Routledge Handbook of the History of Global Economic Thought* (Abingdon/New York: Routledge, 2015).

Barr, James, *A Line in the Sand: Britain, France and the Struggle that Shaped the Middle East* (London: Simon & Schuster, 2011).

Beckles, Hilary, *Britain's Black Debt: Reparations for Caribbean Slavery and Native Genocide* (Kingston: University of West Indies Press, 2013).

Beckles, Hilary, *How Britain Underdeveloped the Caribbean: A Reparations Response to Europe's Legacy of Plunder and Poverty* (Kingston: University of West Indies Press, 2021).

Beker, Avi (ed), *The Plunder of Jewish Property during the Holocaust* (Hampshire: Palgrave Macmillan, 2001).

Belmessous, Saliha (ed), *Native Claims: Indigenous Law Against Empire 1500–1920* (Oxford: Oxford University Press, 2012).

Benkler, Yochai, Faris, Robert and Roberts, Hal, *Network Propaganda: Manipulation, Disinformation and Radicalization in American Politics* (Oxford: Oxford University Press, 2018).

Benyera, Everisto, *Breaking the Colonial Contract: From Oppression to Autonomous Decolonial Futures* (London: Lexington Books, 2021).

Bhabha, Jacqueline, Matache, Margareta and Elkins, Caroline, *Time for Reparations: A Global Perspective* (Philadelphia: University of Pennsylvania Press, 2021).

Bhandar, Brenna, *Colonial Lives of Property: Law, Land and Racial Regimes of Ownership* (Durham, NC: Duke University Press, 2018).

Birks, Peter, *Unjust Enrichment*, 2nd edn (Oxford: Clarendon Law Series, 2005).

Bloch, Roland, Mitterle, Alexander, Paradeise, Catherine and Peter, Tobias (eds), *Universities and the Production of Elites: Discourses, Policies, and Strategies of Excellence and Stratification in Higher Education* (Switzerland: Palgrave Macmillan, 2018).

Brendese, Philip J., *Segregated Time* (Oxford: Oxford University Press, 2023).

Brennan, Fernne and Packer John, *Colonialism, Slavery, Reparations and Trade: Remedying the Past?* (London: Routledge, 2012).

Brenton, Paul and Chemutai, Vicky, *The Trade and Climate Change Nexus: The Urgency and Opportunities for Developing Countries* (Washington, DC: World Bank Publications, 2021).

Brockington, Dan, Duffy, Rosaleen and Igoe, Jim, *Nature Unbound: Conservation, Capitalism and the Future of Protected Areas* (London: Taylor & Francis, 2012).

Bruckner, Pascal, *The Tyranny of Guilt: An Essay on Western Masochism* (Princeton, NJ: Princeton University Press, 2010).

Carrière, Jean-Claude and Nelson, Richard, *The Controversy of Valladolid* (New York: Dramatists Play Service, Inc., 2005).

Carroll, Matthew and Gill, Tim, *Uptake of GCSE Subjects* 2017 updated 2019.

Castellino, Joshua, *International Law & the Reconceptualization of Territorial Boundaries: In Pursuit of Perpetual Peace* (Routledge, 2025 forthcoming).

Castellino, Joshua and Allen, Stephen, *Title to Territory in International Law: A Temporal Analysis* (Dartmouth: Ashgate, 2003).

Castellino, Joshua and Cavanaugh, Kathleen A., *Minorities in the Middle East: A Comparative Legal Analysis* (Oxford: Oxford University Press, 2013).

Cervantes, Fernando, *Conquistadores: A New History* (London: Penguin, 2020).

Charrington-Hollins, Seren, *A Dark History of Tea* (Barnsley: Pen & Sword Books, 2020).

Chilcote, Ronald M., *The Political Economy of Imperialism: Critical Appraisals* (New York: Springer Science, 1999).

Churchill, Winston, *The Story of the Malakand Field Force* (London: Longmans, Green and Co., 1898).

Cohen, Joshua, *The Arc of the Moral Universe and Other Essays* (Cambridge, MA: Harvard University Press, 2010).

Craig, Jonathan, Gerali, Francesco, MacAulay, Fiona and Sorkhabi, Rasoul, *The History of the European Oil and Gas Industry (1600s–2000s)* (London: Geological Society, 2018).

Criscuoli, Giovanni and Pugsley, David, *Italian Law of Contract* (Napoli: Jovene, 1991).

Crowe, Sybil Eyre, *The Berlin West Africa Conference 1884–1885* (Plymouth: Longmans, Green & Co., 1942).

Curzon, George, *Persia and the Persians, Vol. 1* (London: Frank Cass & Co. 1966).

Dalrymple, William, *The Anarchy: The Relentless Rise of the East India Company* (London: Bloomsbury Publishing, 2020).

Dalrymple, William and Anand, Anita, *Kohinoor: The Story of the World's Most Infamous Diamond* (New Delhi: Juggernaut Books, 2016).

Das, Pallavi V., *Colonialism, Development and the Environment: Railways and Deforestation in British India 1860–1884* (Springer, 2016).

De Greiff, Pablo (ed), *The Handbook of Reparations* (Oxford: Oxford University Press, 2006).

Dekker, Ige F. and Werner, Wouter, *Governance and International Legal Theory* (The Hague: Brill, 2004).

Deutsch, Karl and Folz, William, *Nation Building* (New York: Atherton Press, 1963).

Di Blasé, Antonietta and Vadi, Valentina, *The Inherent Rights of Indigenous Peoples in International Law* (Rome: Roma Tre Press, 2020).

Diamond, Jared, *Guns, Germs and Steel: A Short History of Everybody for the Last 13,000 Years* (London: Vintage, 1998).

Dietler, Michael, *Archaeologies of Colonialism: Consumption, Entanglement and Violence in Ancient Mediterranean France* (Berkeley, CA: University of California Press, 2015).

Dirdeiry, M. Ahmed, *Boundaries and Secession in Africa and International Law: Challenging* Uti Possidetis (Cambridge: Cambridge University Press, 2015).

Düffler, Jost and Frey, Marc (eds), *Elites and Decolonization in the Twentieth Century* (London: Palgrave Macmillan, 2011).

Economides, Michael J., Oligney, Ronald E. and Izquierdo, Armando, *The Colour of Oil: The History, Money and the Politics of the World's Biggest Business* (East Nynehead: Round Oak Publishing Company, 2000)

Eggers, Nicole, Pearson, Jessica Lynne and Almada e Santos, Aurora (eds), *The United Nations and Decolonization* (Abingdon/New York: Routledge, 2020).

Eggington, William and Wren, Helen, *Language Policy: Dominant English, Pluralist Challenges* (Amsterdam: John Benjamin Publishing, 1997).

El-Ayouty, Yassin, *The United Nations and Decolonization: The Role of Afro-Asia* (The Hague: Martinus Nijhoff, 1971).

Falcón, Sylvanna M., *Power Interrupted: Antiracist and Feminist Activism Inside the United Nations* (Seattle: University of Washington Press, 2016).

Feinstein, Andrew, *The Shadow World: Inside the Global Arms Trade* (London: Penguin, 2011).

Ferstman, Carla, Goetz, Mariana and Stephens, Alan (eds), *Reparations for Victims of Genocide, War Crimes and Crimes Against Humanity: Systems in Place and Systems in the Making* (Leiden: Brill, 2009).

Fichtner, Paula S., *Terror and Toleration: The Hapsburg Empire Confronts Islam 1526–1850* (London: Reaktion Books, 2008).

Fukuyama, Francis, *The End of History and the Last Man* (Penguin, 2020, original edn 1992).

Ganguly, Varsha Bhagat (ed), *Land Rights in India: Policies, Movements and Challenges* (New York: Routledge, 2016).

Garnsey, Peter, *Social Status and Legal Privilege in the Roman Empire* (London: Clarendon Press, 1970).

Gatheru, R. Mugu, *Kenya: From Colonization to Independence 1888–1970* (Jefferson, NC: McFarland Incorporated Publishers, 2005).

Gertel, Jörg, Rottenburg, Richard and Calkins, Sandra, *Disrupting Territories: Land, Commodification and Conflict in Sudan* (London: James Currey, 2014).

Getachew, Adom, *Worldmaking After Empire: The Rise and Fall of Self-determination* (Princeton, NJ: Princeton University Press, 2020).

Goldring, John L., *The Constitution of Papua New Guinea: A Study in Legal Nationalism* (California: Law Book Company, 1978).

Gorbahn, Katja, Grindel, Susanne and Popp, Susanne, *History Education and (Post-)Colonialism: International Case Studies* (Berlin: Peter Land, 2019).

Grasso, Marco, *From Big Oil to Big Green: Holding the Oil Industry to Account for the Climate Crisis* (Cambridge, MA: MIT Press, 2022).

Grove, Richard, *Ecology, Climate and Empire: Colonialism and Global Environmental History, 1400–1940* (Cambs: White Horse Press, 1997).

Gutstein, Donald, *The Big Stall: How Big Oil and Think Tanks are Blocking Action on Climate Change in Canada* (Toronto: James Lorimer Ltd., 2018).

Haery, Mohsen S., *The Legal Implication of the Dispute over the Iranian Nationalization of the Oil Industry* (Berkeley, CA: University of California Press, 1955).

Haller, Tobias, Blöchlinger, Annja, John, Markus, Marthaler, Esther and Ziegler, Sabine (eds), *Fossil Fuels, Oil Companies and Indigenous Peoples* (Berlin: Lit Verlag, 2007).

Hamilton, Clive, Gemenne, François and Bonneuil, Christophe (eds), *The Anthropocene and the Global Environmental Crisis: Rethinking Modernity in a New Epoch* (New York: Routledge, 2015).

Han, Enze and O'Mahoney, Joseph, *British Colonization and the Criminalization of Homosexuality: Queens, Crime and Empire* (London: Taylor & Francis, 2019).

Häussler, Mathias, *The Herero Genocide: War, Emotion and Extreme Violence in Namibia*, trans Elizabeth Janik (New York: Berghahn, 2021).

Hawkins, Edward Kenneth, *The Principles of Development Aid* (London: Penguin, 2007).

He, Zhipeng and Sun, Lu, *A Chinese Theory of International Law* (Singapore: Springer Nature, 2020).

Heinlein, Frank, *British Government Policy and Decolonisation, 1945–1963* (London: Taylor & Francis, 2013).

Herman, Edward S. and Chomsky, Noam, *Manufacturing Consent: The Political Economy of the Mass Media* (New York: Knopf Doubleday Publishing Group, 2011).

Herzog, Tamar, *Frontiers of Possession: Spain and Portugal in Europe and the Americas* (Boston: Harvard University Press, 2015).

Hicks, Dan, *The Brutish Museums: Benin Bronzes, Colonial Violence and Cultural Restitution* (London: Pluto Press, 2021).

Hino, Hiroyuki, Langer, Arnim, Lonsdale, John and Stewart, Frances (eds), *From Divided Pasts to Cohesive Futures: Reflections on Africa* (Cambridge: Cambridge University Press, 2019).

Hitchens, Christopher, *The Parthenon Marbles: The Case for Reunification* (London: Verso, 2008).

Hochschild, Adam, *King Leopold's Ghost: A Story of Greed, Terror and Heroism in Colonial Africa* (London: Pan Macmillan, 2019).

Holden, Paul, *Indefensible: Seven Myths that Sustain the Global Arms Trade* (London: Bloomsbury Publishing, 2017).

hooks, bell, *Feminist Theory: From Margin to Center* (London/New York: Routledge, 2015).

Houtte Hans Van, Das, Hans, Delmartino, Bart and Yi, Lasson, *Postwar Restoration of Property Rights under International Law* (Cambridge: Cambridge University Press, 2008).

Howard-Hassmann, Rhoda E., *Reparations to Africa* (Philadelphia: University of Pennsylvania Press, 2008).

Hulme, David and Murphree, Marshall, *African Wildlife and Livelihoods: The Promise and Performance of Community Conservation* (London: James Currey, 2001).

Jones, Carwyn, *New Treaty, New Tradition: Reconciling New Zealand and Maori Law* (Vancouver: University of British Columbia Press, 2016).

Kellogg, Susan, *Weaving the Past: A History of Latin America's Indigenous Women from the Prehispanic Period to the Present* (Oxford: Oxford University Press, 2005).

Korieh, Chima J. and Njoku, Raphael Chijioke (eds), *Missions, States and European Expansion in Africa* (New York: Routledge, 2007).

Koskenniemi, Martti, *The Gentle Civilizer of Nations: The Rise and Fall of International Law 1870–1960* (Cambridge: Cambridge University Press, 2004).

Koujianou Goldberg, Pinelopi and Larson, Greg, *The Unequal Effects of Globalization* (Michigan: MIT Press, 2023).

Kowaleski-Wallace, Elizabeth, *The British Slave Trade and Public Memory* (New York: Columbia University Press, 2006).

Kreike, Emmanuel, *Scorched Earth: Environmental Warfare as a Crime Against Humanity and Nature* (Princeton, NJ: Princeton University Press, 2022).

Kull, Andrew, *Restatement (Third) of Restitution and Unjust Enrichment* (St. Paul, MN: American Law Institute Publishers, 2011).

Kutchesfahani, Sara, *Global Nuclear Order* (New York: Routledge, 2019).

Lantigua, David M., *Infidels and Empire in a New World Order: Early Modern Spanish Contributions to Legal Thought* (Cambridge: Cambridge University Press, 2020).

Laurie, Alexandre Charles, *The Land Reform Deception: Political Opportunism in Zimbabwe's Land Seizure Era* (Oxford: Oxford University Press, 2016).

Levene, Mark and Roberts, Penny, *The Massacre in History* (New York/Oxford: Berghahn Books, 1999).

Li, Shaomin, *The Rise of China Inc.* (Cambridge: Cambridge University Press, 2022).

Linnerooth-Bayer, JoAnne, Bouwer, Laurens M., Mechler, Reinhard, Surminski, Swenja and Schinko, Thomas (eds), *Loss and Damage from Climate Change: Concepts, Methods and Policy Options* (Cham: Springer International Publishing, 2018).

López Escarcena, Sebastian, *Indirect Expropriation in International Law* (Cheltenham: Edward Elgar, 2014).

Lüdert, Jan, Heise, Julius and Ketzmerick Maria, *The United Nations Trusteeship System: Legacies, Continuities, and Change* (London: Taylor & Francis, 2022).

Mamdani, Mahmood, *When Victims Become Killers: Colonialism, Nativism and Genocide in Rwanda* (Princeton, NJ: Princeton University Press, 2001).

Manning, Patrick (ed), *Slave Trades, 1500–1800: Globalization of Forced Labour* (eBook, Routledge, 2015).

Marboe, Irmgard, *Calculation of Compensation and Damages in International Investment Law* (Oxford: Oxford University Press, 2017).

Martinek, Michael and Reuter, Dieter, *Ungerechtfertigte Bereicherung* (Tübingen: Mohr Siebeck GmbH, 1983).

Matsa, Winniefridah, *Marginality, Migration and Education: Educational Experiences of Migrants' Children in Zimbabwe* (Switzerland: Springer AG, 2020).

Maugeri, Leonardo, *The Age of Oil: The Mythology, History and Future of the World's Most Controversial Resource* (Guildford, CT: Lyons Press, 2017).

Mbembe, Achille, *Out of the Dark Night: Essays on Decolonization* (New York: Columbia University Press, 2021).

Mhango, Nkwazi N., *How Africa Developed Europe: Deconstructing the His-Story of Africa, Excavating Untold Truth and What Ought to Be Done and Known* (Bamenda: Langaa Research & Publishing CIC, 2018).

Mikhail, Alan, *Under Osman's Tree: The Ottoman Empire, Egypt and Environmental History* (Chicago: University of Chicago Press, 2017).

Miller, David Hunter, *The Peace Pact of Paris: A Study of the Kellogg-Briand Treaty* (New York: GP Putnan & Sons, 1929).

Min, Pyong Gap, *Korean 'Comfort Women': Military Brothels, Brutality and the Redress Movement* (New Brunswick, NJ: Rutgers University Press, 2021).

Monchalin, Lisa, *The Colonial Problem: An Indigenous Perspective on Crime and Injustice in Canada* (Toronto: University of Toronto Press, 2016).

Mondon, Aurelien and Winter, Aaron, *Reactionary Democracy: How Racism and the Far Right Became Mainstream* (London: Verso, 2020).

Moretti, Marco, *International Law and Nomadic Peoples* (Milton Keynes: AuthorHouse, 2012).

Mueller, John Theodore, *Great Missionaries to Africa* (Grand Rapids, MI: Zondervan Publishing House, 1941).

Mushanga, Mwene, *Slavery and Colonialism: Man's Inhumanity to Man for which Africans Demand Reparations* (Nairobi: Law Africa Publishing, 2011).

Newbury, Colin, *Patrons, Clients and Empire: Chieftaincy and Over-rule in Asia, Africa and the Pacific* (Oxford: Oxford University Press, 2003).

Nielsen, Marianne and Robyn, Linda M., *Colonialism Is Crime* (New Brunswick, NJ: Rutgers University Press, 2019).

Nkopo, Athinangamso, Kwoba, Brian and Chantiluke, Roseanne (eds), *Rhodes Must Fall: The Struggle to Decolonise the Racist Heart of Europe* (London: Bloomsbury Publishing, 2018).

Nwokeji, Stella, *The Nigerian History: The Pre-colonial Era, Colonial Amalgamation, and Analysis of the Earlier Nigerian Federal Polity* (Independently published, 2019).

Olajide, Olayanju, *The Complete Concise History of the Slave Trade* (Bloomington, IN: AuthorHouse, 2013).

Olusoga, David and Erichsen, Casper W., *The Kaiser's Holocaust: Germany's Forgotten Genocide and the Colonial Roots of Nazism* (London: Faber & Faber, 2010).

Owolabi, Olukunle P., *Ruling Emancipated Slaves and Indigenous Subjects: The Divergent Legacies of Forced Settlement and Colonial Occupation in the Global South* (Oxford: Oxford University Press, 2023).

Panagariya, Arvind, *Free Trade and Prosperity: How Openness Helps Developing Countries Grow Richer and Combat Poverty* (Oxford: Oxford University Press, 2019).

Phillips, Barnaby, *Loot: Britain and the Benin Bronzes* (London: Simon & Schuster, 2021).

Pollard, Duke E., *The Caribbean Court of Justice: Closing the Circle of Independence* (Kingston: Ian Randle Publishers, 2004).

Proglio, Gabriele, *Decolonising the Mediterranean* (Cambridge: Cambridge University Press, 2016).

Proulx, Rose Marie, *Iranian Oil Nationalization and International Law* (Pullman, WA: State College of Washington, 1952).

Raaflaub, Kurt A., Ober, Josiah and Wallace, Robert W., *Origins of Democracy in Ancient Greece* (Berkeley, CA: University of California Press, 2007).

Rabinowitz, Beth S., *Defensive Nationalism: Explaining the Rise of Populism and Fascism in the 21st Century* (Oxford: Oxford University Press, 2023).

River, Charles (ed), *The East African Slave Trade: The History and Legacy of the Arab Slave Trade and the Indian Ocean Slave Trade* (CreateSpace Independent Publishing Platform, 2017).

Rudall, Jason, *Compensation for Environmental Damage Under International Law* (London: Taylor & Francis, 2020).

Saito, Natsu Taylor, *Settler Colonialism, Race and the Law: Why Structural Racism Persists* (New York: New York University Press, 2020).

Salomone, Rosemary, *The Rise of English: Global Politics and the Power of Language* (Oxford: Oxford University Press, 2022).

Sandford, Victoria, *Buried Secrets: Truth and Human Rights in Guatemala* (London: Palgrave Macmillan, 2003).

Sarkin-Hughes, Jeremy, *Germany's Genocide of the Herero: Kaiser Wilhem II, His General, His Settlers, His Soldiers* (Cape Town: University of Cape Town Press, 2011).

Sharkey, Heather, *A History of Muslims, Christians and Jews in the Middle East* (Cambridge: Cambridge University Press, 2017).

Sherry, James, *The Oligarch: Rewriting Machiavelli's* The Prince *for Our Time* (New York: Palgrave Macmillan, 2018).
Shiva, Vandana, *Protect or Plunder* (London: Bloomsbury Academic, 2001).
Shiva, Vandana, *Soil Not Oil: Environmental Justice in an Age of Climate Crisis* (Berkeley, CA: North Atlantic Books, 2015).
Shiva, Vandana and Mies, Maria, *Ecofeminism* (London: Bloomsbury Academic, 2023).
Short, Damian and Crook, Martin, *The Genocide–Ecocide Nexus* (London: Taylor & Francis, 2022).
Simon, Joshua, *The Ideology of Creole Revolution: Imperialism and Independence in American and Latin American Political Thought* (Cambridge: Cambridge University Press, 2017).
Sureda, Rigo Sureda, *The Evolution of the Right of Self-determination* (Leiden: Sijthoff, 1973).
Swart, Mia and van Marle, Karin eds, *The Limits of Transition: The South African Truth and Reconciliation Commission 20 Years On* (Leiden/Boston: Brill Nijhoff, 2017).
Táíwò, Olúfẹ́mi O., *Reconsidering Reparations* (Oxford: Oxford University Press, 2022).
Tamale, Sylvia, *Decolonization and Afro-Feminism* (Wakefield QC: Daraja Press, 2020).
Terretta, Meredith, *Nation of Outlaws, State of Violence: Nationalism, Grassfields Tradition, and State Building in Cameroon* (Athens, OH: Ohio University Press, 2014).
Thakur, Ramesh Chandra, Popovski, Vesselin and Kemp Walter A. (eds), *Blood and Borders: The Responsibility to Protect and the Problem of the Kin-State* (Tokyo: United Nations University Press, 2011).
Tharoor, Shashi, *The Struggle for India's Soul* (London: Hurst & Co., 2021).
Thiranagama, Sharika and Kelly, Tobias (eds), *Traitors: Suspicion, Intimacy and the Ethics of State Building* (Philadelphia: Penn University Press, 2010).
Vasquez, Patricia I., *Oil Sparks in the Amazon: Local Conflicts, Indigenous Populations and Natural Resources* (Athens, GA/London: University of Georgia Press, 2014).
Vattel, Emmerich, *The Law of Nations or the Principles of Natural Law* (1758).
Whyte, David, *Ecocide: Kill the Corporation Before It Kills Us* (Manchester: Manchester University Press, 2020).
Wijkman, Anders and Rockström, Johan, *Bankrupting Nature: Denying Our Planetary Boundaries* (London: Taylor & Francis, 2013).
Woolaston, Kate, *Ecological Vulnerability: The Law and Governance of Human–Wildlife Relationships* (Cambridge: Cambridge University Press, 2022).
Yamada, Nakaba, *Genkō Kassenki: Battle Records of the Mongol Invasions* (English translation) (Tokyo: Publish Drive, 2019).

Yamazaki, Jane, *Japanese Apologies for World War II: A Rhetorical Study* (London: Routledge, 2012).

Yoshimi, Yoshiaki, *Comfort Women: Sexual Slavery in the Japanese Military During World War II* (New York: Columbia University Press, 2000).

Zhao, Weili, Popkewitz, Thomas S. and Autio, Tera (eds), *Epistemic Colonialism and the Transfer of Curriculum Knowledge Across Borders: Applying a Historical Lens to Contest Unilateral Logics* (London: Routledge, 2022).

Articles and chapters

[Special Issue] 9(5) *Africology: Journal of Pan African Studies* (2016).

Acevedo, Jairo Ramos, 'El "Uti Possidetis" un principio americano y no europeo', 5(5) *Misión Jurídica* (2012) 145–63.

Anyango-van Zwieten, Nowella, Lamers, Machiel and van der Duim, René, 'Funding for Nature Conservation: A Study of Public Finance Networks at World Wide Fund for Nature (WWF)', 9 *Biodiversity Conservation* (2019) 3749–66.

Atiles-Osoria, José, 'Colonial State Crimes and the CARICOM Mobilization for Reparation and Justice', 7(2) *State Crime Journal* (Autumn 2018) 349–68.

Baldwin, Simeon E., 'The International Congresses and Conferences of the Last Century as Forces Working towards the Solidarity of the World', 1(3) *American Journal of International Law* (1907) 808–29.

Barsh, Russell L., 'Indigenous Peoples in the 1990s: From Object to Subject in International Law?', 7 *Harvard Human Rights Journal* (1994) 33–62.

Castellino Joshua, 'Territorial Integrity and the "Right" to Self-determination: An Examination of the Conceptual Tools', 33(2) *Brooklyn Journal of International Law* (2008) 503–68.

Castellino, Joshua, 'The Rise of Majorities and Emerging Existential Threats to India and China', 8 *Chinese Journal of Comparative Law* (December 2020) 538–77.

Chetail, Vincent, 'Sovereignty and Migration in the Doctrine of the Laws of Nations: An Intellectual History of Hospitality from Vitoria to Vattel', 27(4) *European Journal of International Law* (2016) 901–22.

Cooper, Allan D., 'Reparations for the Herero Genocide: Defining the Limits of International Litigation', 106(422) *African Affairs* (January 2007) 113–26.

Cowled, Brendan D, Bannister-Tyrrell, Melanie, Doyle, Mark, Clutterbuck, Henry, Cave, Jeff, Hillman et al, 'The Australian 2019/2020 Black Summer Bushfires: Analysis of the Pathology, Treatment Strategies and Decision Making About Burnt Livestock', 9 *Frontiers in Veterinary Science* (2022) 790556.

Crook, John R., 'Applicable Law in International Arbitration: The Iran–U.S. Claims Tribunal Experience', 83(2) *American Journal of International Law* (1989) 292–3.

Crook, Martin, Short, Damian and South, Nigel, 'Ecocide, Genocide, Capitalism and Colonialism: Consequences for Indigenous Peoples and Glocal Ecosystems Environments', 22(3) *Theoretical Criminology* (2018) 298–317.

Dickson, Brice, 'Unjust Enrichment Claims: A Comparative Overview', 54 *Cambridge Law Journal* (1995) 100–26.

Domínguez, Lara and Luoma, Colin, 'Decolonising Conservation Policy: How Colonial Land and Conservation Ideologies Persist and Perpetuate Indigenous Injustices at the Expense of the Environment', 9(3) *Land* (2020) 65.

Elias, Taslim Olawale, 'The Doctrine of Intertemporal Law', 74(2) *American Journal of International Law* (1980) 285–307.

El Amouri, Sarah and Smis, Stefaan, 'Inter-State Apologies for Colonial Injustices from an International State Responsibility Perspective: A Commentary on the Belgian Controversy', 27(4) *American Journal of International Law* (April 2023).

Fagan, David N., 'Achieving Restitution: The Potential Unjust Enrichment Claims of Indigenous Peoples Against Multinational Corporations', 76 *New York University Law Review* (2001) 626.

Fombad, Charles Manga, 'The Principle of Unjust Enrichment in International Law', 30(2) *Comparative & International Law Journal of South Africa* (1997) 120–30.

Forrester, Katrina, 'Reparations, History and Global Justice', in Duncan Bell (ed), *Empire, Race and Global Justice* (Cambridge: Cambridge University Press, 2019) 22–51.

Friedman, W., 'The Principle of Unjust Enrichment in English Law', 16 *Canadian Bar Review* (1938) 384.

Gallo, Paolo, 'Unjust Enrichment: A Comparative Analysis', 40(3) *American Journal of Comparative Law* (1992) 431.

Garnett, S.T., Burgess, Neil D., Fa, Julia E., Fernández-Llamazares, Álvaro, Molnár, Zsolt, Robinson, Cathy J. et al, 'A Spatial Overview of the Global Importance of Indigenous Lands for Conservation', 1 *Nature Sustainability* (2018) 369–74.

Gathii, James Thuo and Ntina, Tzouvala, 'Racial Capitalism and International Economic Law: Introduction', 25(2) *Journal of International Economic Law* (2022) 199–206.

Geldman, Jonas, Manica, Andrea, Burgess, Neil D. and Balmford, Andrew, 'A Global-Level Assessment of the Effectiveness of Protected Areas at Resisting Anthropogenic Pressures', 116(46) *PNAS* (2019) 23209–15.

Hamilton, J. B., 'The Evolution of the Dum-Dum Bullet', *British Medical Journal* (14 May 1898) 1250–1.

Hoffman, Kira M., Davis, Emma L., Wickham, Sara B., Schang, Kyle, Johnson, Alexandra, Larking, Taylor et al, 'Conservation of Earth's Biodiversity is Embedded in Indigenous Fire Stewardship', 18(32) *PNAS* (2021) 1–6.

Kupisch, Berthold, 'Ungerechtfertigte Bereicherung', in E.J.H. Schrage (ed), *Unjust Enrichment: The Comparative Legal History of the Law of Restitution*, Vol. 15, 2nd edn (Duncker & Humblot GmbH, 1999) 237–74.

Mc Cartney, Ann M., Head, M.A., Tsosie, K.S., Glas, J.R., Paez, S., Geary, J. and Hudson, M., 'Indigenous Peoples and Local Communities as Partners in the Sequencing of Global Eukaryotic Biodiversity', 2(8) *NPJ Biodiverse* (2023).

Mitchell, Charles and Oliver, Peter, 'Unjust Enrichment and the Idea of Public Law', in Robert Chambers, Charles Mitchell and James Penner (eds), *Philosophical Foundations of the Law of Unjust Enrichment* (Oxford: Oxford University Press, 2009) 406.

Murdock, Esme G., 'Conserving Dispossession? A Genealogical Account of the Colonial Roots of Western Conservation', 24(3) *Ethics, Policy & Environment* (2021) 235–49.

Murphy, Kaitlin M., 'Fear and Loathing in Monuments: Rethinking the Politics and Practice of Monumentality and Monumentalization', 14(6) *Memory Studies* (2021) 1143–58.

O'Bryan, Christopher J., Garnett, Stephen T., Fa, Julia E., Leiper, Ian, Rehbein, Jose A., Fernández-Llamazares, Álvaro et al, 'The Importance of Indigenous Peoples' Lands for the Conservation of Terrestrial Mammals', 35(3) *Conservation Biology* (2021) 1002–8.

Prăvălie, Remus, 'Nuclear Weapons Tests and Environmental Consequences: A Global Perspective', 43(6) *Ambio* (2014) 729–44.

Ratner, Steve R., 'Drawing a Better Line: Uti Possidetis and the Borders of New States', 90 *American Journal of International Law* (1996) 590.

Reyes-García, Victoria, Fernández-Llamazares, Álvaro, Aumeeruddy-Thomas, Yildiz, Benyei, Petra, Bussmann, Rainer W., Diamond, Sara K. et al, 'Recognizing Indigenous Peoples' and Local Communities' Rights and Agency in the Post-2020 Biodiversity Agenda', 51 *Ambio* (2022) 84–92.

Robinson, Darryl, 'Ecocide – Puzzles and Possibilities', 20(2) *Journal of International Criminal Justice* (2022) 313–47.

Schrage, E.J.H., 'Restitution in the new Dutch Civil Code', in P.W.L. Russell (ed), *Unjustified Enrichment: A Comparative Study of the Law of Restitution* (Vrije Universiteit, 1996) 10–53.

Sherwin, Emily, 'Restitution and Equity: An Analysis of the Principle of Unjust Enrichment', 79 *Texas Law Review* (2001) 2083–104.

Smith, Lionel, 'Unjust Enrichment', 66(1) *McGill Law Journal* (2020) 165–8.

Stahn, Carsten, 'Reckoning with Colonial Injustice: International law as Culprit and as Remedy?', 33(4) *Leiden Journal of International Law* (2000) 823–35.

Sundberg, Ulrika, 'Durban: The Third World Conference against Racism, Racial Discrimination, Xenophobia and Related Intolerance', 73 *Revue Internationale de Droit Pénal* (2002) 301.

Tan, Eugene K.B., 'Law and Values in Governance: The Singapore Way', 30(1) *Hong Kong Law Journal* (2000) 91–119.

Tharoor, Shashi, 'Saying Sorry to India: Reparation or Atonement?', *Harvard International Law Journal* 1–5, available at https://journals.law.harvard.edu/ilj/wp-content/uploads/sites/84/Tharoor-Reparations.pdf.

Theurer, Karina, 'Minimum Legal Standards in Reparation Processes for Colonial Crimes: The Case of Namibia and Germany', *German Law Journal* posted 26 June 2023 on *SSRN*.

Uga, Nishant, 'India Launches Offshore Licensing Round in Latest Exploration Push', *Upstream: Energy Explored* (12 October 2022).

Veraat, Wouter, 'Two Rounds of Postwar Restitution and Dignity Restoration in the Netherlands and France', 41(4) *Law & Social Inquiry* (2016) 956–72.

Wagner, Kim A., '"Calculated to Strike Terror": The Amritsar Massacre and the Spectre of Colonial Violence', 233 *Past & Present* (November 2016) 185–225.

Weinrib, Ernest J., 'Correctively Unjust Enrichment', in Robert Chambers, Charles Mitchell and James Penner (eds), *Philosophical Foundations of the Law of Unjust Enrichment* (Oxford, Oxford University Press, 2009).

Wessels, B., 'Civil Code Revision in the Netherlands: System, Contents and Future', 41 *Netherlands International Law Review* (1994) 163.

Wong, Gerrit W., 'Standards of Civilization Today', in Mehdi Mozaffari (ed), *Globalization and Civilizations* (London: Routledge, 2002) 77–96.

ANNEX

Regional Groupings of Countries

Africa (54)

North Africa (6 +1)
Algeria, Egypt, Libya, Mauritania, Morocco, Tunisia, *Saharan Arab Democratic Republic*

West Africa (15)
Benin, Burkina Faso, Cabo Verde, Côte d'Ivoire, The Gambia, Ghana, Guinea, Guinea-Bissau, Liberia, Mali, Niger, Nigeria, Senegal, Sierra Leone, Togo

Central Africa (9)
Burundi, Cameroon, Central African Republic, Chad, Democratic Republic of Congo, Republic of Congo, Equatorial Guinea, Gabon, São Tomé and Príncipe

East Africa (14)
Comoros, Djibouti, Eritrea, Ethiopia, Kenya, Madagascar, Mauritius, Rwanda, Seychelles, Somalia, South Sudan, Sudan, Tanzania, Uganda

Southern Africa (10)
Angola, Botswana, Eswatini, Lesotho, Malawi, Mozambique, Namibia, South Africa, Zambia, Zimbabwe
NB: *African States have been classified as per the African Union listing. The following are not listed because they are dependencies: St. Helena (UK), Mayotte and Reunion (France)*

The Americas (35)

North America (3)
Canada, Mexico, United States of America
Also: Saint Pierre and Michelon (France)

Caribbean and Central America (22)
Antigua and Barbuda, The Bahamas, Barbados, Belize, Costa Rica, Cuba, Dominica, Dominican Republic, El Salvador, Grenada, Guatemala, Guyana, Haiti, Honduras, Jamaica, Nicaragua, Panama, Saint Kitts and Nevis, Saint Lucia, Saint Vincent and the Grenadines, Suriname, Trinidad and Tobago
Also Aruba, Curacao, Bonaire Sint Eastatius and Saba, Sint Maarten (all Netherlands) Anguilla, Bermuda, British Virgin Islands, Cayman Islands, Montserrat, Turks and Caicos Islands (all United Kingdom), Puerto Rico, US Virgin Islands, Guadeloupe, Martinique, Sant Barthelemy, Sant Martin (all France)

South America (10)
Argentina, Bolivia, Brazil, Chile, Colombia, Ecuador, Paraguay, Peru, Uruguay, Venezuela
Also see: Bouvetøya (Norway), The Malvinas/Falklands, South Georgia and the South Sandwich Islands (UK), French Guiana (France)

Asia (48)
East Asia (5)
Democratic People's Republic of Korea, China, Japan, Mongolia, Republic of Korea
Also see: 'Republic of China' (Taiwan), Hong Kong Special Administrative Region, Macau Special Administrative Region (both China)

Southeast Asia (11)
Brunei Darussalam, Cambodia, Indonesia, Laos, Malaysia, Myanmar, Philippines, Singapore, Thailand, Timor Leste, Vietnam

South Asia (8)
Afghanistan, Bangladesh, Bhutan, India, Maldives, Nepal, Pakistan, Sri Lanka

Central Asia (6)
Azerbaijan, Kazakhstan, Kyrgyzstan, Tajikistan, Turkmenistan, Uzbekistan

Western Asia (including the Gulf) (17 +1)
Armenia, Bahrain, Cyprus, Georgia, Iran, Iraq, Israel, Jordan, Kuwait, Lebanon, Oman, Qatar, Saudi Arabia, *Palestine*, Syria, Turkiyë, United Arab Emirates, Yemen

Europe (42)
Central and Eastern Europe (17)
Albania, Bosnia and Herzegovina, Croatia, Belarus, Bulgaria, Czech Republic, Hungary, Poland, Moldova, Montenegro, North Macedonia, Romania, Russian Federation, Serbia, Slovenia, Slovakia, Ukraine

Western Europe (25 +1)
Andorra, Austria, Belgium, Denmark, Estonia, Finland, France, Germany, Greece, *Holy See*, Iceland, Italy, Ireland, Latvia, Liechtenstein, Lithuania, Luxembourg, Malta, Netherlands, Norway, Portugal, San Marino, Spain, Sweden, Switzerland, United Kingdom

Also see: Aaland Islands (Finland), Faroe Islands (Denmark), Gibraltar, Guernsey (incl. Sark), Jersey, Isle of Man, (UK) Svalbaard and Jan Mayen Islands (Norway), Monaco (France)

Australasia and the Pacific (16)

Australia and the Pacific (14 +2)
Australia, Aotearoa/New Zealand, *Cook Islands*, Federated States of Micronesia, Fiji, Kiribati, Marshall Islands, Nauru, *Niue*, Palau, Papua New Guinea, Samoa, Solomon Islands, Tonga, Tuvalu, Vanuatu

Also see: Christmas Island, Cocos, Heard Island and McDonald Islands, Norfolk Island (Australia), French Polynesia, New Caledonia/Kanak, Wallis and Futuna (France), American Samoa, Guam, Northern Mariana Islands, United States Minor Outlying Islands – Baker, Howland, Jarvis, Johnston Atoll, Kingman Reef, Midway Atoll, Palmyra Atoll, Wake Island plus Navassa Island in the Caribbean Sea (USA), Pitcairn Islands (UK), Tokelau (New Zealand)

Index

A

Aboriginal knowledge 114–15
acceptance of wrongfulness 53, 76–81, 89
access, to reparation process 77, 92, 130
Accra Proclamation on Reparations (2023) 76
Africa
    artefacts stolen from 54–7
    crimes and compensation to 90–2
    genocide 52–4, 91–2, 130
    slave trade 38, 55–6, 76, 83
    territorial acquisition 43–6
    UN Working Group of Experts on People of African Descent 79–80
aid 69
Akufo-Addo, Nana Addo Dankwa 75
alliances/collaboration 9, 147, 148–9
Americas 38, 55, 64–5
Ammoun, Fouad 42–3
Amritsar massacre 50–2
Ancient Greece 40–1
Anglo-Iranian Oil Company 87
anthropocentricity 4, 24, 29, 35–6, 37, 63, 142, 149
antiquities *see* cultural artefacts
Aotearoa (New Zealand) 33, 47–9, 101
apologies 12, 32, 80, 83
archives 91
arms, dum-dum bullets 38–40
arms deals 68, 73, 111–12
arms industry 104
Australia 47, 59, 114–15

B

Barbados 75
Battle of Waterberg 52
Bedjaoui, Mohammed 42–3
Belgium 23, 79–80, 94, 102–3
Benin 55, 56
Benin Bronzes 54–7, 78, 85
Berlin West Africa Conference (1884–1885) 23–4, 55
biodiversity *see* protected areas
#BlackLivesMatter movement 15, 109–10

BRICS countries 104
Bridgetown Initiative 75, 82
British colonial powers
    acknowledgement and reparation by 77, 90–1, 94
    ammunition used by 38–40
    assets misappropriated by 85–6, 87
    crimes of 43–9, 50–2, 55–7, 101
    enduring impact of 59, 103, 137
    laws 23, 28
    legal influence 112
British Museum 56–7
Brown, Imani Jacqueline 114

C

Canada 59
carbon sinks 71
Caribbean States 75, 82–4
Caricom Reparation Commission (CRC) 82–4
China 11, 37, 64, 65, 103, 104
Chorzów Factory case (1928) 89
Christianity 37, 102
Churchill, Winston 39
circular economies 103, 106
civilization 36, 89, 102, 103
climate change
    Bridgetown Initiative 75
    and fossil fuel extraction 63
    ineffective responses to 98–9, 107
    law as enabler of colonization and 107–13
    link with colonial crime 97–8, 101–7, 124–5
    need for governance change 145–9
    and protected areas 71–2, 99, 113–18, 129
    see also environmental crime
climate guardians 114
collaboration/alliances 9, 147, 148–9
collusion in colonial crime 72–3
colonial crime
    academic engagement with 126
    categories
        collusion 72–3
        decolonization-oriented crimes 64–9
        episodic crime 49–57
        legacy crimes 69–72

subjecthood and objecthood 35–40
systemic practices 57–64
territorial acquisition 40–9
ineffective responses to 98–9
link with climate change 97–8, 101–7, 124–5
myths preventing action 4–8
practical difficulties in addressing 7–8
reluctance to address 147
solutions 74–6
  acceptance of wrongfulness 76–81
  barriers to justice *see* justice
  compensation 12, 84, 88–93
  reparations 81–5
  restitution 27–8, 85–8
  solidarity-oriented remedies 93–4
colonial powers
  CRC assertions against 82–3
  European and beyond 10–11
  relationship with post-colonial States 73, 147
  reparation by *see* reparation
  role in arms industry 111–12
  role in global lawmaking 112
  see also specific countries
colonial rule, legacies of 8–10, 69–72, 103
colonization
  law as enabler 107–13
  status as crime 22–4
commercial activities 68–9, 102, 103–4, 111
  see also private/corporate entities
communities *see* native populations
compensation (financial) 12, 84, 88–93, 139
Conference of Parties (CoP) 107, 146–7
conservation *see* environmental regeneration; protected areas
consumption 105, 144, 145
contracts/treaties 28, 44–5, 46, 47–9, 87, 101, 109–10
corporations *see* private/corporate entities
CRC (Caricom Reparation Commission) 82–4
Creoles 65
crime *see* colonial crime; environmental crime
cultural artefacts 12, 28, 50, 54–7, 78, 83, 85

D

Dalrymple, William 86
debt 68, 73, 84
decolonization 1, 62, 108–9, 110, 111–12
  crimes related to 64–9
defence spending *see* arms deals
Democratic Republic of Congo 80, 103
development aid 69
development banks 75
development programmes 74, 83
development through technology 84
dum-dum bullets 38–40

Durban Conference *see* World Conference against Racism
Dyer, Reginald (General) 50–2

E

ecocide 122–3
economic activities *see* commercial activities
economies
  colonial impact on 102–3
  see also circular economies; extractive economic model
education, and reparation 79, 80, 83–4
education systems 58–60
Egypt 12
empathy 149–50
English language 59
entrepreneurs 44, 45, 105–6, 144
environment, objecthood of 127
environmental crime 124–30
  ecocide 122–3
  and unjust enrichment 133–9
environmental destruction
  and colonial legacy crimes 70–2
  see also climate change
environmental regeneration
  role of native populations 117, 118–19
  see also protected areas
episodic colonial crime 49–57
  compensation for 90–3
equality 144
  see also inequality
European colonial powers 10–11, 37–8, 82–3
  see also specific countries
European colonization 102
extraction of fossil fuels 60–4, 81, 86–8, 139, 146–7
extractive economic model
  architecture supporting 142–3
  colonial imposition of 58
  disrupting cycle of 143–5
  need for governance change 145–9
  in post-colonial States 115, 122, 127–8, 146–7
  in protected areas 115

F

financial architecture 75
financial asset restitution 85–8
financial compensation 12, 84, 88–93, 139
Floyd, George 15, 120–1
fortress conservation *see* protected areas
fossil fuels 60–4, 81, 86–8, 139, 146–7
free trade 111
French colonial powers 23, 47, 55, 70, 94, 112, 134

G

genocide 52–4, 91–2, 130
German colonial powers 52–4, 91–2, 130, 134
global economy 75, 105–6

INDEX

global governance 106–7, 146–9
  see also United Nations
global lawmaking 112
governance
  global 106–7, 146–9
  need to change 145–9
  in post-colonial States 9–10, 66–70, 108–9
Greece (Ancient) 40–1
Grotius, Hugo 65

H

#BlackLivesMatter movement 15, 109–10
health 83
Herero genocide 52–4, 91–2, 130
historical narratives
  of former colonial powers 13–16, 52
  as partial 30–1, 34–5, 52, 54
  of post-colonial States 126
  of territorial acquisition 44–5
  verification of 30–1, 76–8, 91–2
history, colonial crime dismissed as 5
homosexuality 57–8
human rights 2–3
human rights violations in protected areas 115–17, 125
Hunter Commission (1919) 51, 52
hunting (sport) 70, 117–18, 129

I

identity politics 2, 3, 140
  see also national identity
independence movements 9, 67
India 9, 11, 39, 50–2, 54, 64, 85–6, 102, 103
Indigenous peoples see native populations
inequality 2–3, 105–6, 144
  see also structural discrimination
Intergovernmental Panel on Climate Change (IPCC) 97–8, 124
international governance 106–7, 146–9
international law (laws of nations)
  and armed conflict 111–12
  as enabler of colonization 107–13
  and free trade 111
  and global lawmaking 112
  and legal personhood 25–6
  limitations of 65, 126–7
  and property rights 110
  and protected areas 113–18
  and territorial acquisition 99–101
  and territorial regimes 108–9
  and treaty-making 109–10
International Monetary Fund 75
intertemporal rule of law 22–4, 100, 101, 126, 134, 137, 145
IPCC (Intergovernmental Panel on Climate Change) 97–8, 124
Iran 60, 87–8
Iraq 9

Israel 11
Italy 134

J

Jallianwala Bagh massacre 50–2
jus resistendi 1, 65, 109
justice 21, 107
  barriers to 120, 134–5
  calculating tort 31–2
  establishing victimhood 29
  general versus specific 29–30
  historical verification 30–1
  intertemporal rule of law 22–4
  legal personality 24–6
  property rights 27–8
  statutes of limitations 26–7
  validity of contracts 28
  wider remedies 32–3

K

Kenya 90–1
Khan, Genghis 11
knowledge, traditional 114–15
knowledge exchanges 84

L

land, blank (*terra nullius*) 38, 42–3, 99–101
land acquisition see territorial acquisition
land cultivation 41–2
land rights 9, 27–8, 69, 81–2, 110
land rights claims 138
land tenure systems 57
language 59
law
  barriers to justice see justice
  international see international law
  non-application abroad 23
laws of nations see international law
legacy crimes 69–72
legal bias 57
legal personality 24–6, 40
  see also subjecthood
legal systems 9, 58, 69–70
Lena Goldfield Arbitration Award 133
loans 73
Lobengula, King of Ndebele people 44–5

M

Māori people 47–9
maps 59, 126
Marquez, Francia 75
massacres 50–2, 91
Mau Mau uprising 90–1
memorials 79, 91
Middle East 60–2, 87–8
mining rights 44–5
moral obligations 79
Mottley, Mia 75–6
museums 56–7

171

N

Nama genocide 52–4, 91–2, 130
Namibia 52–4, 91–2, 94, 130
nation-building 62, 66, 67
national governance 9–10, 66–70, 108–9, 146
national identity 33, 67–8
nationalism 3
native populations
  dual victimization of 118
  involvement in decolonization process 108
  involvement in reparation process 77, 92, 130
  in protected areas 70–2, 113–14, 115–17
  resistance to extractive model 129
  role in environmental regeneration 114, 117, 118–19
  subjecthood and objecthood of 24–6, 36–40, 101, 118, 128
  and territorial acquisition 44–9
  traditional knowledge of 114–15
Ndebele Kingdom 44, 46
Netherlands 23, 32, 94, 134
New Zealand (Aotearoa) 33, 47–9, 101
Nigeria 9, 55, 56, 57, 139
non-discrimination 35
nuclear weapons 70

O

objecthood 24–5, 35–40, 101, 127–8
Ogoni people 139
oil extraction 60–4, 87–8, 139, 146–7
Organization of Petroleum Exporting Countries (OPEC) 147
Ovaherero genocide 52–4, 91–2, 130

P

Papua New Guinea 9
patriarchy 59
political power 106
political systems 70
politics 139–40
Portuguese colonial powers 23, 37–8, 55, 65, 94, 101
post-colonial States
  arms and defence spending 68, 73, 111–12
  collusion crimes 72–3
  commercial exploitation of 104
  extractive economy 115, 122, 127–8, 146–7
  governance 9–10, 66–70, 108–9
  histories 126
  land rights 9, 27–8, 69, 81–2, 110
  legacies of colonial rule 8–10, 69–72, 103
  legal systems 9, 69–70
  responses to colonialism–climate link 125
  responsibility of 1–2, 10, 72–3
  self-determination 64–5, 68, 109, 110
  territories 55, 108, 147
  unity and division 9–10, 66, 67–8, 108–9

  wealth and fossil fuel extraction 62–3
  see also specific countries
private/corporate entities
  colonial role of 86, 87
  culpability and reparation 119, 135–6, 137
  litigation against 138–9
  in post-colonial States 104
  see also entrepreneurs
private/corporate wealth 63–4, 103, 105–6, 135–6, 137, 144–5
property appropriation *see* cultural artefacts; territorial acquisition
property rights 9, 27–8, 69, 81–2, 110
protected areas 70–2, 99, 113–18, 129
psychological rehabilitation 84
public health 83
public response to colonialism–climate link 125

R

race 3, 11–12, 24, 38
racism 23, 24, 38, 40, 93
recognition of crimes 53
  see also acceptance of wrongfulness
reconciliatory justice 82
regional approach 148–9, 166–8
religion 3, 37, 57, 102
reparation
  apologies 12, 32, 80, 83
  barriers to justice *see* justice
  Bridgetown Initiative 82–4
  calculating tort 31–2, 92–3
  calls for 75–6
  community involvement in 77, 92, 130
  culpability of colonial states 136–7
  difficulties of 120, 134–5
  financial compensation 12, 84, 88–93, 139
  forms of 12, 83–4
  for fossil fuel extraction 81–2
  for genocide 53–4
  limited action 6, 57, 94, 122, 130
  restitution *see* restitution
  return of cultural artefacts 12, 28, 54–7, 78, 83, 85
  role of private/corporate entities 119, 135–6, 137
  solidarity-oriented remedies 93–4
  varied discourses of 29–30
repatriation 83
research 91
resistance
  jus resistendi 1, 65, 109
  see also independence movements; social movements
restitution 27–8, 85–8
  of cultural artefacts 12, 28, 54–7, 78, 83, 85
retrospective application *see* intertemporal rule of law
Reuters Concession (1872) 87
revisionist history 13–16, 31

INDEX

Rhodes, Cecil 43–6
Roman territory 42, 100–1
Rowlatt Acts 50
Rudd Commission 44–5, 46
Rudd Concession 44, 45
Rwanda 9

S

Saito, Natsu Taylor 43
Scramble for Africa 56
self-determination 1, 64–5, 68, 109, 110
Shell Oil 139
Singapore 9
slave trade 38, 55–6, 58, 76, 83
slavery (contemporary) 128
Smith, Lionel 131
social movements 145–6
  see also independence movements
solidarity-oriented remedies 93–4
South Africa 43–4
Spanish colonial powers 23, 37–8, 65, 94, 101
sport hunting 70, 117–18, 129
States see colonial powers; post-colonial States
statutes of limitations 26–7, 90–1
structural discrimination 77, 120–1, 126, 136–7
subjecthood 24–6, 35–40, 101, 118, 127–8
supply chains 103, 119, 144
system change
  crime of unjust enrichment 136, 138
  cycle disruption 143–5
  governance change 145–9
  need for 121–2
systemic colonial crimes 57–64

T

Táíwò, Olúfẹ́mi 82
tax havens 144
technology 84, 118–19
terra nullius 38, 42–3, 99–101
territorial acquisition
  examples 43–9
  law relating to 40–3, 99–101
  methods 99–101
territorial regimes, law as enabler 108–9
territories
  blank (*terra nullius*) 38, 42–3, 99–101
  and oil extraction 62
  of post-colonial states 55, 108, 147
  return of 118
  see also land rights

testimonies 91–2
Tharoor, Shashi 85–6
theft
  of artefacts see cultural artefacts
  and European colonization 102
30×30 plan 71–2, 113, 115, 129
time see intertemporal rule of law; statutes of limitations
tort
  calculating 31–2, 92–3
  prolonged 106
traditional knowledge 114–15
treaties/contracts 28, 44–5, 46, 47–9, 87, 101, 109–10
Treaty of Waitangi 47–9, 101
truth and reconciliation commissions 77, 80

U

UN Working Group of Experts on People of African Descent 79–80, 84
United Nations 64, 65, 75
United Nations Security Council 112
United States of America 15, 59, 65, 104, 114, 121, 131
unjust enrichment
  concept of 131–3
  crime of 133–9, 145

V

Valladolid Controversy 37–8
Vattel, Emmerich 41–2
verification 30–1, 76–8, 91–2
victimhood 29
von Trotha, General 52–3, 91

W

Waitangi Treaty 47–9, 101
Waitangi tribunal 49
wealth accumulation 102–4, 105–6, 135–6, 137, 144–5
  related to oil extraction 61, 62–4
weapons see arms; arms deals; arms industry; nuclear weapons
Western Sahara case 100
women, subjecthood of 24–5
World Bank 75
World Conference against Racism (Durban 2001) 5, 29, 93
World Wildlife Fund (WWF) 115–17, 125
wrongfulness, acceptance of 53, 76–81, 89

Z

Zimbabwe 9, 43–6

www.ingramcontent.com/pod-product-compliance
Lightning Source LLC
Chambersburg PA
CBHW051549020426
42333CB00016B/2168